MARTIN CLASSICAL LECTURES

〜 〜

The Martin Classical Lectures are delivered annually at Oberlin College through a foundation established by his many friends in honor of Charles Beebe Martin, for forty-five years a teacher of classical literature and classical art at Oberlin.

John Peradotto, *Man in the Middle Voice: Name and Narration in the* Odyssey

Martha C. Nussbaum, *The Therapy of Desire: Theory and Practice in Hellenistic Ethnics*

Josiah Ober, *Political Dissent in Democratic Athens: Intellectual Critics of Popular Rule*

Anne Carson, *Economy of the Unlost (Reading Simonides of Keos with Paul Celon)*

Helene P. Foley, *Female Acts in Greek Tragedy*

Mark W. Edwards, *Sound, Sense, and Rhythm: Listening to Greek and Latin Poetry*

SOUND, SENSE, AND RHYTHM

LISTENING TO GREEK AND LATIN POETRY

Mark W. Edwards

PRINCETON UNIVERSITY PRESS

PRINCETON AND OXFORD

Copyright © 2002 by Princeton University Press
Published by Princeton University Press, 41 William Street,
Princeton, New Jersey 08540
In the United Kingdom: Princeton University Press, 3 Market Place, Woodstock,
Oxfordshire OX20 1SY
All Rights Reserved

Library of Congress Cataloging-in-Publication Data

Edwards, Mark W.
Sound, sense, and rhythm : listening to Greek and Latin poetry / Mark W. Edwards.
p.   cm. — (Martin classical lectures. New series)
Includes bibliographical references and index.
ISBN 0-691-08666-4 (alk. paper)
1. Classical languages—Metrics and rhythmics.   2. Classical poetry—History
and criticism.   3. Oral communication—Greece.   4. Oral communication—
Rome.   I. Title.   II. Martin classical lectures (Unnumbered). New series.

PA185.E39 2001   880′21—dc09   2001021989

British Library Cataloging-in-Publication Data is available

This book has been composed in Janson Typeface

Printed on acid-free paper. ∞

www.pup.princeton.edu

Printed in the United States of America

10 9 8 7 6 5 4 3 2 1

μαθεῖν θέλεις; δίδασκε. δός, κτᾶσθαι θέλων

CONTENTS

PREFACE

W<small>HEN</small> I received the invitation to give the Martin Classical Lectures, I felt that I did not want to devote the whole series to what has been my main research subject, the poetry of Homer. During my life as a university teacher I have also developed a number of other interests, usually arising from courses I have taught, and about two of them in particular I thought I had something to say that might be useful to my peers in the profession: the ways in which Aeschylus uses lyric meters in his choruses to convey a meaning and a mood, and the ways Roman poets (Propertius in particular) availed themselves of the special characteristics of the Latin language to produce certain effects. These topics, it seemed to me, could be linked with two others from Homeric studies that were much in my mind at the time: the order and positioning of words in the verse, and the interconnection of successive scenes (and hence the significance of the book divisions). All four were centered upon the way one should try to imagine oneself listening to ancient poetry, rather than reading it from the page; and all four had strongly affected my teaching of these and other authors in undergraduate classes, and might be of interest to others in such circumstances.

When I delivered the lectures in Oberlin in February 1998, I gave them in the chronological order of authors discussed. In preparing them for publication I at first thought of abandoning this simple sequence in favor of one that progressed from word order in Homer to word order in Latin poetry, then on to word rhythm (or meter) in Aeschylus, and finally to larger-scale issues of Homer's ways of keeping his hearers' attention while passing from one scene to another. However, readers of this version were not impressed by this arrangement of the material, and complained that the transitions between the chapters were weak—they were obviously thinking the book should be a unified whole, and wanted a better synthesis of the parts. I have therefore returned to the sequence of the lectures, which (besides having the advantage of familiarity) produces another, perhaps clearer, progression of topics. Now our examination moves from Homer's art in arranging the sequence of his words to his skill in linking the succession of his scenes, and then on to how Aeschylus drives home his meaning by his use of meter (i.e., music and dance) and how Roman poets use the quite different features of the Latin language for their own poetic purposes. Since most Classics teachers are involved with all the authors I discuss, I hope they will read through the whole volume; but the chapters can be read independently if desired.

Though I hope that the following chapters make a scholarly contribution to their topics, I am in the first instance aiming at a readership of Classics professors at large who teach Greek and Latin literature to undergraduates—who spend much of their working lives teaching students to translate ancient poetry in class. There are still many of them in the United States, especially in the numerous liberal arts colleges of Ohio and Virginia. This kind of work is characteristic of our discipline, and essential for training the future teachers who will ensure its continuance; and—though possibly ranking below the cultural, political, and social lessons that should be drawn from the ancient Greek and Latin civilizations—the education of students in the immense possibilities of language is an important part of the value of the study of Classics. The most enjoyable part of my own past teaching experience has been reading and translating classical authors, both Greek and Latin, with undergraduates, and my research and scholarly reading have both contributed to this work and profited from it. If the content of this volume seems polymorphous and disconnected—"And now for something completely different"—it is partly because much of it arises from my past teaching assignments, the daily kaleidoscopic workload that we classicists enjoy.

I hope that my approach to the three authors (and the two languages, besides English) I focus on in this book will refresh readers' insights into these and similar texts and give them renewed interest in showing their students *how to translate*—how best both to understand the intonations and implications of the original language and to see why it can be so difficult to reproduce it in the different norms of English idiom. Most university Classics teachers, in their careers from teaching assistant to full professor, seldom discuss their everyday classroom word-for-word-translation experience with their peers, and it is not often that a student produces an insight into the intent of the author's wording that gives the teacher a new idea. New ideas and renewed excitement is what I hope to inspire in this volume.

For the same purpose, that of augmenting and perhaps reinvigorating the teaching of Greek and Latin authors in the original language, I have included a good many illustrations from English literature, in particular to show Tennyson's adoption of Homeric style and word order and the effective use of the rhythms of ancient lyric meters by some twentieth-century poets. I think such parallels provide a good means of familiarizing students with the classical models—and probably of improving their knowledge of English literature, too. Examples like these are further elaborated in the appendixes, which include material extending the main subjects that I think could be both interesting and useful to a teacher.

I also hope that to some extent the points I make here may be of interest to nonclassicists, and to that end I have translated Greek and Latin quotations, except in a few cases where an understanding of the original is essential for the argument. Such readers may well be more aware of the short-comings in my knowledge of English literature than of any contribution I make to its appreciation, but many well-known authors, past and present, have had a familiarity with classical literature far surpassing that of some modern-day critics, and can be better valued if the qualities they observed (knowingly or not) in ancient writers are better known.

These chapters were first written in a style suitable for public lectures, and in refashioning them for publication I have added footnotes and made a number of other changes. Sometimes, however, I think something of my lecturing manner may have survived, and I hope this more personal touch will not be found offensive.

I am grateful to the Martin Classical Lectures Committee of Oberlin College, and to the members of the Oberlin Classics Department, for inviting me to give the Lectures in 1998 and for their generous hospitality during the week I visited their campus. In producing this volume, my old friend Tom Van Nortwick has given me very valuable support and criticism, and Jim Helm has helped me with Princeton University Press. Thorough, useful, and constructive comments on my text (at various stages) have been made by John Heath, Edward Spofford, Thomas Van Nortwick, and Oberlin's anonymous reader, and I am very much in their debt. Professor Charles O. Hartman and the late Professor John F. Nims were very helpful in answering my queries about their work, and my colleagues Andrew Devine and Paul Kiparsky gave me generous assistance with relevant parts of their own research.

The content of chapter 1 owes much to the research of Professor Egbert J. Bakker; chapter 2 to the work of Professor Scott Richardson; chapter 3 to the long-ago lectures of the late Professor H.D.F. Kitto, my teacher when I was an undergraduate at Bristol University (though he would not have agreed with some of my basic principles); and chapter 4 to the insights of the late Craig A. Manning, who as an undergraduate at Brown University in my first years of teaching taught me more about Latin poetry than I ever taught him.

A modified version of the Aeschylus chapter was given as the Carl Deppe Memorial Lecture at the University of California at Santa Cruz on 22 April 1999. I am grateful to those who chose to honor me with this invitation.

The book's epigraph is taken from a typewritten card I used to see in my early years of teaching at Brown on the door of my then-colleague C. Arthur Lynch. I never asked him its origin. It means: "You want to learn? Then teach. Give, if you wish to receive."

SOUND, SENSE, AND RHYTHM

Chapter One

HOMER I: POETRY AND SPEECH

Mostly, we *read* the Homeric epics; despite the existence of modern recordings, few of us *listen* to them. In the last seventy years, scholars have devoted a great deal of time to studying the poems as oral *compositions*, but—as the term suggests—have very largely concentrated their investigations on the techniques by which poems of such metrical complexity and length could be composed and adjusted to the occasions of performance. Not much attention has been paid to the listeners, and what demands were imposed on *them* by the need to understand the recitations, what capacities they had to employ if they were in any way to appreciate the enormous depth of artistic skill that we readers identify in Homer.

Yet two great advances made about seventy years ago much improved our understanding of what the characteristics of oral poetry meant to the listener, as well as to the singer. Only quite recently, however, has this become clear. The two scholars responsible for the older discoveries, Hermann Fränkel and Milman Parry, though unaware of each other's work, shared a common and largely original insight: that Homer's verse should be analyzed into larger units than dactyls and spondees, and his sentences should be analyzed into larger units than words. And now, within the last fifteen or twenty years, there have been two other advances, in the field of linguistics, that have provided a much better theoretical understanding than we had before of why this is the case. They have revealed that the now-well-known compositional techniques of the oral poet not only provide the resources for the singer to present a song adapted to the occasion of performance: they are also developed so that the song will be as accessible as possible to the listening audience.

In what follows I first quickly explain the "larger units" upon which Hermann Fränkel in 1926 and Milman Parry in 1928 focused attention. Then I describe the two more recent and less-well-known theories I mentioned. Finally, I demonstrate the advantages of emphasizing this kind of approach to Homer by commenting in detail on one passage from the *Iliad*—not a well-known speech or a highly wrought emotional scene, but one of the descriptions of Achilles' battles soon after his return to the fighting. Battle scenes are sometimes neglected, because there are so many of them, and because their brutality may discourage and perhaps disgust the modern reader; but just as Homer lavishes all his poetic powers on the speeches of his hero Achilles, so, if one pays proper attention, his account of Achilles' battles, too, brings before our eyes the superb skills of this greatest of poets.

THE OLDER DISCOVERIES: FRÄNKEL AND PARRY

In 1926 Hermann Fränkel published a monumental article in a German periodical[1] demonstrating that the Homeric hexameter should be viewed not simply as a succession of six metrical feet, heavy and light syllables arranged as dactyls (DUM DE DE) or spondees (DUM DUM), but as a series of four (or occasionally just three) word groups whose syllables certainly add up to a hexameter, but which should be regarded as entities separated by word-end and often by a pause in sense.[2] This means a typical hexameter might be DUM DE DE DUM (word break) DE DE DUM DE (word break) DE DUM DE DE (word break) DUM DE DE DUM DUM (verse-end)—or (with some dactyls replaced by spondees) οὐλομένην ἢ μυρί᾽ Ἀχαιοῖς ἄλγε᾽ ἔθηκε (Iliad 1.2). The four units in this example include interior word breaks as well, but the sense pauses (often the punctuation points) would fall *between* the units, not *within* them. Occasionally a verse occurs that illustrates this by presenting strong and obvious breaks between each of the units, as in ἀλλὰ σοί, ὦ μέγ᾽ ἀναιδές, ἅμ᾽ ἑσπόμεθ᾽, ὄφρα σὺ χαίρῃς (Iliad 1.158:[3] "But you—you shameless thing—we followed you, to do you a favor"). It is highly significant that all the units are of different metrical shapes—a vital matter for avoiding monotony—and, of course, further variety is added both because the units in other verses will be different in shape from those given in the example, and because each group of two light syllables may be replaced by a single heavy one.

Here is a further illustration, from a couplet that will concern us again later. In the second book of the *Iliad*, after Agamemnon finishes addressing the assembly, the Greek troops move off and fix themselves a meal, which as always includes a sacrifice. Then come the lines (*Iliad* 2.402–403):

αὐτὰρ ὃ βοῦν ἱέρευσε ἄναξ ἀνδρῶν Ἀγαμέμνων
πίονα πενταέτηρον ὑπερμενέϊ Κρονίωνι.

[1] *Göttinger Nachrichten* (1926), 197–229, revised in Fränkel 1968b: 100–156. Fränkel's ideas are easily accessible in G. S. Kirk's "The Structural Elements of Homeric Verse" (Kirk 1985: 17–37, esp. 19–20). Note, however, that Kirk's designations (ibid.: 18) of the three main word breaks (A; M, F; B) differ rather confusingly from those of Fränkel (1968b: 104; A; B; C), which are normally used.

[2] Fränkel calls the dividing points "sense breaks" (*Sinneneinschnitte*), characterizing them as "strong" or "weak" (Fränkel 1968b: 103–104). G. S. Kirk says, "The cola are not therefore units of meaning, although they tend to comprise organic word-groups" (1985: 19), but I do not understand what distinction he is making here.

[3] This example is used in Edwards 1966: 118 and Kirk 1985: 22. The punctuation is that of Allen's Oxford Classical Text (1920); the breathing on ἑσπόμεθ᾽ follows West 1998: xvii.

The orthodox prose translation is, "But Agamemnon, king of men, slew a fat bull of five years to the son of Cronos, supreme in might."[4] If we follow the examples Fränkel gives (1968b: 112–113), we would divide the lines into word groups like this:

αὐτὰρ ὃ | βοῦν ἱέρευσε | ἄναξ ἀνδρῶν | Ἀγαμέμνων
πίονα | πενταέτηρον | ὑπερμενέϊ | Κρονίωνι.

Most of the breaks are obvious, and they divide the sentence into separate sense-units. In the first half of the first verse, however, there is a problem—should the break fall before or after βοῦν?—and in such cases it is best not to force the issue but (as Kirk pointed out, 1985: 19) to take the half-verse as a virtually continuous whole. We might note (though this is surely accidental) that the two verses are similar in rhythm, each composed of the different metrical units *DUM DE DE   DUM DE DE DUM DE   DE DUM DUM DUM* (or *DE DUM DE DE DUM*)   *DE DE DUM DE.*

In the past I have tried to give nonclassicists an idea of the effect of Homeric verse, when looked at in this way, by quoting Longfellow's "Hiawatha."[5] If one runs two "Hiawatha" verses together, they add up to something roughly like a Greek hexameter in length, divided by three heavy word breaks and sense pauses into four parts, each usually *DUM DE DUM DE:*

Shoúld yoù ásk mè, | whénce thèse stóriès? | Whénce thèse légènds | ànd tràdítiòns,
Wìth thè ódoùrs | òf thè fórèst, | Wìth thè déw ànd | dámp òf meádòws,
Wìth thè cúrlìng | smóke òf wígwàms, | Wìth thè rúshìng | òf gréat rívèrs . . .

(Here and elsewhere I use an acute accent to mark a stressed syllable, a grave to mark an unstressed one.[6]) The replacement of a heavy syllable by a light one does little to vary the movement—particularly as many readers might tend to maintain the metrical stress and hear (for instance), "Wìth thè ódoùrs | óf thè fórèst. . . ." Only occasionally is there a noticeable reversal of stress, as above in ". . . òf gréat rívèrs," or the running over of a word from one unit to the next, as in:

Wìth theìr fréquènt | répètítiòns, | Ànd theìr wíld rè- | vérbèrátiòns . . .

---

[4] Version of A. T. Murray in the Loeb Classics series (London and New York, 1928). E. V. Rieu in the 1950 Penguin Classics translation brings out the emphasis rather better: "King Agamemnon himself sacrificed a fatted five-year-old ox to the almighty Son of Cronos."

[5] In Edwards 1987: 45–49.

[6] More on these markings in chapter 3, note 9. I would disagree with T. Steel's suggestion (Baker 1996: 242) that in such verses as the last, Longfellow would have wished us to follow regular scansion (cf. R. Wallace, in ibid.: 336–337).

This meter soon becomes monotonous, because so many of Longfellow's component metrical units and sense units have (or are liable to be forced into) the same rhythm, *DUM DE DUM DE*. This trochaic meter is very natural to English ("a staple of English prosody," says J. F. Nims, referring to Poe's eighteen-stanza "The Raven" as well as "Hiawatha," Baker 1996: 193) and is very easy to compose: anyone, with little effort, knowing nothing about rhythm, can go rambling on forever in this free and easy meter. But the Homeric Greek hexameter is very different, because of its constant variation. Usually, like Longfellow's verses when quoted in pairs, it has a pause in the middle; but the position can vary by a syllable either way, which changes the length of the two adjacent metrical units. More than this: again as with the doubled Longfellow verses, the Greek hexameter often has two further pauses, one in each half of the verse, but their position varies a good deal, and sometimes they are not present (or at least not noticeable) at all. Here are the first few verses of the passage I shall be discussing later (*Iliad* 20.455–59), divided by pauses into the kinds of unit identified by Fränkel:[7]

ὣς εἰπὼν | Δρύοπ' οὖτα | κατ' αὐχένα μέσσον | ἄκοντι· | 455
ἤριπε δὲ | προπάροιθε ποδῶν· | ὃ δὲ τὸν μὲν | ἔασε, |
Δημοῦχον δὲ | Φιλητορίδην | ἠΰν τε μέγαν τε |
κὰγ γόνυ | δουρὶ βαλὼν | ἠρύκακε. | τὸν μὲν ἔπειτα |
οὐτάζων | ξίφει μεγάλῳ | ἐξαίνυτο θυμόν. |

Translated into English in the same rhythm, substituting stressed and unstressed syllables for the heavy and light syllables of the Greek (and retaining as far as possible the same word order, if necessary in violation of the normal idiom), this becomes:[8]

Speakíng só, | hè hìt Drýòps, | hìt straíght ìn thè gúllèt |
    bỳ speárpoínt; | 455
Fállèn hè láy | òn thè groúnd àt hìs feét; | ànd hè léft hìm |
    tò líe thére; |
Démūchús thèn, | Phìlétòr's yoùng heír— | goód fíghtèr, gìgántíc— |
Kneé bèing | strúck wìth thè speár— | héld fást wàs hè; | thén tò thè
    néxt mán, |
Woúndíng hím | wìth hìs pówèrfùl swórd | hé tóre oùt hìs spírìt. |

The first line consists of four differently shaped units, the third of which is longer than usual and the last of which is shorter (in fact, a break between αὐχένα and μέσσον would be normal, but the two words go together in

---

[7] Some scholars might omit a few of the breaks I have indicated.

[8] I admit to lots of infelicities in this, but I hope it is worth it to make the point for the Greekless. In particular, I know it is not very natural to stress the second syllable of "speaking" (and not that of "being"), and that "young" is a heavy word to leave unstressed (would the lighter "kìd heír" have been more acceptable?).

sense); the second is questionable (the feminine caesura (i.e., a word break between the two light syllables of a dactyl) traditionally identified between προπάροιθε and ποδῶν splits two words connected in sense, and ὃ δὲ τὸν μὲν ἔασε might be taken as one unit or two); the third unarguably falls into three units, not four, with the usual word break in the middle bridged by the long patronymic;[9] the fourth has four units, all of them of a different shape from any occurring in the previous lines, and a strong break before the fourth unit (at the bucolic diaeresis, a word break before the fifth dactyl); and the last verse again is formed of three units only, the midpoint of the verse falling at the break between the two closely connected words ξίφεϊ μεγάλῳ, "with his sword [the] powerful [one]."

Note also that the stronger pauses in these five verses, as marked with English punctuation by the editor of the Greek text, fall at different positions: the first at verse-end; the next a little after the midpoint of the second verse (at the caesura or word break in the fourth foot) closely followed by another at verse-end; the next comes late in the fourth verse (at the bucolic diaeresis); the last at verse-end again. I think it is seldom realized that this continual change in the positions of the major and minor pauses in sense, which constantly alters the shape of the component units (and hence the rhythm), and the location of the breaks between clauses and sentences, contributes much more to the variety of the Homeric line than the admission of either dactyls or spondees in the first four feet (and the occasional spondee in the fifth). Homer's listeners would not have experienced the monotony that might well afflict those exposed to Longfellow's seldom-changing cadences.

Fränkel's work was apparently not known to Milman Parry, studying a few years later in Paris, but Parry discovered the same divisions in the Homeric hexameter while developing his own enormously important contribution: the demonstration of the prevalence and dominance of the "formulas," the traditional systems of expression in Homer, especially the combinations of proper names with epithets. This need not be recapitulated in detail here; most classicists accept that whether Achilles is described as "brilliant," "swift-footed," or "Peleus' son" in one of Lattimore's lines depends on the metrical circumstances of the particular Homeric verse, not on the physical or emotional circumstances of the hero.[10] Here it need only be noted that the formulas or conventional expressions in Homer fall between the sense pauses just mentioned—after all, they naturally begin and end at sense breaks.

[9] On such "threefolders," see Kirk 1985: 20–24; and Minton 1975: 33–34.

[10] See (for instance) the articles by E. Bakker, M. W. Edwards, and J. Russo in Morris and Powell 1997; Hainsworth 1993: 1–31; and A. Parry's introduction to Parry 1971. Russo (Morris and Powell 1997: 253–254) discusses some critics of Parry's theories, to whom Shive (1987) may be added (see reviews of this work, e.g., by G. Nagy in *Phoenix* 42 [1988]: 364–366).

Through Parry's eyes, our demonstration couplet at *Iliad* 402–403 would look like this:

αὐτὰρ ὃ βοῦν ἱέρευσε ἄναξ ἀνδρῶν Ἀγαμέμνων
πίονα πενταέτηρον ὑπερμενέϊ Κρονίωνι.

This is following Parry's technique, in his archetypal analysis of formulae in *Iliad* and *Odyssey* 1–25, of marking word groups that recur unchanged by a solid underline and using a dotted underline for "phrases which are of the same type as others . . . limit[ing] the type to . . . those in which not only the metre and the parts of speech are the same, but in which also at least one important word or group of words is identical."[11] In the first line we note that its first half recurs with slight modifications (and again followed by a noun-epithet formula) at *Iliad* 7.314 and *Odyssey* 13.24, and that its second half is the standard name-epithet formula for Agamemnon when the second half of the verse is to be filled. The second verse recurs at *Iliad* 7.315 with the minor change of ἄρσενα ("male") for πίονα ("fat").[12] The concluding phrase ὑπερμενέϊ Κρονίωνι is also a name-epithet formula in the dative, recurring four times in *Iliad* in this case and twice in the accusative. For both name-epithet formulas, the "economy" that was one of Parry's most significant discoveries is observed—no alternative word group for this character in this metrical position and in this grammatical case is found.[13]

Longfellow of course discovered proper-name formulas, too, and he invented the same kind as the Greek tradition provided for Homer (remember, he spoke of "stories . . . with their frequent repetitions"). Thus the name "Hiawatha" fits neatly within one of Longfellow's metrical units (i.e., between the sense pauses), and so do "Minnehaha," "Mudjekeewis," and others; some other names are padded to fit by adding an epithet, like "*old* Nokomis" and "*lazy* Kwasind," or expanded to cover two units, like "Gitche Manito the Mighty" and "Chibiabos the musician." So Longfellow constructed passages like:

Thus it was that | Hiawatha | to the lodge of | old Nokomis |
Brought the moonlight, | starlight, firelight, | brought the sunshine | of his people, |
Minnehaha, | Laughing Water, | handsomest of | all the women |

[11] Parry 1971: 301–304 (quotation from 301).

[12] Actually πίονα πενταέτηρον and ἄρσενα π. also occur at verse-end (*Odyssey* 14.419, 19.420), but Parry's restricted definition of a formula, stipulating that the word group must be employed "*under the same metrical conditions*" (Parry 1971: 272), would not include these instances; a better guide is now Hainsworth 1993: 1–31.

[13] Though when an initial consonant is required for "Zeus" in the dative, there exist the alternatives κελαινεφέϊ Κρονίωνι (three times in the *Iliad*) and Διὶ Κρονίωνι ἄνακτι (four times in the *Iliad*). On such "good and bad formulae," see J. B. Hainsworth in Fenik 1978: 41–50, and on "economy" and violations of it, Hainsworth 1993: 24–26.

In the land of | the Dakotahs, | in the land of | handsome women. |

In the Greek, such formulas occur mainly in the second half of the verse, where the pauses tend to fall at more regular positions.

Since the focus here is on word units and word positioning in Homeric verse, there is no need to summarize the later extension and development of Parry's theories by his student Albert Lord in particular.[14] The world of classical scholarship was slow in applying—or in some cases even acknowledging—Parry's work, and it was more than thirty-five years before study was made of the ways in which the formulas that Parry had identified and studied corresponded to the divisions in the hexameter identified by Hermann Fränkel. In 1966 this was done, independently, in articles published by G. S. Kirk and myself.[15] Kirk compared the metrical units with the units of sense, finding a good many discrepancies. He also studied the "internal stops" and "enjambment" (runover of sentence and sense from one verse to the next) in Book 16 of the *Iliad*, emphasizing—this is particularly relevant to the development of the analyses discussed here—that very often Homer "sings a verse potentially complete in itself, then he qualifies or adds to it in a succeeding verse connected by progressive enjambment. . . . Each new piece of information, as the story proceeds, can be envisaged as being heaped upon its predecessor" (Kirk 1966b: 114). My own article took a different approach, studying in turn the word groups that begin the Homeric verse or occur as the second, third, and fourth units in it, and identifying the most common units of *meaning* (such as proper names, adjectives, dependent nouns in the genitive, appositional phrases, and so on) that tend to fall within each of the *metrical* units established by Fränkel's pauses in the verse. This naturally led me to the sense units and metrical units presented by Parry's formulas, and not surprisingly I found that they were the same as Fränkel's: Parry's traditional compositional units fitted between Fränkel's pauses in the verse, just as did the other sense groups.

I also noted that in Homer a given sense unit, such as a clause, or a phrase, or an adjective and a following noun in agreement, is not usually divided between two verses, as often happens in (for instance) Virgil; and that even where a sentence runs over from one verse to the next (i.e., enjambment occurs[16]), there is rarely an actual *overlapping* of sense—one or more component units of the sentence, such as subject, object, verb, has already been completed before the verse-end, so that the listener knows where he stands in the sentence even if it is not yet complete. (Homer's style is very far removed from "Of Man's first disobedience, and the fruit | of that forbidden

---

[14] Post-Parry work is summarized in Edwards 1986–1988.

[15] Kirk 1966a and 1966b; Edwards 1966.

[16] Much work has been done on enjambment in Homer since that time; see especially Higbie 1990; Clark 1997 and 1994.

tree, whose mortal taste | . . . ," and so on for another four verses before we reach Milton's first main verb, "Sing!") It also became obvious that a word in the runover position, that is, standing in the initial place in the verse but syntactically connected with the preceding verse and followed by a strong pause, usually received strong emphasis.[17] This is in fact often the case with any verse-initial word, even if it begins or is in the middle of its sentence.[18]

I attributed these Homeric phenomena both to the poet's technique of composition, his fitting the component blocks between the usual pauses in the hexameter, and to his development of an easy sequence of thought, because of his consideration for the hearer's powers of comprehension. Forty years earlier, S. E. Bassett had said much the same in an article on runover words, speaking of Homer's "*civilité*" or "courtesy," by which he "minimizes the listener's intellectual effort, and leaves his soul free to find a more purely artistic pleasure in the poetry," as well as his "continuity," by which "the interlacing of Homer's ideas is so nearly perfect, and at the same time so unobtrusive, that no part of the reader's attention is lost by the effort required to bridge even a slight chasm of thought."[19] My own comments (in 1966) on our test couplet αὐτὰρ ὁ βοῦν ἱέρευσε ἄναξ ἀνδρῶν Ἀγαμέμνων | πίονα πενταέτηρον ὑπερμενέϊ Κρονίωνι, besides of course noting that the breaks between Fränkel's word groups and Parry's formulas coincided, would have been that as usual in Homer the basic sense becomes clear early in the sentence (subject, verb, and object: "He sacrificed a bull"), and the elaboration (". . . a fat one . . . to . . . Kronos") is added later; that the initial adjective πίονα in the second verse is significant (acclaiming the animal and Agamemnon's munificence), though not technically a "runover" word, since it is not followed by a strong pause or the commonly following exegesis (as, for example, οὐλομένην, ἣ μυρί᾽ Ἀχαιοῖς . . . , *Iliad* 1.2); that the technique of using an adjective to fill the second block of the verse (like πενταέτηρον here) is very common; and that the employment or omission of a formulaic epithet like ὑπερμενέϊ in the third block of the verse is common (though actually Κρονίωνι and Κρονίωνα are not found in the final position without a preceding epithet, except in Hesiod).[20] I would also have noted that, though formulaic, the adjectives and name-epithet phrase in the second verse add a significant meaning, emphasizing the superior nature of the sacrifice. From this viewpoint, once again an examination of the structure and sequence of the sentence reveals how easy it is for a listener to follow and appreciate the sense.

---

[17] Edwards 1966: 138–148.
[18] I have given some examples of this in Edwards 1991: 42–44.
[19] Bassett 1926: 126, 144, 145.
[20] καθεζομένη Κρονίωνι (*Works and Days* 259). Cf. Edwards 1966: 138–144, 149–152, 159.

THE NEW THEORIES: FUNCTIONAL GRAMMAR
AND THE GRAMMAR OF SPEECH

Despite the advent of computers, after 1966 nothing much happened to our knowledge of Homeric word order for some time. Meanwhile, new theories about language were developing. One, known as Functional Grammar or Pragmatics, was developed primarily by Dutch scholars, especially Simon Dik in a book first published in 1978; the other, the grammar of spoken language, was developed primarily by the American scholar Wallace Chafe in the late 1970s and 1980s. Functional Grammar conceives of language as "in the first place an instrument of social interaction between human beings, used with the primary aim of establishing communicative relations between speakers and addressees."[21] From my point of view, its essential contribution is in studying the word order in a sentence: instead of starting from the traditional elements of syntax—Subject, Verb, Object, or Subject, Object, Verb, or whatever sequence seems to appear most often in the language in question—it focuses on the function or use of the parts of a sentence, on what purpose they are serving *in their context*. As a result, instead of grammatical categories like subject and object, a sentence is analyzed according to its presentation of: what is already in the minds of the speaker and the addressee (the "Topic"); what new information is given about it in this particular sentence (the "Focus"); and whatever else is left over (the "Remainder," including predictable items and elements that point forward to the following sentence). When I say: "Functional Grammar analyzes a sentence pragmatically," the "Topic" of the sentence is "Functional Grammar," which is what both you and I already know we are talking about; "analyzes a sentence" is the verb or predicate, again containing nothing very surprising; and "pragmatically" is the Focus, the new information about Functional Grammar that the sentence is communicating from me to you.

In English, a clause usually begins with the Topic (sometimes preceded by a question word, a relative pronoun, or the like); then comes the verb; and the new information, the Focus, usually comes at the end.[22] In Greek, this is not the case. For Greek prose, the work of H. Dik on word order in Herodotus, based on this approach, suggests—this will not surprise those who have taught Greek prose composition—that the fundamental word order is: Topic, Focus, Verb (if it is not Topic or Focus), Remainder.[23] So in ancient Greek, the normal word order would be not "Functional Grammar analyzes a sentence pragmatically," as we noted above for English, but

---

[21] S. C. Dik 1981: 1.
[22] For more details, see Hannay 1991.
[23] H. Dik 1995.

the equivalent of "Functional Grammar *pragmatically* analyzes a sentence"—and we remember our Homeric demonstration sentence began αὐτὰρ ὃ βοῦν ἱέρευσε, with the stressed word "bull" in second place (after the Topic "But he . . ."), in contrast with the normal English word order "But he sacrificed a *bull*." Using the Functional Grammar approach, we can observe how far Homer seems to be following the normal ancient Greek pattern of emphasis.

The second innovation in linguistic studies, related to Functional Grammar, is the study of the grammar of spoken language. In a series of articles beginning in the early 1970s and a book published in 1994, Wallace Chafe, working not from written texts but from tape-recorded spoken narrative and conversations, suggests that first in consciousness, then in speech, discourse appears in chunks, each containing only one new piece of information together with an orientation point to indicate where it fits. (This is, of course, much like the identification of a clause's Focus and Topic.[24]) These chunks Chafe calls "idea units"; and these in turn, for both physical and intellectual reasons, are verbalized in "spurts," and appear in speech as what he calls "intonation units," usually separated by pauses. Consciousness, says Chafe, both that of the speaker and that of a listener, can only focus on one idea at a time; and (again like the Functional Grammar people) he investigates carefully the extent to which information is new, or has already been shared between speaker and listener about the subject in question (and is therefore already active or semi-active in their minds), and the effects that this has upon the words used and the word-order sequence. Chafe refers to the syntactical subject (coming first, in English) as the "point of departure," and defines a "light subject constraint," that is, the subject has a light information load (there's nothing very new about it); and these, of course, are also the characteristics of the "Topic" (normally in the initial position) of Functional Grammar. He also speaks of a "one new idea constraint," pointing out that an intonation unit usually conveys only one new idea, and this is usually in the predicate, which makes it correspond to the "Focus" element of the Functionalists.

For Homerists, the final highly significant step was taken by Egbert Bakker in an article published in 1990.[25] He pointed out that study of the grammar of spoken language was highly relevant to the orally delivered poems of Homer, and applied Chafe's insights to the Homeric text. Bakker proposed to "accept the ultimate linguistic and cognitive consequences of what it means to speak of oral poetry," and went on to "resort to modern linguistic research on orality outside the sphere of Homeric philology or

---

[24] See Chafe 1994: 53–70, 108–119; H. Dik 1995: 24; Slings 1997: 194.

[25] Bakker 1990 (quotations in this paragraph are from p. 2). He has followed up on this in a series of valuable articles and a recent book (Bakker 1997a).

even oral poetry." He noted that what I called in my 1966 article the "component units" of the sentence, which are not divided by the end of the verse, are in fact the "chunks," the "idea units" and "intonation units," of Chafe and the Functionalists. Bakker has placed a foundation of up-to-date theory beneath facts that had been *observed* previously but not properly *explained.*[26]

Bakker shows that the intonation units of spoken discourse correspond to the metrical units of Homeric verse; the pauses or caesurae in the Homeric hexameter, identified in 1926 by Fränkel, are similar to the pauses that continually interrupt our spoken language—in his own words, "The segmentation of Homeric discourse, as evidenced by the length of the linguistic units of which it consists, can be seen as the manifestation in speech of the flow of the speaker's consciousness, each unit being the verbalization of a focus of consciousness. The length and duration of the units fits the acoustic short-term memory of the performer, or in other words, that ability to process linguistic expressions as wholes."[27] The traditional Homeric formulas also appear in a new light, as "stylized intonation units." This enables us to see better *why* the pauses that mark off the units fall where they do, and to understand this not just as the poet's following of tradition and routine, but as the result of his desire to communicate orally with his audience in the most effective way possible. Bakker has, I think, made us understand for the first time what the well-worn expression "oral poetry" really signifies.

It was Bakker who made good use of the *Iliad* couplet we have been using to demonstrate different approaches to Homeric verse.[28] In contrast to the normal English prose order of "Agamemnon, lord of men, sacrificed a fat ox, five years old, to the almighty son of Kronos,"[29] Bakker's rendering of our αὐτὰρ ὁ βοῦν ἱέρευσε ἄναξ ἀνδρῶν Ἀγαμέμνων | πίονα πενταέτηρον ὑπερμενέϊ Κρονίωνι follows the sequence of the word groups (or intonation units) of the Greek, and runs, "But he, he sacrificed a bull, ruler of men Agamemnon, fat, five years old, to the all-mighty son of Kronos." Adding a little more continuity and word-order emphasis, this might become, "But *he* sacrificed a *bull*, Lord Agamemnon did—a fat one, five years old, to the almighty son of Kronos." This is obviously conversational English, an exact parallel to "He's a nice chap, your brother is"—and much more vivid and vital than the usual prose translations: this is the way a bard would address

---

[26] The classical linguistics scholars Andrew Devine and Laurence Stephens did the same kind of thing for our understanding of the structure of the hexameter (Devine and Stephens 1984).

[27] Bakker 1997a: 52. He gives an example in Bakker 1999: 39–40. See also Bakker 1997b and 1997c.

[28] Bakker 1997a: 92, 95. He quotes many such examples.

[29] Translation of M. Hammond (Penguin ed. [Harmondsworth, 1987], 29).

his audience, the kind of rendering one could read aloud to students and hope to keep them awake.

Agamemnon is already in our minds (i.e., he is the Topic), since he has been speaking in the assembly, and so ὅ, "he," serves to refer to him and stands first. The bull is the Focus, because this is the new, significant information—the ordinary troops would have poured libations or sacrificed smaller creatures—so βοῦν falls in the second place in Greek (and at the end of the main clause in English). The verb, "sacrificed," again is already in our minds, because that's what all the troops have been doing, so it falls in the unemphatic place—at the end of the clause in Greek, in the middle in English. Finally, the conventional name-epithet formula ἄναξ ἀνδρῶν Ἀγαμέμνων, "Lord Agamemnon," is what in Functional Grammar is called the "Tail," like "your brother" in the English equivalent. Then, now that we have the facts straight, come the details, the qualities—and hence the great importance—of the offering to the supreme god. The matter is properly dignified, epic, and religious; but the style is *conversational*, or oral.[30]

The new understanding given by these two theories can be illustrated by a simple example. An accomplished Homeric scholar recently sent me the draft of an article he was preparing, in which the first words of *Iliad* 6.460, "Ἕκτορος ἥδε γυνή . . ." (literally "'Hector's this the wife'"), were translated "This was the wife of Hector" (the words are those of Hector himself, telling his wife Andromache the kind of thing people will say of her when, after his own death and the fall of Troy, she has become a slave). Classicists in general would see no problem with this translation. But at that time I was working on significant word order in Horace (to be taken up in chapter 4), and my ideas were dominated by the notion that the sequence of ideas in a translated version should be, as closely as possible, the same as that in the original language, so that each new thought should reach the listener or reader in the same order as it reached the original speaker's intended audience. So I objected to the way in which this translation, "This was the wife of Hector," had shifted Hector's name from first to last position in the phrase. Then I reflected further, and I realized that in fact the translation was correct: because in Greek (as Functional Grammar has shown), the Focus, the new information that a speaker wishes to convey to a listener—in this case, the heroic stature of this particular slave-woman's dead husband—is put early in the sentence, normally in second place after an initial reference to the general Topic of discourse already known to both of them. In the present instance, the Topic is not expressed, but is clearly understood by the two onlookers as they both look at the passing woman, and is picked up by the demonstrative pronoun ἥδε, "this [woman]." So the new infor-

---

[30] The origin of these characteristics of Homeric style is discussed in Devine and Stephens 1999: 206–209.

mation,"Εκτορος, "Hector's," comes first in the sentence. But in English, the new information is normally reserved for the *end* of the sentence. (Cf. the immediately preceding sentence!) So it can well be argued that the emphasis of "'Εκτορος ἧδε γυνή . . .'" is very properly preserved in English in, "'This was the wife of *Hector*.'"[31] It only remains to add that in English the Focus is occasionally put at the start of the sentence, for special emphasis,[32] and so an English onlooker might well say, as the slave-woman walked by with her water-pot, "*Hector's* wife, that is" (adding what is in Functional Grammar called a "Tail," "that is," the sentence paralleling Dik's example "He's a nice chap, *your brother*"[33]). So this short phrase shows that in translating, and a fortiore in appreciating, Greek poetry, we must be conscious not only of the sequence of ideas presented, but also of the different positions for stressed (i.e., new) information in Greek and in English, and always of the fact that Homer, drama, and much other Greek poetry was intended to be heard, not read from the page.

[31] Though I have not seen any explicit mention of it in the considerable number of articles I have read on the art of translation, this essential difference in the nature of the ancient Greek and the English languages, the one normally placing new information in the second position in the sentence, the other at its end, automatically makes it hard or impossible to achieve both the same *emphasis* and the same *sequence* in transmission of ideas in the two languages. This must often be the unacknowledged—and perhaps unrealized—cause of a translator's difficulties. (It must be a constant problem for simultaneous translators of spoken modern languages.) I have not been able to find a discussion of this in George Steiner's *After Babel: Aspects of Language and Translation* (2d ed., Oxford, 1992), but I have not checked the bibliographical material in the massive footnote on his p. 126. M. Clark in his appendix on "Problems of Translation" (Clark 1997: 239–248) has a good treatment of translators' problems with enjambing (runover) words, and some others, but does not go into this point. None of the contributors to Brower 1966a, though they cover many angles—philosophical and linguistic, as well as practical—of the topic of translation, mentions word order or position emphasis.

It is noteworthy that by instinct, Tennyson might change the natural Greek word order to the natural English one, using Homeric verses like τὴν δὲ μέγ' ὀχθήσας προσέφη νεφεληγερέτα Ζεύς (*Iliad* 1.517, etc.: Focus words second in order) as a model for his "To whom replied King Arthur, *much in wrath*" (*Morte d'Arthur* 118, Focus words italicized at end; see below).

[32] See Hannay 1991: 147. In passing, I might note that placing the Focus *first* in the sentence is the hallmark of one of the best-known contrived violations of normal English word order, flourishing in the early years of *Time* magazine ("Into family chapels went he, robbery of the dead intent upon"—parodied by Wolcott Gibbs in his profile of Henry Luce in a 1936 *New Yorker*, "Backward ran sentences until reeled the mind"). Virginia Woolf allowed herself a similar mannerism, presumably liking the effect: "He had thrown himself from a window. Up had flashed the ground" (*Mrs. Dalloway*, [Harcourt Brace, 1997], 200); "Gravely sounded the voices; wisely the organ replied"; "Dim was the cow parsley in the meadows"; "Listless is the air in an empty room"; "Melancholy were the sounds on a winter's night"; "Violent was the wind now rushing down" (*Jacob's Room*, pp. 29, 35, 36, 51, 152 in the Penguin edition [Harmondsworth, 1965]).

[33] S. Dik 1981: 153. In written English, the "Tail" is usually set off by a preceding comma, as here.

HOMERIC STYLE IN TENNYSON'S *MORTE D'ARTHUR*

Our better understanding of where the new information is normally posi-
tioned in an ancient Greek sentence, and of the nature of the intonation
units of speech (and hence of the metrical and formulaic units of Homeric
verse), leaves us with a better realization of why Homeric word order is the
way it is, and a greater opportunity to appreciate the emphasis and tone of
a phrase or sentence. But there is another hugely important element to be
taken into consideration when we analyze the text of Homer, which may
overrule the practices of ordinary speech: the Homeric hexameter verse,
and how sentences are fitted within it. The beginning and end of each verse
are immediately noticeable, whether to hearer or reader, and words placed
at those points may receive special emphasis for that reason; enjambment—
the running over of sentence and sense from one verse to the next—may
derive great importance by exploiting this possibility of stressing words that
are in mid-sentence but at verse-initial or verse-final position; and the additional strong pauses in sense that frequently occur not at the end of a verse
but within it (see above), create a constant interplay of rhythm and sense
that is characteristic of Homer (but usually lacking in Longfellow!).[34] This
can best be made clear, I think, not by description but by illustration, and
fortunately there exists an English poem that provides a fine example of
Homeric style.[35]

Tennyson began studying Greek at the age of seven, and before going to
Cambridge had already written an epic in Greek as long as a book of
Homer; later in his life Homer was among the poets he used to read aloud
to his wife.[36] His *Morte d'Arthur*, written in 1833 when he was twenty-four
years old, shows more clearly than any other poem I know the characteristic Homeric features of name-epithet formulas, formulaic speech introductions, variation of major sense pauses, enjambment, parataxis (linking
clauses without subordination, i.e., by "and," as with the Greek δέ), and
many more. It is also an oral poem, in the sense that it would of course have
been intended to be read aloud: it is in fact framed by sections in which the
"author" of the piece, after modestly disparaging his "faint Homeric echoes,
nothing-worth, | Mere chaff and draff, much better burnt," is persuaded to

---

[34] For examples in Greek, see Edwards 1991: 42–44.

[35] As Kipling illustrates Latin word order (though by parody), in his "There are whose
study is of smells . . ." in *Stalky & Co.* (reprinted by Oxford University Press [Oxford, 1987],
180); see S. Medcalf, "Horace's Kipling," in Martindale and Hopkins 1993: 217–239.

[36] My source is Levi 1993: 26–27. Levi writes (115), "'Tiresias' . . . has more immediate
roots in an epic poem as long as a book of Virgil which Tennyson wrote in Greek before going
up to Cambridge"—I presume this was in Homeric hexameters—and (222) "he read Theocritus and Shakespeare and Dante and Homer aloud to his wife." On *Morte d'Arthur* and Virgil, see Gray 1998.

read it to a few friends late on a Christmas Eve, ". . . mouthing out his hollow oes and aes, | Deep-chested music." Not only the music, but also Tennyson's Homeric sentence structure, emphasize his concern for his listeners. Even the following short excerpt (lines 133–146—a mere fourteen of its 272 verses) exhibits many Homerisms, as the commentary indicates.[37]

Then quickly rose Sir Bedivere, and ran,

The poetic inversion of subject and verb places the name at phrase-end, the position of the Focus word in English, establishing it strongly in preparation for the following coordinate clauses. The sense is complete at the comma; then a new phrase begins, and the sense is again complete before the verse-end. If the poet had wished, he could have filled out the verse with the name-epithet formula he uses five times elsewhere,[38] writing, "Then quickly rose the bold Sir Bedivere." Similarly, Homer often begins a new phrase (either complete within the line or enjambing) at the bucolic diaeresis (five syllables before the verse-end), sometimes cutting short the line-ending name-epithet formula in order to do so: *Iliad* 2.179 begins ἀλλ' ἴθι νῦν κατὰ λαὸν Ἀχαιῶν . . . , "But go now through the host of the Greeks . . . ," and Homer could well have completed the verse by completing the familiar formula Ἀχαιῶν χαλκοχιτώνων, "bronze-clad Greeks," but instead he ignores the easy solution and (like Tennyson here) adds a new complete clause, μηδ' ἔτ' ἐρώει, "no longer hold back."[39]

And, leaping down the ridges lightly, plunged

A connective and a participial phrase continue the sense, the new main verb coming later in the sentence and the verse and gaining emphasis from the line-end. Homer often uses a similar construction (e.g., σπερχόμενος δὲ . . . , *Iliad* 11.110).

Among the bulrush-beds, and clutch'd the sword,
And strongly wheel'd and threw it. The great brand

The enjambing phrase completes the sense of the preceding verb, and the second half of the verse contains a new complete clause. There are more connective "ands" (Greek δέ)—poor English style, but good Homeric parataxis—common in conversation, easy for a listener to follow. At the end of the second verse a new sentence begins, and this time the sense runs over. The new phrase for "sword" adds weight both from the archaic nature of the word "brand" (very Homeric style) and from the two successive stressed syllables ("greát bránd")—which give something of the effect of the occa-

[37] See Appendix A for the full text of the poem, with a commentary.
[38] In lines 39, 69, 120, 156, 231.
[39] See Edwards 1966: 170 and 172–174.

sional Homeric spondaic ending. Tennyson may have in mind the frequency of ἔγχος, "spear," at the end of a Homeric line, often before enjambment like this.

Made lightnings in the splendour of the moon,

The line-initial verb, as often in Homer, gains emphasis from its position. Tennyson is copying Homer's word for Zeus hurling thunderbolts, ἀστράπτει, used three times to begin a verse (*Iliad* 2.353, 9.237, 17.595).

And flashing round and round, and whirl'd in an arch,

More verbs linked by "and." A metrical variation near the end of the verse ("ìn àn árch," two short syllables in place of one) perhaps reflects the swiftness of the movement.

Shot like a streamer of the northern morn,
Seen where the moving isles of winter shock

The sharp monosyllabic runover verb "shot," imitating the abruptness of the action, is copied from a common Homeric verse-initial effect (e.g., | βάλλ', | νύξ', both meaning "he struck"). The simile is extended into a natural scene, in the Homeric manner—an unchanging fact of human experience common to bard and audience (even if the aurora and the iceberg collisions are actually as unfamiliar to us as the lions common in Homeric similes were to his audience).[40] The abrupt monosyllabic verb "shock" at the end of the second verse is probably without parallel in Homer (because of the Greek personal verb-endings), but possibly Tennyson had noticed the line-endings expressing sudden nightfall, ἀμβροσίη νύξ, οὐρανόθεν νύξ.[41]

By night, with noises of the northern sea.

Notice that Tennyson's generous punctuation marks off the intonation units, the places where a reader would naturally pause.

So flash't and fell the brand Excalibur:

A characteristically Homeric return to the narrative after the simile. And the verse ends with another Homeric name-epithet formula: "the brand Excalibur" recurs twice at verse-end (lines 52, 147), once with "my" for "the" (27), and the name alone at verse-end three times (36, 108, 136).

But ere he dipt the surface, rose an arm

The sword now becomes masculine in gender. The most common word for "sword" in Homer (φάσγανον) is actually neuter in gender; the most famous

[40] There is a huge bibliography on Homeric similes. Here I seek forgiveness for referring only to my own contribution, Edwards 1991: 24–41 (with references there to the earlier work of others).

[41] Each three times in the *Odyssey*.

Homeric weapon, Achilles' spear (Πηλιάδα μελίην), is feminine, but it is not personified like this. Perhaps the female sex of the nymph led (consciously or not) to Tennyson's masculinization of her weapon. Again a new sentence—a highly significant one—begins late in the verse and is already complete in sense at verse-end. The inverted word order (he could have said "àn árm róse," matching for rhythm "thè greát bránd" of line 136) places the most significant word in the final "Focus" position and immediately before the enjambing adjectives. (It also brings the sonorous long *o* between the short *a*'s.)

    Clothed in white samite, mystic, wonderful,

This use of runover adjectives, beginning the verse and in agreement with a noun in the previous verse, is very Homeric; five times in the *Iliad* and once in the *Odyssey* ἔγχος, "weapon," is followed in this way (in the next verse) by βριθὺ μέγα στιβαρόν, "heavy, huge, stout," once with an added κεκορυθμένον, "tipped [with bronze],"[42] at other times with descriptive relative clauses to complete the verse. The whole-verse amplification slows down the movement and adds to the impressiveness. Tennyson repeats this verse verbatim—another Homeric technique—at 31 (where Arthur describes how he obtained the sword) and 164 (where the bold Sir Bedivere reports its return to its owner).

    And caught him by the hilt, and brandish'd him,

The pronouns are masculine again. "Brandish'd" is a play on words (cf. "the brand Excalibur," 142) of the kind Homer loves;[43] perhaps the best parallel is *Iliad* 16.102–105, where missiles (root *bel-*) are hurled (root *bal-*, used three times) against Ajax.

    Three times, and drew him under in the mere.

Here is more easy-to-listen-to paratactic construction (three more "ands" adding new clauses), and a very Homeric verse-beginning, "Three times. . . ." In his translation of *Iliad* 18.228–229,[44] where τρὶς μὲν . . . | τρὶς δὲ . . . occurs in successive verses, Tennyson rendered it "Thrice . . . | Thrice . . . ," keeping the adverb in the initial position. In another familiar Homeric technique, these last three lines are repeated at 159–161, with the (Homeric) minor change "that" for "and" before "caught."[45]

    Tennyson's observation of the movement of Homeric verse was acute,

---

[42] After κεκορυθμένον, the expected verse-ending formula αἴθοπι χαλκῷ ("with bright bronze") is here (*Iliad* 16.802) rather oddly omitted and replaced by the enjambing phrase αὐτὰρ ἀπ᾽ ὤμων |. . . .

[43] Cf. (for instance) Edwards 1987: 117–123.

[44] Published in response to Matthew Arnold's remark (in 1861): "If blank verse is used in translating Homer . . . it must not be Mr Tennyson's blank verse" (quoted in Levi 1993: 235).

[45] Printed in Appendix A, p. 142.

and his imitation of it is both impressive in English and good "oral" poetry, clearly marked off (usually by punctuation) into short sense-units ideal for recitation, that is, for oral communication to listeners. Both authors illustrate the importance of realizing the difference between the style of the written and the spoken languages; Milton's much more periodic style presents an eloquent contrast.[46]

HOMERIC STYLE IN THE DUELS OF ACHILLES

Finally, to demonstrate some of these current methods of analyzing and appreciating the small-scale, finely detailed craftsmanship of the *Iliad*, I want to study a passage that has probably not drawn the attention of most readers. Everyone knows that the speeches of Achilles in the *Iliad*—for instance, his passionate response to Odysseus's account of Agamemnon's offer (9.308–429), or his emotional, self-reproachful words with his mother after the news of Patroclus' death (18.78–126)—are among the most carefully wrought parts of the poem;[47] but less attention has been paid to details of the descriptions of Achilles' battles when, after Patroclus' death, he returns from his encampment to fight again with the Trojans. Achilles, after all, is the greatest fighter among the Greeks; but the battles of the *Iliad* begin in Book 3 and last, on and off, until Book 20 before the superhero himself gets involved; then, after only two further books, comes the last battle of the poem, his duel with Hector. The poet arranges matters so that Achilles, longing to fight Hector, must first spend a good deal of time (and talk) in an abortive encounter with Aeneas, whose life is saved by the god Poseidon; then he has a short series of duels in which he kills just four Trojans, the last of them Priam's son Polydorus. Polydorus' death is used immediately to introduce a short exchange of words and weapons between Achilles and Hector, Polydorus' grieving brother, who, like Aeneas, is then rescued by a god (this time Apollo). After Achilles' short, disgusted speech to the vanished Hector, there follows a second series of duels, in which the Greek hero kills ten Trojans, none of them ever heard of elsewhere (their names and patronymics tend to sound unusually fictitious). This is the passage I am going to examine.[48] Afterward, two similes describe Achilles' unstoppable rage and the bloodshed beneath his horses' feet, leading to a passage of general description, two long-drawn-out episodes with the Trojans Lycaon and Asteropaeus, Achilles' battle with the river-god Scamander, the farcical bat-

---

[46] For further commentary on *Morte d'Arthur*, see Appendix A.

[47] On Achilles' speeches, see Griffin 1986: 50–57, and Edwards 1992b.

[48] *Iliad* 20.455–489. Bakker (1997a: 104–105) and Scully (1986: 140–142) have commented on parts of this scene. My interest in it developed when I was writing my commentary on it (Edwards 1991: 340–343), and some of my points were adumbrated there.

tle of the gods themselves, and finally the encounter with the Trojan Agenor that leads into the final duel between Achilles and Hector.

The structure is careful, many themes preparing the way so that following episodes may have maximum effect, though we do not realize it until later. Aeneas' rescue by Poseidon prefigures Hector's rescue by Apollo—and anticipates Athena's standing beside him in his final moments, when she will *not* save him; the death of Priam's son Polydorus prepares for the scene in which old Priam, his father, will implore Hector not to fight Achilles, saying that he has lost many sons at Achilles' hands already and fears the deaths of yet two more, Polydorus and Lycaon—*their* deaths *we* already know about, though *he* does not. Beyond that, the poet is preparing for the great scene at the end of the poem, where the poet will bring Priam and Achilles face to face and the old king will again speak of the deaths of his sons, by then including that of Hector himself. Agenor's confrontation with Achilles closely parallels on a smaller scale the much longer narrative of Achilles' final meeting with Hector. Another striking small-scale anticipation of a theme later given more expanded treatment we shall see in a few moments.

So our passage, *Iliad* 20.455–489, is one of only two in which Achilles participates in the series of successive short duels that forms most of the many battle scenes in the *Iliad*.[49] How is Homer going to make it a very special, Achilles-sized description? We can study his techniques for doing that, and at the same time check on how well we can find conversational "intonation units" that fulfill the "one new idea" constraint and the general sequence "Topic: Focus: Predicate: Remainder." In what follows, I have printed the Greek with the intonation units separated (i.e., the speech pauses marked) by vertical bars (in doubtful cases, within parentheses),[50] together with a translation in an "oral" English, English as it is spoken (as nearly as I can contrive), matching intonation unit for unit, printed with the intonation units separated for emphasis. Sometimes for comparison, or where they are of particular interest, I have added the translations of Lattimore 1951 (for its familiarity and line-for-line format: marked "La."), Fagles 1990 (for its conversational vividness—frequent dashes often represent the jerkiness of ordinary informal discourse: marked "F."), and Lombardo 1997 (marked "Lo.": because he says his translation "began as scripts for

---

[49] For analysis of the patterns appearing in these scenes, the essential work is of course Fenik 1968. Morrison 1999 (which appeared after this chapter was written) studies Homer's inventiveness in his descriptions of death in duels and includes a good bibliography of previous work.

[50] The text is that of T. W. Allen's Oxford Classical Text (downloaded from the *Thesaurus linguae Graecae*). Van Thiel's (1996) is the same except for the accentuation εὖ in 20.464 and some of the punctuation. I was not able to check the second volume of West 1998, which had not yet appeared.

solo performances. . . . Throughout the period of composing the translation as poetry on the page, I continued reciting it to audiences, voicing the text as I crafted it and crafting it to capture the voice that I heard," x).[51]

Achilles is exasperated by Apollo's rescue of Hector—all the more reasonably since only a few minutes earlier the Trojan leader Aeneas has similarly been rescued from Achilles' attack by another god, Poseidon—and so he is forced to leave his greatest enemy for another day and turn to killing lesser mortals. He has just said to the vanished Hector (*Iliad* 20.449–454; Fagles' version):

> "Now, again, you've escaped your death, you dog,
> but a good close brush with death it was, I'd say!
> Now, again, your Phoebus Apollo pulls you through,
> the one you pray to, wading into our storm of spears.
> We'll fight again—I'll finish you off next time
> if one of the gods will only urge me on as well.
> But now I'll go for the others, anyone I can catch."[52]

Now the narrator continues (455):

Ὣς εἰπὼν | Δρύοπ᾽ οὖτα | κατ᾽ αὐχένα μέσσον (|) ἄκοντι·   455

> *So speaking,*
> *he stabbed Dryops,*
> *right in the neck,*
> *with his spear,*

(La.) He spoke, and with the spear full in the neck stabbed Dryops

(F.) Whirling | he stabbed Dryops, speared him right through the neck—

(Lo.) And he put his spear through Dryops' neck,

The normal end-of-speech formula, "so speaking," not only lets us know that the singer has finished the direct-speech impersonation of Achilles, but

---

[51] Lines quoted are taken from: *The Iliad of Homer* by Richmond Lattimore (Chicago: University of Chicago Press), copyright © 1951 by The University of Chicago; reprinted by permission; from *The Iliad* by Homer, translated by Robert Fagles, copyright © 1990 by Robert Fagles, Introduction and Notes copyright © 1990 by Bernard Knox, used by permission of Viking Penguin, a division of Penguin Putnam Inc.; and from *Homer: Iliad*, translated by Stanley Lombardo, copyright © 1997 by Stanley Lombardo, quoted by permission of Hackett Publishing Company, Inc. For uniformity I have (with the publisher's permission) changed Lombardo's capitals at the beginning of a verse to lower case.

[52] "ἐξ αὖ νῦν ἔφυγες θάνατον κύον· ἦ τέ τοι ἄγχι
ἦλθε κακόν· νῦν αὖτέ σ᾽ ἐρύσατο Φοῖβος Ἀπόλλων,
ᾧ μέλλεις εὔχεσθαι ἰὼν ἐς δοῦπον ἀκόντων.
ἦ θήν σ᾽ ἐξανύω γε καὶ ὕστερον ἀντιβολήσας,
εἴ πού τις καὶ ἔμοιγε θεῶν ἐπιτάρροθός ἐστι.
νῦν αὖ τοὺς ἄλλους ἐπιείσομαι, ὅν κε κιχείω."

gives (in Functional Grammar terms) the Topic to begin the verse and sentence, that is, "what is already in the minds of the communicator and the recipient," in this case Achilles' words. Then in second place (as is normal in Greek) comes the Focus, the salient new item of information, namely, the name of Achilles' first victim, Dryops. Then comes the action, the Verb or Predicate, "he stabbed"—a secondary item here, not the main news, because in this context stabbing does not surprise us at all. Finally, the poet adds the "Remainder"—the subordinate details of where Dryops was stabbed, and with what weapon. Notice that (as usual in Greek) the sequence is: Topic ("he"), Focus ("Dryops"), Predicate/Verb ("[he] wounded"), which is contrary to the normal *English* sequence with Focus at the end, "he stabbed Dryops"—my first version of this line read "Dryops he stabbed," and I altered it when I realized that in an English version I should follow the emphatic order of English, not Greek. This difference in the normal sequence in the two languages, a fundamental translator's problem, shows up in the two familiar translations: Lattimore reverses the whole sentence, and perhaps emphasizes the spear and the neck too much; Fagles produces a more accurate and vivid version—an *oral* version—by reversing just object and verb, Focus and Predicate, to produce the natural English order. Lombardo drops the speech-ending, and produces fair English, much less emphatic, however, than Fagles'.

ἤριπε δὲ προπάροιθε ποδῶν· | ὃ δὲ τὸν μὲν ἔασε,   456

and he dropped before his feet;
and as for him, *he left* him,

(La.) so that he dropped in front of his feet. He left him to lie there
(F.)   he dropped at his feet and Achilles left him dead
(Lo.) dropping him at his feet. He left him there

Dryops is inconsequential, the kind of guy you forget killing, so the next new information is simply the verb "he dropped" describing his death, with a minor detail to follow; then, along with Achilles, we go straight on to the next opponent. "He," "his," and "him" are clear enough, as there are only two men in the picture and we are not likely to get them mixed up. One little word in the Greek makes a lot of difference and is next to impossible to reproduce naturally in English (so I have overtranslated it, "as for him")—the particle μέν, which signals that up ahead we shall find something that will contrast with Dryops' motionless corpse—

Δημοῦχον δὲ | Φιλητορίδην | ἠΰν τε μέγαν τε   457

and Demuchus,
Philetor's son,
huge and powerful,

(La.) and with a spear thrown against the knee stopped the charge of Demou-
chos,

(F.)   and smashed Demuchus' knee, Philetor's strapping son,

(Lo.) and took out Demuchus, Philetor's tall son,

—and yes, the contrasting figure is the charging Demuchus, a really big
man with a significant father, so it takes a little more time, a little more
space, to kill him—but from the Functional Grammar viewpoint, he's not
the Focus but a contrasting Topic, coming first in the phrase.[53] For Demuchus is not really new information, he's just the next on the casualty list,
and the salient feature, the Focus, comes in the next verse:

κὰγ γόνυ δουρὶ βαλὼν | ἠρύκακε. | τὸν μὲν ἔπειτα   458

on the knee with his spear hitting [him],
he stopped [him];
and [as for] him, then,

(La.) Philetor's son, a huge man and powerful. After the spearcast

(F.)   stopped him right in his tracks with a well-flung spear

(Lo.) first hitting him on the knee with his spear.

He's wounded in the knee (Focus), and "stopped in his tracks" (as Fagles
says, with his usual sound grasp of what is emphatic, which is obscured in
Lattimore; I like Fagles' addition of "well-flung," too). And in the final
phrase we have another untranslatable μέν, already looking forward to who-
ever is going to be the next victim when we've finished off Demuchus.

οὐτάζων ξίφεϊ μεγάλῳ | ἐξαίνυτο θυμόν·   459

striking [him] with his great sword,
he stripped away his life.

(La.) with an inward plunge of the great sword he took the life from him.

(F.)   then sprang with his great sword and ripped his life away.

(Lo.) then finishing him off with his sword.

Demuchus is wounded by Achilles' sword (Focus—the action), and is
robbed of his life (Predicate—the unsurprising sequel). Lattimore and Fagles keep the Greek order, perhaps slightly changing the emphasis to the
killing instead of the wounding, but their versions are vivid enough—especially beside Lombardo's, which places "with his sword" in the correct

---

[53] A reader (John Heath) asked if, when the μέν member of the correlative phrases is unemphatic, the δέ member will be unemphatic, too. I'm not sure, but I think that is the case
here: I would say that in 456, ἔασε is the Focus, the new information; ὃ δέ, the Topic of the
whole sentence; τὸν μὲν and Δημοῦχον δὲ (457) Topics of the two members of which it is composed.

position for English emphasis but loses effectiveness (in my opinion) because of the flat choice of words.

αὐτὰρ ὃ Λαόγονον καὶ Δάρδανον | υἷε Βίαντος   460

And he—Laogonus and Dardanus,
the sons of Bias,

(La.) Then Achilleus swooping on Dardanos and Laogonos, sons both
(F.)   Then on he rushed at the sons of Bias—Laogonus, Dardanus—
(Lo.) Bias' two sons, Laogonus and Dardanus,

Sentence and verse begin with αὐτὰρ ὅ, "and he . . . ," picking up the μέν I mentioned a moment ago; but actually "he" turns out to be not the next victim but Achilles himself again, the Topic, followed as usual by the Focus, the new information, the two new names. Notice that already Homer has used three different ways of introducing the next victim, though all three accounts have started at the beginning of the verse. And already we observe that the pauses in the verse are falling in different places.

ἄμφω ἐφορμηθεὶς | ἐξ ἵππων | ὦσε χαμᾶζε,   461

at both of them hurling himself,
out of their chariot
he threw them to the ground;

(La.) of Bias, dashed them to the ground from behind their horses,
(F.)   hurled them off their chariot, slammed them both to ground,
(Lo.) he shoved from their chariot, killing one

After identifying the brothers, immediately we hear "at both of them hurling himself"—a sudden flash of movement in their direction, and the next thing we see, they are tumbled out of their chariot and on the ground—

τὸν μὲν δουρὶ βαλών, | τὸν δὲ σχεδὸν ἄορι τύψας.   462

one with the spear thrown,
the other, close at hand, with his sword striking.

(La.) one with a spearcast, one with a stroke of the sword from close up.
(F.)   one with a spear-thrust, one chopped down with a blade.
(Lo.) with a spearcast, the other in close with his sword.

—and *then* we realize—or rather, Homer the sports commentator tells us—the particulars of their deaths: the final line is very much the narrator's explanation, *his* careful syntactical balancing of Achilles' two actions. Fagles' rendering of the episode has been a good deal more vivid than Lattimore's, because he does not hesitate to use dashes instead of punctuation, that is, he is closer to the style of conversation. None of the translators really brings out the initial-verse emphasis of ἄμφω ἐφορμηθείς, "at *both* of them hurling himself"—Achilles takes on two men at once.[54]

Τρῶα δ᾽ Ἀλαστορίδην, | ὃ μὲν ἀντίος ἤλυθε γούνων,   463

And Tros, Alastor's son—
he came right up to [his] knees,

(La.) Now Tros, Alastor's son: he had come up against Achilleus'
(F.) Then Tros, Alastor's son, crawled to Achilles' knees
(Lo.) And then Tros, Alastor's son, tried to clasp

Now we have yet another variation: here the victim's name stands initially, in the accusative, as the object of the sentence (as previously with De-muchus)—it's what in Functional Grammar would be called a "Theme," placed ahead of the main sentence to "specify the universe of discourse with respect to which the subsequent predication is presented as relevant."[55] In English, *"That guy,* he's really weird"—a very conversational, *oral* kind of expression.

Instead of being stopped by a spearcast, like his predecessor, Tros does something surprising: as soon as we've seen and identified him, in the second half of the verse he immediately dashes toward Achilles' knees. This attempted supplication of Achilles by Tros is a short, preliminary version of an even more pathetic supplication a little later by Priam's son Lycaon, who, like Tros, makes no attempt to fight but immediately catches Achilles' knees and pleads for his life.[56] Lycaon's special plea is that he was previously captured by Achilles and was nominally his guest until he was sold into slavery, ransomed, and brought home to Troy, to fall again into Achilles' hands on his return to battle. Achilles, of course, in his present mood, does not accede to his supplication, but in this later scene (*Iliad* 21.34–135) the poet gives Lycaon a long and emotional speech and also Achilles' reply, which will concern us later.

Tros' action is unexpected—and so is the grammar: the accusative name is left hanging and Tros continues, more actively than we thought, as a nominative pronoun.[57] He is not just the object acted upon, but becomes the active subject of the clause, just as instead of being a powerless victim, he

[54] Lattimore seems to have taken ἄμφω with the phrase preceding it in the previous verse, which is harsh.

[55] S. C. Dik 1981: 19; in detail, 132–141. This kind of usage in Greek is studied by Slings 1997: 193–202.

[56] On this characteristic Homeric technique of repeating a theme in shorter and longer versions, see Fenik 1968: 213–214; Edwards 1991: 19–23; Edwards 1987: 50–60.

[57] There is a similar kind of unexpected grammar matching unexpected sense at *Iliad* 1.194, where the traditional line-end epithet ἀργυρόηλον after ξίφος is ignored and Athena suddenly bursts on to the scene and into the line: ἦλθε δ᾽ Ἀθήνη | ..., "But Athena arrived ..." (see Edwards 1987: 180).

initiates an action in the hope of saving his life. Lattimore keeps the irregular grammar better than Fagles and Lombardo, but hardly does justice to the vividness and abruptness of this verse. We might perhaps have taken the pronoun ὃ (μὲν), "he," to refer to Achilles, but as the clause is completed, we realize from the sense that it is Tros approaching Achilles' knees, not the other way around. And what happens then?

εἴ πώς εὐ πεφίδοιτο | λαβὼν | καὶ ζωὸν ἀφείη   464

if perhaps he might spare him,
taking [him prisoner],
and release him alive,

(La.) knees, to catch them and be spared and his life given to him
(F.)   and clutched them, hoping he'd spare him,
        let Tros off alive,
(Lo.) Achilles' knees to see if he would spare him,
        take him captive and then let him go

But before we hear what happens to Tros, Homer the omniscient narrator lets us see into his mind, telling us his thoughts; in the later repetition of this scene, Lycaon will tell us his thoughts himself, in moving direct speech. There is also a transient ambiguity in the line,[58] because it would be easy to understand λαβών to refer to Tros himself, the subject of the main clause, temporarily giving the very fair sense "taking [Achilles' knees]" (the phrase καὶ λάβε γούνων, "and he clasped his knees," occurs eight times in Homer). This ambiguity attracts our attention because of its unexpectedness. Fagles recovers the speed, but Lattimore is rather verbose.

μηδὲ κατακτείνειεν | ὁμηλικίην ἐλεήσας,   465

and might not kill him,
his agemate, pitying [him].

(La.) if Achilleus might take pity upon his youth and not kill him;
(F.)   no cutting him down in blood,
        he'd pity Tros, a man of his own age—
(Lo.) and not kill him because they were the same age.

Tros' thoughts run on, and at an even deeper level of focalization (to use the narratological term),[59] for now Homer tells us Tros' thoughts about *Achilles'* thoughts—that he may pity him because they are of the same age; and we know that such an "age class" tie in Greece was strong, much

---

[58] On the term, see chapter 4, pp. 106–108.
[59] See de Jong 1987a: esp. 31–33; Rimmon-Kenan 1983: 71–85. The "focalizer" is (in simple terms) the one through whose eyes the action is seen.

stronger than that between classmates in an American high school or university, perhaps because of shared community puberty rituals. Earlier in the poem, Helen has lamented the loss of *her* agemates, back home in Greece, and in the *Odyssey* their similar age is mentioned as a tie between Telemachus and Nestor's son Peisistratus.[60]

Lattimore loses the "agemate" point; Fagles takes an extra line, but manages it well enough, placing the exclamatory "Fool!" of the following verse at the end of this line instead of the beginning of the next, which is a good way to bring out the emphasis in English. Lombardo loses the force of "pitying."

νήπιος, | οὐδὲ τὸ ἤδη | ὃ οὐ πείσεσθαι ἔμελλεν·   466

The fool!
He didn't know this,
that he was not going to persuade [him];

(La.) fool, and did not see there would be no way to persuade him,
(F.)   —the young fool,
        he'd no idea, thinking *Achilles* could be swayed!
(Lo.) He actually thought that he would persuade him,

Suddenly Homer the narrator, in his own voice, gives us his own comment on Tros and his hopes and on Achilles' present frame of mind. Homer often emerges like this in the narrator's persona, and besides telling us how the poet himself regards his characters' thoughts, of course it effectively increases our intimacy with *him*, the narrator.[61] Fagles conveys the author's personal address and the immediacy, at the expense of some distancing from the original wording. Lombardo loses some of the narrator's intimacy.

Later, in Lycaon's version of the scene, it is not the narrator but Achilles himself who begins his response with "Fool!" (21.99), and then goes on to explain, in an almost equally intimate and friendly tone, that this time Lycaon has no chance of ransom, as now Patroclus is dead and Achilles is taking no prisoners. He concludes with a superb adaptation of the familiar trope, "Even Heracles died, though he was son of Zeus." Achilles, however, doesn't say exactly this: he says, "Even *Patroclus* died, a far better man than you" (*Iliad* 21.107), and goes on to the climax:

"And look, you see how handsome and powerful I am?
the son of a great man, the mother who gave me life

[60] Cf. R. Sallares, *The Ecology of the Ancient World* (Ithaca, N.Y., 1991), 127: "However, the concept of age as a principle of social organization, age class organization as it may be termed, is indeed fundamental to understanding the social organization of the ancient Greek world," and his pp. 160–192 = §2.5 (I thank F. S. Edwards for this reference). See also Edwards 1991: 341.

[61] See Edwards 1991: 4–7 and references there. This verse recurs at *Odyssey* 3.146.

a deathless goddess. But even for me, I tell you,
death and the strong force of fate are waiting.
There will come a dawn or sunset or high noon
when a man will take my life in battle too—
flinging a spear perhaps
or whipping a deadly arrow off his bow."

(Iliad 21.108–113, trans. Fagles)

So Achilles predicts his own imminent death—one of many such predictions—as his victorious exploits against the Trojans continue. Achilles, the archetypical Greek warrior hero, was also the first in surviving Western literature to declare, "The paths of glory lead but to the grave."

οὐ γάρ τι γλυκύθυμος ἀνὴρ ἦν | οὐδ᾿ ἀγανόφρων,   467

this was no kind-hearted man,
nor amiably disposed,

The narrator's comments continue. The two compound adjectives are very rare in Homer and elsewhere in Greek; one wonders if they are new, invented by the poet, or just colloquialisms that were never accepted into dignified poetic language. Even if they were unfamiliar to the audience (we don't know if they were or not), they are simple and eminently easy to understand—as immediate and directly appreciated as the similes are.

ἀλλὰ μάλ᾿ ἐμμεμαώς· | ὃ μὲν ἥπτετο χείρεσι γούνων   468

but utterly furious;
he was reaching with his hands for his knees,

Ἐμμεμαώς, "furious," is the word that was applied to Achilles as he dashed at Hector a little earlier (20.442), perhaps an intended reminder that his mood has not changed. It has been pointed out[62] that Tros is killed before he has established actual physical contact with Achilles, so he has a much weaker claim on Achilles' mercy (Lycaon *will* grasp his knees, but it won't help him). The change of subject back to Tros is easy enough, and returns us to his action in 463, just as after a simile Homer always carefully returns us to the narrative line; that the change comes at mid-verse seems to juxtapose even more strongly the fury of the one character and the fear of the other. Like a good movie director, Homer has given us a close-up of Tros, then a wide shot (the narrator's comment on the folly of his hopes), then another close-up (Achilles' furious face), then a return to focus on the ongoing action between the two characters.[63]

ἱέμενος λίσσεσθ᾿, | ὃ δὲ φασγάνῳ (|) οὖτα κατ᾿ ἧπαρ·   469

[62] In Gould 1973: 80.
[63] Based on an observation by John Heath.

hoping to make a prayer;
but he with his sword,
stabbed him in the liver.

Again we hear a summary of poor Tros' thoughts; but then we see Achilles' sword dart forward, and that's the end of Tros' consciousness. The second half of the verse might be divided into intonation units after either φασγάνῳ or οὖτα—in which case it may be best not to divide the phrase at all.

ἐκ δέ οἱ ἧπαρ ὄλισθεν, | ἀτὰρ μέλαν αἷμα κατ' αὐτοῦ   470

His liver slid out,
and black blood from it

κόλπον ἐνέπλησεν· | τὸν δὲ σκότος ὄσσε κάλυψε   471

drenched his lap.
And darkness covered his eyes,

But the poet continues to tell us about Tros—after all, he's had more personality given him than any of the other slain Trojans. So we hear about his abdominal wound, and a regular death formula concludes the verse and (we think) the episode.

θυμοῦ δευόμενον·

his life leaving him.

To our surprise, the narrator stays a little longer still with the dying Tros—unexpectedly, for of the thirteen times that Homer uses this phrase τὸν δὲ σκότος ὄσσε κάλυψε, "and darkness covered his eyes," this is one of only two instances where it does not end the sentence and the verse. Here, enjambing into the following verse, we have two more words to end the life of Tros. The poet keeps us attentive by deceiving our expectations, and again avoids the coincidence of the end of the verse and the end of the sentence; in the eighteen verses since the episode began, the editor of the·Oxford Classical Text has only once marked a period at verse-end (after 462).

On the other occasion when the sentence does not end after this "darkness . . ." phrase, the continuation is even more striking, for the poet adds, at the dramatic death of Asteropaeus, killed while trying to wrench Achilles' own spear out of the ground and hurl it back at him, the single word ἀσθ-μαίνοντ(α), "gasping" (*Iliad* 21.182), suggesting the desperate man's long-drawn-out effort and death struggle. There may well be something like that intended here, too, for the phrase we have, θυμοῦ δευόμενον, is also once used of lambs killed for a sacrifice gasping out their lives (*Iliad* 3.294).

Achilles' duels resume:

ὃ δὲ Μούλιον οὖτα (|) παραστὰς   472

And he stabbed Moulius,
standing beside [him],

(La.) Next from close in he thrust at Moulios
(F.)   And Mulius next—
(Lo.) Achilles was already upon Mulius,

Tros gone, the pronoun returns us naturally to Achilles, and for a further variation his tale begins in the middle of the verse—the first time this has happened in this group of duels. As usual, the Greek sequence is: Topic ("he"), Focus ("Moulius"), Verb ("stabbed"), Remainder ("standing beside"), and English order of emphasis reverses Verb and Focus, placing Moulius' name at clause-end.

δουρὶ κατ᾽ οὖς· | εἶθαρ δὲ δι᾽ οὔατος ἦλθ᾽ ἑτέροιο   473

with his lance through the ear;
right through the ear it went, the other ear,

(La.) with the pike at his ear, so the bronze spearhead pushed through and
       came out
       at the other ear.
(F.)   he reared and jammed his lance through the man's ear,
       so the lance came jutting out through the other ear,
(Lo.) Putting his bronze javelin through one ear
       and all the way out the other, while,
       in almost the same motion, he struck

For yet further variation, this is the first time that there has been a major sense-pause at this early point in the verse. For Achilles' weapon I have used "lance," like Fagles: Lattimore used "pike," and Lombardo "javelin"; and we all avoided "standing near" for παραστάς. We English-speakers were all frightened of the jingle "standing *near* . . . with a *spear* through the *ear*." But *Homer* seems to *like* that kind of echo—he cheerfully repeats the -*ou*- sound over and over: ὃ δὲ Μούλιον οὖτα παραστὰς | δουρὶ κατ᾽ ους· εἶθαρ δὲ δι᾽ οὔατος ἦλθ᾽ ἑτέροιο. . . .[64] Translators are too cowardly to follow him. (I don't know why Fagles wrote "he *reared*" (my italics)—presumably because of the sound, since there is nothing in the Greek to suggest that sense.) The last word, ἑτέροιο, "the *other* ear," comes as a surprise—if you like, you can think it's like the surprise of seeing the spear-point suddenly appear on the other side of poor Moulius' head. All three translators sound prosaically verbose compared with the tautness of the Greek.

αἰχμὴ χαλκείη· | ὃ δ᾽ Ἀγήνορος υἱὸν Ἔχεκλον   474

[64] On sound effects in Homer, see Edwards 1991: 57–58 and references there.

the bronze point [did].
And he, Agenor's son Echeclus,

(La.)   Now he hit Echeklos the son of Agenor
(F.)   bronze point glinting. Echeclus son of Agenor next—
(Lo.) Agenor's son Echeclus full on the head

The runover words "the bronze point" are not necessary to the sense, but add to the picture—very like conversation, even English conversation; Fagles does well to add "glinting." Then, as in the case of Moulius two lines above (472), the next killing begins in the middle of the verse, with a resumptive pronoun for Achilles next to the name of the next victim; but the poet here adds the Trojan's father's name, too. This is not accidental, because an Echeclus has already been killed several books back (16.694) by Patroclus, along with another Moulius; and the prominent position of the father Agenor's name both serves to differentiate this Echeclus from his dead namesake and to give prominence to Agenor, who has played a considerable role in the fighting and will himself soon be facing Achilles in an important scene.

μέσσην κὰκ κεφαλὴν | ξίφει ἤλασε | κωπήεντι,   475

right on top of his head,
with his sword he drove through,
with the hilted [sword],

Certainly the adjective κωπήεντι, "hilted," is added for metrical reasons, to fill up the space to the end of the line, as it is on one other occasion (16.332). But the epithet is not entirely otiose, because it draws a little more attention to the sword, which we are to hear more about in the next verse; and perhaps mention of the hilt conjures up the depth of the wound.[65]

πᾶν δ᾽ ὑπεθερμάνθη | ξίφος αἵματι·

and all over it grew warm,
the sword [did], with the blood.

Here the verb is clearly the Focus. This kind of vivid close-up detail is a frequent feature of Homeric style, and often memorable: one thinks of Hector's tall shield knocking against his neck and ankles as he runs to Troy with it slung over his back (*Iliad* 6.117–118), and the sweat-soaked strap supporting Diomedes' shield chafing his shoulder after his mighty exertions (5.796–797).[66] Who is observing this warmth—Achilles? Homer? All of us?

[65] I owe this idea to John Heath.
[66] See further Edwards 1987: 85, and references at ibid.: 87.

| τὸν δὲ κατ᾽ ὄσσε   476

And for him, down over his eyes

ἔλλαβε πορφύρεος θάνατος (|) καὶ μοῖρα κραταιή.   477

[there] seized him bright-red death
and [his] invincible fate.

The solemn and evocative expression for Echeclus' death recurs occasionally elsewhere. Here the color adjective is especially well-suited to the previous verse.

Δευκαλίωνα δ᾽ ἔπειθ᾽, | ἵνα τε ξυνέχουσι τένοντες   478

Deucalion next,
just where the tendons meet,

(La.)   Now Deukalion
        was struck in the arm, at a place in the elbow where the tendons
(F.)   Deucalion next—he lanced his arm with a bronze-shod spear,
(Lo.)   Deucalion was next, Achilles' spearpoint

Here is yet another different grammatical structure. Deucalion's name is
placed first, like that of Tros in line 463 above, as a Theme—"specif[ying]
the universe of discourse with respect to which the subsequent predication
is presented as relevant"(see above, p. 24)—but here immediately after
Deucalion's name, the place of his *wound* is identified—almost as though
we watch through Achilles' own eyes as he identifies his target and prepares
to strike, or through those of the radio commentator: "Now it's Duke's
turn—right where the tendons meet—the elbow tendons—*there* he's got
him—right through the arm he's drilled him!" (Lovers of the Homeric
Greek language will notice the wonderful Homeric particle τε in the second phrase, the "generalizing" *te* that tells us that tendons *always* meet at
this place, in everybody's arm, not just in Deucalion's: there is nothing like
this *te* in English—unless one were to translate "where the tendons are
wont to meet.")

ἀγκῶνος, | τῇ τόν γε φίλης διὰ χειρὸς ἔπειρεν   479

at the elbow,
there *[he got him], right through the arm he spitted him,*

(La.) come together. There through the arm Achilleus transfixed him
(F.)   he spitted the Trojan through where the elbow-tendons grip
(Lo.) piercing his elbow just where the sinews join.

My "he got him" is an attempt to render the Greek γε, another more-or-
less untranslatable particle lending emphasis to the preceding pronoun

"him." None of the translators attempts to match the runover genitive noun "at the elbow."

αἰχμῇ χαλκείῃ· | ὃ δέ μιν μένε | χεῖρα βαρυνθεὶς   480

with his spear of bronze;
and he waited for him,
his arm hanging useless,

(La.) with the bronze spearhead, and he, arm hanging heavy, waited
(F.)   and there he stood, waiting Achilles, arm dangling heavy,
(Lo.) His arm hung uselessly as he stood there

As in 474 above, the runover words "with his bronze spear" are not necessary to the sense but add color, as well as avoiding both end-stop and a break in the first half of the verse. As usual, the meaning of the pronouns "he" and "him" is clear enough from the sense.

πρόσθ᾽ ὁρόων θάνατον·

in front of him seeing—death;

(La.) and looked death in the face.
(F.)   staring death in the face—
(Lo.) staring death in the face.

The phrase draws our attention because of its pathos. It is also effectively imprecise—is it really *Deucalion* who *knows* death is before him? Or is it the narrator who is telling us that death, namely Achilles, is before Deucalion? Either of these—or preferably both.[67] The translators keep the effective simplicity.

ὃ δὲ φασγάνῳ αὐχένα θείνας   481

and he, with his sword striking his neck,

(La.)   Achilleus struck with the sword's edge
(F.)   and Achilles chopped his neck
(Lo.)   Achilles closed in
      and sliced into his neck,

τῆλ᾽ αὐτῇ πήληκι κάρη βάλε·

far away, along with the helmet, hurled his head;

Here the *action* comes first, and then (again) one close-up detail—

μυελὸς αὖτε   482

the spinal fluid back

---

[67] R. Renehan points out that the poet portrays helplessness rather than defiance ("The *Heldentod* in Homer: One Heroic Ideal," *Classical Philology* 82 [1987]: 108).

(La.) at his neck, and swept the helmed head far away, and the marrow
(F.)   and his sword sent head and helmet flying off together
(Lo.)   sending the head,
       helmet and all, flying through the air.
       Marrow spurted up

σφονδυλίων ἔκπαλθ', | ὃ δ' ἐπὶ χθονὶ | κεῖτο τανυσθείς.   483

out of the vertebrae it spurted out;
and he, on the ground,
lay stretched out.

(La.) gushed from the neckbone, and he went down to the ground at full length.
(F.)   and marrow bubbling up from the clean-cut neckbone.
       Down he went, his corpse full length on the ground—
(Lo.)   through his spinal cord,
       and then the corpse was lengthwise on the ground.

which you might prefer to have been omitted (Fagles is more gruesome
even than Homer—and both he and Lattimore should have been wary of
describing a headless trunk as lying "full length"!). "He lay stretched out"
occurs many times (in varying forms), always of the dead except when it is
applied to the grieving (and himself doomed) Achilles lying beside Patroclus' corpse (*Iliad* 18.26–27).

αὐτὰρ ὃ | βῆ ῥ' ἰέναι | μετ' ἀμύμονα Πείρεω υἱὸν   484

But the other [guy],
he went [watch this!]
after Peires' noble son,

(La.) Now he went on after the blameless son of Peires,
(F.)   just as Achilles charged at Piras' handsome son,
(Lo.) Rhigmus, Peiros' peerless son, had come

This is yet another different way to introduce the next victim; there was a
verse beginning αὐτὰρ ὃ . . . ," But he . . . ," back in 460, but there it was
immediately followed by the names of the next victims. Here the "But he
. . . ," contrasting with the ὃ δ', "and he . . . ," in the previous verse (the dead
Deucalion), refers to the continuing Topic, Achilles (as was the case in 460,
too), and is followed directly by the verb βῆ, "[he] went"; and the verb is
followed by the particle ῥ(α), whose purpose is to summon the listener's attention (I have overtranslated it as "watch this!") and emphasize the word
that precedes it.[68] Then Achilles surges forward, and we see who he is pur-
suing this time:

[68] On how this postpositive particle marks an intonational boundary, see especially Bakker
1997a: 101, and his General Index s.v. *Ára*.

Ῥίγμον, | ὃς ἐκ Θρῄκης ἐριβώλακος | εἰληλούθει·　　485

Rhigmus;
who from Thrace, that fertile land,
had come;

(La.) Rhigmos, who had come over from Thrace where the soil is rich. This man
(F.)　Rhigmus who'd sailed from the fertile soil of Thrace
(Lo.) from farm country in Thrace.

This is the first time in this massacre that the poet has used this common grammatical structure of name followed by relative clause. He tells us something about Rhigmus' origins as a touch of pathos, because we know the man won't be going home again now. As usual he places the new information, "from fertile Thrace," in the second position in the sentence, and the unsurprising verb at the end—and as usual I wondered whether to keep the same word order (as given above) or the proper English sequence with the Focus word last (". . .he'd come from *Thrace*"). Fagles uses a number of dashes here, which well convey the oral nature of the sentences; Lattimore is perhaps a little wordy and slow, but (by enjambment here) he manages to begin the next line with the emphatic verb.

τὸν βάλε μέσσον ἄκοντι, | πάγη δ᾽ ἐν νηδύϊ χαλκός,　　486

he struck him in the middle with his spear,
and it stuck in his belly, the bronze [weapon did],

(La.) he stabbed in the middle with the spear, and the spear stuck fast in his belly.
(F.)　Achilles pierced his belly, the bronze impaled his guts
(Lo.)　　　　　　　　　　　　　Achilles' spear
　　　　transfixed him and stuck in his belly.

Both halves of the verse might well be subdivided.

ἤριπε δ᾽ ἐξ ὀχέων· | ὃ δ᾽ Ἀρηΐθοον θεράποντα　　487

and he fell from his chariot;
and he—Areïthoüs his driver,

(La.) He dropped from the chariot, but as Areïthoös his henchman
(F.)　and out of his car he pitched as his driver Areithous
(Lo.) He fell from his chariot, and as his driver,

As already in lines 472 and 474, with Moulius and Echeclus, the next report begins in mid-verse with a pronoun for Achilles and the name of his victim as object. The variety here comes from the fact that the next sufferer is the charioteer of the last man killed, and a swiftly moving new action is described in rapid, jerky speech units:

ἂψ ἵππους | στρέψαντα | μετάφρενον | ὀξέϊ δουρὶ   488

backward the horses
he's turning—
his back
with his sharp spear

(La.) turned the horses away Achilleus stabbed him with the sharp spear
(F.)   swung the horses round but Achilles speared his back
(Lo.) Areïthous, was turning the horses around
      Achilles hit him in the back, the blow

It is literally a "blow-by-blow" description. On three other Iliadic occasions, charioteers are killed as they try to turn their horses around; one can
well imagine it was a hazardous procedure in the midst of a battle. Here
Areïthoüs turns the horses and exposes his vulnerable, possibly unarmored
back—and Achilles, and we too, focus on it at once. We all know what's
going to happen:

νύξ', | ἀπὸ δ' ἅρματος ὦσε· | κυκήθησαν δέ | οἱ ἵπποι.   489

he struck [it],
and thrust [him] from the chariot;
and they bolted,
his horses [did].

(La.) Achilleus stabbed him with the sharp spear
      in the back, and thrust him from the chariot. And the horses bolted.
(F.)   and the spearshaft heaved him off the chariot too
      and the panicked stallions bolted.
(Lo.) pushing him from his car. The horses ran wild.

There's a sudden monosyllabic blow, *nux'* (we may remember Tennyson's
"Shot . . . ," p. 16 above), and Areïthoüs is out, and down (but both Lattimore and Fagles lose the abruptness and bury the verb "struck" in the middle of their verses). In the closing view of the scene we see the spooked
horses take off across the plain. *Cut.* The horses are firmly in our minds, so
Homer can put the emphatic verb "[they] bolted," the Focus word here,
first in the sentence, without a linking Topic.

Homer continues with two longish similes, both perhaps linked to this
view of Rhigmus' panicked horses dashing off over the plain: the first likens
Achilles' charge to a windswept forest fire, the second compares his chariot horses to oxen trampling grain on a threshing-floor. This leads to a general description (nowadays interrupted by the end of this book and the beginning of the next—see chapter 2) of his pursuit of the Trojans to the River
Scamander, on whose banks he comes upon Priam's son Lycaon, and enters

upon a scene I have already mentioned. During this time all the other Greeks remain offstage, forgotten while we watch the exploits of the one superhero who has now at last returned to the battlefield.

When reading the *Iliad* with students, either in Greek or in translation, one tends to avoid—or at least pay less attention to—the battle scenes. This is understandable, perhaps even advisable. But it is worthwhile occasionally to examine some such scene as the above in detail, so that we can see how, in the hands of a master, the content of its narrative can be diversified, and the slaughter, if not disguised, at least given pathos, by the insights the poet gives us into the minds of his cannon fodder. Above, we have seen Achilles hewing, slashing, stabbing, with spear and with sword; various ways of death by injury to various body parts; the names of his victims, their ancestry, glimpses of their personality, the ways they face their death; one man's futile supplication (Tros') preparing us for a much more fully told (and equally futile) supplication still to come (Lycaon's); the narrator's own sympathy, directly expressed, for a man so misguided as to hope for mercy from an enemy depicted as being in Achilles' present frame of mind. On this small scale, as in the entire poem, a close reading reveals the poet's humanity, not a glorification of warfare or the joy in victory he sometimes portrays in his characters.

In the battle scenes, too, one can readily identify Homer's superb art, in the range of techniques he uses to diversify his narrative and keep his listeners' attention. We have seen above how he avoids the monotony of assigning interchangeable segments, each a few verses long, to each victim, but instead constantly varies the position of the pauses in the verse, the places where sentences begin and end, and their grammatical structures. Again and again the listeners' expectations are deceived by Homer's avoidance of the mechanical operations that might, in the hands of a lesser poet, mark tradition-based composition. And if we look closely, it becomes clear that the essential element of the uniqueness and impressiveness of Homer's style is his word order—notable in two ways: both for his skill in placing significant words in the emphatic position at the beginning of the verse, and for his maintenance of the normal Greek sequence of Topic/Focus/Predicate. This is the oral style, the style that made his verse easy for a listening audience to understand.

These observations are not new, but thanks to recent research we now understand better than previously the reasons behind them. Homer has been compared to a cameraman moving his viewfinder over the battlefield.[69] Here, I'd sooner compare him to a ring-side commentator giving

---

[69] E.g., by Bakker 1997a: 69 n. 36; Edwards 1987: 178.

us *literally* a "blow-by-blow" description of a battle, communicating *orally* (through his microphone) with us, his audience. Observing the nature and technique of oral discourse, of conversation, enables us to realize this better—and perhaps to translate the poem better, and better to appreciate the exceptional genius of this poet.

Chapter Two

HOMER II: SCENES
AND SUMMARIES

I N THE LAST CHAPTER we observed Homer's infinite variety in describing what might have been a routine, standardized series of killings by his hero: how he changes the positions where sentences and clauses end, how he makes use of the emphasis given by the beginning and the end of the verse, how the duels are diversified—all adaptations within the framework of the traditional language and style. This avoidance of monotony must have been an aid in retaining his listeners' attention. Now we will look at one of the poet's larger-scale techniques for continually holding their interest: his ways of moving from one location (or scene) to another without interrupting their focus on the action.

We don't listen to Homer: we read him. And the text we see before us, whether it is printed in Greek or in English, misleads us all the time. For the pages we read, whether printed with verse or prose, are marked with paragraph indents, which we immediately notice and absorb; furthermore, from time to time there comes white space at the end of a book and a heading at the beginning of the next, just as at the chapter divisions of a novel. The constantly interrupting, visually striking paragraph breaks and book divisions force themselves upon our attention as the apparent articulation points of the narrative. Close examination reveals that very often the impression we thus receive from the printed page is wrong: Homeric narrative is indeed articulated, but the poet treats the junctures quite differently from the breaks in the novels with which we are most familiar.

First we will look at the book divisions, which have recently received a good deal of scholarly attention. Commentaries always respect them, publishers depend upon them, teachers set readings and plan lectures based upon them. My own heavily annotated old hardback copy of Richmond Lattimore's *Iliad* translation (fifth impression, 1956) prints the book number on each page as a heading, and for many years the first thing I used to tell teaching assistants to do in my courses in translation was to write these book numbers at the top of each right-hand page of their Homer for easy reference, since the University of Chicago Press long ago ceased to provide us with that convenience (which goes back to at least the fourth century

C.E.).[1] But few modern scholars believe that these breaks were made by Homer.

Similarly, no one thinks that the ubiquitous paragraph divisions of modern texts and translations[2] are authentic, but probably most editors feel that teachers, readers, and students alike would abhor a text (whether in Greek or English) that was not articulated by paragraph indents every twenty lines or so. But such breaks obscure the poet's technique for moving from one scene to another—particularly since few editors venture to place a paragraph break in mid-verse, where consistency would often position it.[3] Homer's narrative runs smoothly from one scene to another, but he takes great care at the articulation points to make clear to his listeners exactly what he is doing—what is ending, and what is beginning. An examination of the circumstances in which these modern breaks in our text occur will make it easier to determine what kind of break in continuity they actually represent, to what extent they were regarded as articulation points by the poet himself, and how they were felt by a listener in antiquity. Finally, we will see how Homer manages major transitions between the episodes of his narrative.

The Book Divisions

Any attentive reader of a translation of the *Iliad* or *Odyssey* notices that the division into books sometimes falls at unexpected places. In particular, the beginning of a book often does not offer a good starting-place for a reader or a recitation: one would hardly choose to enter upon a recitation with "She came to the ships . . ." when (unless we have read the preceding book) we do not know who "she" is; or with "When they reached the ford . . . , splitting them in two he chased . . . ," where we are obviously breaking into the middle of some violent action between unnamed persons; or even with "So he spoke . . . ," concluding a speech we never heard[4]—and in fact Pope amused himself imitating this oddity in "The Rape of the Lock," where Canto IV ends with the unfortunate victim crying to her ravisher:

---

[1] Haslam 1997: 59 (the date: 63) mentions an *Odyssey* codex of the third or fourth century C.E. that repeats the book number at the top of each right-hand page, just as I recommend.

[2] The only exception I know of is Albert Cook's verse translation of the *Odyssey* (New York, 1967).

[3] J. van Leeuwen's editions of the *Iliad* (1912, 1913) and *Odyssey* (1915) are the exception. (The mid-verse breaks in Fagles' translation [1990] do not necessarily correspond to Homer's scene changes.)

[4] The beginnings of (respectively) *Iliad* 19 (after a couplet confusingly introducing Dawn: see Edwards 1991: 235), *Iliad* 21 (see Edwards 1991: 345; and N. Richardson 1993: 51), *Iliad* 7.

"Oh hadst thou, cruel! been content to seize
Hairs less in sight, or any hairs but these!"

and Canto V begins:

She said: the pitying audience melt in tears.
But Fate and Jove had stopp'd the Baron's ears.

(Virgil may have imitated it, too: *Sic fatur lacrimans . . .* [*Aeneid* 6.1].[5])

It must be admitted that positioning an obvious (white-space) break in the middle of a continuing action is not uncommon in a modern novel. Novelists of any period vary considerably in their use of chapter divisions. Henry Fielding said that chapter divisions are for the convenience of the reader, not the author, and should be regarded as "an Inn or Resting-Place" that gives a chance to reflect upon the preceding chapter—a work without such occasions for rest and reflection, he says, "resembles the Opening of Wilds or Seas, which tires the Eye and fatigues the Spirit when entered upon."[6] The Homeric poems, as we have them, give the listener no such respite—nor do many well-known English novelists. In Kipling's *Kim*, which on the analogy of his *Just So Stories*—ideal for reading aloud and full of phrases repeated in quasi-Homeric style—one might expect to have many convenient stopping-points, it is often impossible to pick up the tale at the beginning of a chapter because the narrative has continued without interruption from the last, so that chapters start with "Behind them an angry farmer brandished a bamboo pole," "Followed a sudden natural reaction," and the like.[7] In Conrad's *Heart of Darkness*, which has only three chapters, the second chapter ends with the conclusion of a direct speech and the third begins with a kind of speech conclusion—"I looked at him, lost in astonishment."[8] However, for many reasons it would be unwise to use such modern analogies to justify the divisions in our Homeric text.

Recently the origin and significance of the book divisions in our *Iliad* and *Odyssey* texts have received a good deal of attention from Homeric scholars. In particular, a recent article (Jensen 1999) includes a full survey of the ev-

[5] But it may have been the editors Varius and Tucca who moved the line here from the end of the previous book: see the critical apparatus. It may be relevant that *Odyssey* 13 similarly begins with a phrase ending the hero's long tale, whereas Virgil differed, placing his equivalent at the *end* of his corresponding book (*Aeneid* 3.716–718).

[6] Quoted in Stevick 1970: 25.

[7] Wender (1977: 343) claims that "The Elephant's Child" has a higher percentage of repetition than James Notopoulos found in the *Iliad*. I well remember how much we used to enjoy listening to our schoolmistress reading—beautifully—the *Just So Stories* to us at the close of Friday afternoons in my one-room village school in England.

The Kipling examples come from the beginnings of chapters 3 and 11 (pp. 90 and 233 in the 1989 Penguin edition).

[8] Stevick 1970: 57–63 has many similar examples. On Virginia Woolf's *Mrs. Dalloway*, see below.

idence and scholars' opinions and is followed by a number of comments by others. In this article, the author suggests that the poems were first written down from dictation by the prize-winning bard in Athens at a Greater Panathenaia festival in the time of Peisistratus, and that the book division represents as much as the bard could manage to sing in one day's performance. Some Homerists (including S. West) would agree that the division is earlier than the work of the Alexandrian scholars, whereas others still tend to credit the Alexandrians (Janko, N. Richardson). Still others have recently suggested that the commercial book trade may be responsible, demanding the isolation (for publication) of popular excerpts (Olson), or that Aristarchus reestablished a former division into twenty-four units made for performances at Athens (Nagy).[9] Considerations of the size of papyrus rolls and the needs and interests of the publishing trade may well be relevant, but seem not to be conclusive.[10] At the moment it seems impossible to find a consensus.

The fullest recent discussion of the extent to which the book divisions in the *Iliad* fall at pauses in the action, or interrupt a continuous narrative, is Oliver Taplin's (1992), and his work provides a good starting point. Taplin argues for a division of the *Iliad* into three parts, with the breaks falling after Book 9 (he omits Book 10) and at Book 18, line 354. The book division (which he is inclined to attribute to the school of Aristarchus in the mid-second century B.C.E.) he discusses in an appendix, examining each and considering why it is placed where it is and where else it might have been put. He does not explain his principles or his methodology, but seems to be basing his remarks on a division into narrative units of some kind.

On the whole, Taplin finds the present *Iliad* book divisions rather unsatisfactory. Four of them he approves: that between Books 7 and 8 (both armies go to sleep, and then after the break Zeus at dawn calls an assembly of the gods); that between 8 and 9 (he calls this "a memorable moment of closure," though the famous simile at the end of 8, describing the Trojan campfires on the plain, is followed at the beginning of 9 by the balancing simile depicting the storm-tossed hearts of the panicky Greeks); that between 9 and 11 (the Greeks retire to sleep; then dawn breaks and Strife summons them to battle), which is one of his "two fundamental divisions of the

---

[9] For references and further details, see Jensen 1999 (to her listings should now be added Haslam 1997: esp. 58–59) and Burgess 1996: 87–89 (on book divisions in the Epic Cycle). There is also a full up-to-date bibliography in Heiden 1998: 68 n. 2, and a fine summary of the very limited evidence in Richardson 1993: 20–21. The "Comments" by other scholars on Jensen 1999 in the same volume of *Symbolae Osloenses* (74: 35–73), which I saw only after this chapter had been completed, give valuable insights into the diversity of current opinions, but (except for my own) do not touch upon the main issue of this chapter, the "paragraph" divisions.

[10] See (in particular) Haslam 1997; Olson 1995; van Sickle 1980.

Iliad"; and that between 12 and 13 (the Trojans break through the Greek wall, and Zeus turns his attention elsewhere), which he calls "the most significant dividing-point between book 11 and 15."[11] Taplin is content with, but can find equally good alternatives for, another eight book divisions (including the "So he spoke . . ." mentioned above);[12] at two places he can find a better place for the division than the conventional one;[13] and he objects to the placing of the book division at eight places.[14] It is noteworthy that Taplin can find preferable or equally acceptable alternatives to the traditional book division at all but four of the twenty-two positions, which suggests that the divisions do not fall at especially significant points.

Taplin does not discuss the phraseology that occurs immediately before and immediately after either the existing book divisions or the alternative breaks he sometimes prefers. This, however, has been done by Keith Stanley (1993). Stanley's book offers an immensely thorough exploration of instances of ring form in the composition of the *Iliad*, and includes a section on the book division. He points out that usually "a new book begins with a change of scene, a shift from a general view to a close-up (and the reverse), or a transfer of attention from one character to another—rarely a discontinuity in time. Beyond marking these shifts, the new beginnings generally provide both formal and verbal closure for the previous narrative and, even more consistently, an introduction to the ensuing action."[15] He goes on to identify four major types of transition between books, emphasizing the extent of the summarizing of the action—retrospective and prospective, that before and that to come—in each case and the strength of the consequent continuity.

Stanley does not, however, study in detail the phrases the poet uses in making these transitions. If we expect to find a new book beginning a new episode, we would look for books of the *Odyssey* opening with the phrase that Odysseus pronounces five times to introduce his successive adventures: ἔνθεν δὲ προτέρω πλέομεν ἀκαχήμενοι ἦτορ, "Then further on we sailed, with grief in our hearts." But actually this verse always occurs *within* a book.[16] We might expect to find one book closing with a sunset and the

---

[11] Taplin 1992: 289–290. However, concerning the break between Books 12 and 13, he criticizes G. S. Kirk's remark that it has "strong organic authority," and feels "it is rather unfortunate that it marks the single great break in two-volume editions."

[12] After Books 1, 2, 5, 6, 11, 13, 19, 23 (this is my categorization of Taplin 1992: 287–293).

[13] After Books 3 and 21.

[14] After Books 4, 14, 15, 16, 17, 18, 20, and 22 (since Taplin omits Book 10, he deals with only twenty-three books and thus with a total of twenty-two book divisions).

[15] Stanley 1993: 249. Stanley refers to van Groningen's earlier work on retrospective and prospective links in Greek literature, but does not mention or list his main publication on the subject (van Groningen 1960: 36–53).

[16] Though once it stands as the penultimate line, expanded by the following ἄσμενοι ἐκ θανάτοιο, φίλους ὀλέσαντες ἑταίρους, "glad to have escaped death, having lost our beloved companions" (*Odyssey* 9.565–566); the other occurrences are 9.62, 9.105, 10.77, 10.133.

next beginning with a sunrise; and in fact one of the two most common ways to begin a book is with the coming of Dawn, found nine times. These cases are, however, only a few among many: as de Jong has pointed out, "The *Iliad* has thirteen sunrises, of which three are found at the beginning of a book (Books 8, 11, 19); and fourteen sunsets, of which four occur at the end of a book (1, 7, 8, 9). The *Odyssey* has eighteen sunrises, of which six are found at the beginning of a book (2, 3, 5, 8, 16, 17); and twenty-nine sunsets, of which nine occur at the end of a book (1, 2, 3, 5, 7, 16, 17, 18, 19)."[17]

The same is true, however, of the other equally common beginning for a book in the two poems (which Stanley notices). This is the phrase ὣς οἱ μὲν . . . (including ὣς ὁ μὲν . . . , ὣς αἱ μὲν . . . , ὣς τὼ μὲν . . .) followed by δὲ or αὐτάρ: "So they . . . ; but the others. . . ." This phrase begins seven books of the *Iliad* (9, 12, 16, 18, 20, 22, 23) and two of the *Odyssey* (6, 7). But as with sunsets and sunrises, these nine instances at book division are a minority of the total occurrences of the phrase, which number thirty-four in the *Iliad* and thirty-five in the *Odyssey*. So we must note that the phraseology, and the structure—the retrospective and prospective links—of *every* book division can be paralleled at other positions within the books (usually where modern editors mark a paragraph division). This makes it clear that there is little or no point in studying and categorizing the forty-six breaks that occur at the book divisions of the two poems while ignoring (as Stanley does) the hundreds of similar breaks found elsewhere *within* the books. The analyses of the book divisions by Taplin and Jensen similarly suffer from their failure to consider this.

To repeat: *The book divisions are merely a few among the many similar breaks in the poems.* And since the phraseology used most commonly at book divisions, signaling sunset-dawn or summarizing the preceding action ("so they . . ."), is far more common at other places in the text, it is clear why Taplin could so often find alternative positions for the book divisions. It must also be noted that these phrases do not indicate any heavy break in the continuity of the narrative. Of course, sunset and sunrise represent a boundary of sorts, a time of rest for the characters, and potentially for the audience and singer, too. But though the characters retire to rest and then rise again to take up the business of the day, at only three of the book divisions listed above is there a change of setting (from earth to Olympus, beginning *Iliad* 8 and 11 and *Odyssey* 5): in the remaining six cases there is no change in location or characters, so the narrative break is slight and easy for the listener

---

[17] De Jong 1996: 22–23 (I have replaced her roman numerals with arabic). I have followed de Jong (ibid.: 23) in including *Odyssey* 16 among those books beginning with a sunrise, though the reference to it is slight (16.2: . . . ἅμ' ἠόϊ . . .)—as is that to the preceding nightfall (15.556–557: . . . συβώτης . . . | ἐνίαυεν). On dawn and dusk as breaking points in other epics, see van Sickle 1984. De Jong also remarks (1996: 24–25) on the use of the ὣς ὁ μέν . . . formula, and has contributed many useful observations on the book-division breaks to the *Symbolae Osloenses* debate (de Jong 1999).

to follow. We do not lose the continuity when Telemachus goes to bed in
the last verses of *Odyssey* 1 and gets up and dresses at the start of *Odyssey* 2
(he does the same at *Odyssey* 16–17, and so does Alcinous at 7–8).[18]

The same is true of scene changes introduced by ὣς οἱ μὲν . . . ; the demands on the listener's attention and acuteness are similarly light. In fact,
van Groningen, in his masterly study of such cases, considered the phrase
to signify not a break at all, but a *link* (French *cheville*). He included it in the
cases that he found to be the most common connection between sections,
his "mixed link" (*cheville mixte*), which combines both a retrospective and a
prospective view, summarizing both what has just happened and what is to
come.[19] Two examples will illustrate this. The first (*Iliad* 13.671–675) has
a line break between μέν and δέ:

τὸν βάλ᾽ ὑπὸ γναθμοῖο καὶ οὔατος· ὦκα δὲ θυμὸς
ᾤχετ᾽ ἀπὸ μελέων, στυγερὸς δ᾽ ἄρα μιν σκότος εἷλεν.
ὣς οἳ μὲν μάρναντο δέμας πυρὸς αἰθομένοιο·
Ἕκτωρ δ᾽ οὐκ ἐπέπυστο Διῒ φίλος, οὐδέ τι ᾔδη
ὅττι ῥά οἱ νηῶν ἐπ᾽ ἀριστερὰ δηϊόωντο.

Him he [Paris] struck under the jaw and the ear; swiftly the life
left his limbs, and dreadful darkness overcame him.
So *they* fought, looking like a fire blazing;
But *Hector* had not heard, he Zeus' favorite, and did not know
that his men by the ships to the left were being slaughtered.

The second (*Iliad* 20.73–76) breaks between what is past and what is to
come at the strong pause position (the bucolic diaeresis) near the line-end:

ἄντα δ᾽ ἄρ᾽ Ἡφαίστοιο μέγας ποταμὸς βαθυδίνης,
ὃν Ξάνθον καλέουσι θεοί, ἄνδρες δὲ Σκάμανδρον.
ὣς οἳ μὲν θεοὶ ἄντα θεῶν ἴσαν· αὐτὰρ Ἀχιλλεὺς
Ἕκτορος ἄντα μάλιστα λιλαίετο δῦναι ὅμιλον.

Against Hephaestus the mighty swirling river [took his stance],
"Xanthos" the gods call him, and men, "Scamander."
So *they*, gods against gods, advanced; but *Achilles*,
Hector most of all he was longing to meet in the throng.

In both cases the present general situation is summarized, concluding the
past action, and then our attention is directed toward (i.e., the poet zooms
in on) a particular individual upon whom will center the action to come.
The summary both confirms the state of the action and signals to the lis-

---

[18] On the special case at the beginning of *Iliad* 19, see below, note 24.

[19] Van Groningen 1960: 44. The Homeric examples he gives are *Iliad* 1.318 and 22.1, with
Odyssey 9.62 ("Then further on we sailed . . . "). Among his other examples is Herodotus 1.92–
93.

tener that a change of focus is coming: it "is always a sign that the action just told is concluded, that we are to expect a change of some kind, and it is very often the harbinger of a scene switch."[20] Two formulas that include the phrase are especially common: ὡς οἳ μὲν τοιαῦτα πρὸς ἀλλήλους ἀγόρευον, "So they were talking like this among themselves; [but ...]" (eight times in the *Iliad*, seventeen in the *Odyssey*), and ὡς οἳ μὲν μάρναντο [δέμας πυρὸς] [αἰθομένοιο], "So they fought, [looking like a fire] [blazing]; [but ...]," which comprises useful variations in length and occurs in some shape fifteen times in the *Iliad*.

The same linking function can be seen in many of the other phrases used at book divisions (as well as within books). Books 2 and 10 of the *Iliad* begin ἄλλοι μὲν ..., "Everyone else ...," summarizing (retrospectively) the preceding few verses, which tell how the rest of the world is asleep, before focusing (prospectively) on the leading character in the episode to come with Δία δ᾽ οὐκ ἔχε νήδυμος ὕπνος (2.2) and ἀλλ᾽ οὐκ Ἀτρεΐδην Ἀγαμέμνονα ποιμένα λαῶν | ὕπνος ἔχε γλυκερός ... (10.3–4), "But sleep did not grip Zeus / Agamemnon...." The same phrase also occurs four times at what are now marked as paragraph breaks in the *Iliad*, and twice in the *Odyssey*, as well as a number of times at mid-paragraph.[21] Four books begin αὐτὰρ ἐπεὶ ... "But when ..." (*Iliad* 3, 15; *Odyssey* 11, 12), in the first three cases introducing a clause that summarizes the preceding action before the coming events are announced in balancing μέν and δέ clauses.[22] Similar, theoretically, are cases where a book begins with a formulaic speech-conclusion summarizing a speech that took place in the preceding book, and the remainder of the sentence looks forward (*Iliad* 7, and *Odyssey* 9 and 13, where a new speaker continues the same scene).[23] Book 24 of the *Iliad* also begins with two verses of general summary of the situation before starting the new topic at the end of verse 3 with αὐτὰρ Ἀχιλλεὺς....

In a few cases, the present book division contrives that the preceding book ends with a retrospective summary, as at the end of *Iliad* 13, and the new book begins with a prospective one (*Iliad* 5, 6, 13, 14). Here we may include the beginning of *Iliad* 4, where the retrospective summary is the speech conclusion ὣς ἔφατ᾽ Ἀτρεΐδης, "So spoke Agamemnon" (3.461), and the prospective summary shifts the scene to Olympus.

In the above cases, the retrospective and prospective summaries form a close link between the end of one book and the beginning of another (as

[20] S. Richardson 1990: 31 (more will be said later about Richardson's work).
[21] At breaks: *Iliad* 1.22, 1.376, 2.211, 24.677; *Odyssey* 1.11, 9.172; mid-paragraph: *Iliad* 5.877, 7.473, *Odyssey* 2.82, 4.285, 5.110 = 133 = 7.251, 17.503, 21.232.
[22] Between the end of *Odyssey* 11 and the start of *Odyssey* 12, there is no break in the action, location, or narrative. A search of the Homer *Thesaurus linguae Graecae* database with Pandora software listed 171 total occurrences of this phrase.
[23] S. Richardson (1990: 32) calls ὣς φάτο "a vestigial summary."

they do elsewhere between scenes or "paragraphs"). But several times no such link is necessary, because there is no change of location, just a change of focalization from one character to another. In *Iliad* 14.1 and 17.1 the character switch is conveyed by οὐκ ἔλαθεν (οὐδ' ἔλαθ'), "This was not unnoticed by . . . ," and in the first lines of *Odyssey* 14, 19, 20, and 22 simply by αὐτὰρ ὁ . . . , "But *he*. . . ." *Odyssey* 24 may also be regarded as separated from the end of 23 by a change in focalization of the same scene, as the location is unchanged and the two actions are alike—from Odysseus' palace, Athena led away (ἐξῆγε) Odysseus and his companions, and Hermes in the following verse called away (ἐξεκαλεῖτο) the ghosts of the dead suitors. Rather similar is the arrival of the beggar Irus in the first line of *Odyssey* 18, joining the characters in the current scene with the same phrase, ἦλθε δ' ἐπὶ . . . , "There came up . . . ," as the successive shades who approach Odysseus in the underworld (*Odyssey* 11.84, 90, 387, 467) and the ghost of Patroclus when it appears to Achilles (*Iliad* 23.65).

Once in the *Iliad* a book division interrupts a continuous narrative (without change of scene or focalization), paralleled elsewhere where editors do not even indent a new paragraph (between *Iliad* 20 and 21);[24] and once in the *Odyssey* a continuing scene, focused on the same character, is broken into by the book division (between *Odyssey* 20 and 21). In the same way, two books of the *Odyssey* begin with the arrival at a new location of the characters already in our minds at the conclusion of the previous book, marking no change in scene or focalization (*Odyssey* 4, 10).

Of the forty-six book divisions in the two poems, we have now discussed forty-five, noting the phrases that bridge the break and the similar phrases that occur *within* the books. The remaining book division is that between *Odyssey* 14 and 15, where at the end of one book Eumaeus, in Ithaca, "made his way out to lie down where his white-tusked pigs, | under a hollow rock, were sleeping, in shelter from the north wind," and at the beginning of the next, "But she to broad-wayed Lacedaimon, Pallas Athena, | went . . . ," where she found Telemachus asleep. This is, it seems, the same night, and the break might just perhaps be fitted into the dusk-dawn group (Page speaks of ". . .the same night, spread above the separated father and son, bringing them together . . . the night in which Telemachus begins his journey blends imperceptibly with the night of Odysseus at Ithaca"[25]). But the

---

[24] The parallel narrative is at *Iliad* 11.169–170; see Edwards 1991: 345. I was delighted to find that Robert Fagles, in his *Iliad* translation (1990), at the end of Book 20 puts no period but just a dash—an eminently fitting indicator of the continuity.

In my view, the division between *Iliad* 18 and 19, which I have mentioned above among the breaks at the coming of dawn, may well belong with these "scene-interrupting" divisions, as the same type-scene of Thetis' divine journey runs over from book to book; see Edwards 1991: 235.

[25] Page 1955: 67–68. Page gives a full account of older treatments of the chronological issue here (77 n. 14).

drastic and unmediated change of characters and location—Athena left Ithaca long ago (13.439–440) and does not carry us with her on her journey to Lacedaimon—is unique, and might better be attributed to the poet's unfamiliarity with handling a narrative taking place simultaneously in two widely disparate locations.[26]

We have seen that in all cases the change of setting, if there is one, is smoothed by one means or another, by some interconnection between the end of one book and the start of the next. The connection is sometimes between the fall of night and the dawn that follows—a pause, a joint, an articulation point, not a break in continuity (at the beginning of nine books).[27] Mostly, retrospective and/or prospective summaries tie the past and future actions together by contrasting the characters in some way ("Some [were doing one thing], the others [did something else]," at the beginning of twenty-four books).[28] Or the same scene may continue, with just a change of focalization to another character (at the beginning of eight books),[29] or even without such a change (at the beginning of four books).[30] If one prints out the last few lines of one book and the first few of the next, with no white space to suggest a division (thanks to computers and databases this can easily be done), it is immediately apparent that Homer is not concerned with providing a convenient ending for one book and a beginning for the next—on the contrary, he joins them together as smoothly as possible, making it as easy as he can for the listener to be unaware of any interruption or transition.

THE PARAGRAPH DIVISIONS

If the narrative breaks at the forty-six book divisions are identical with those at the much greater number of places where modern editors and translators mark paragraph indents, we should look more closely at the latter—do they

---

[26] The only parallel in the *Odyssey*, a reverse change of location from Telemachus in Lacedaimon to the suitors in Odysseus' palace, occurs in the middle of a book and is eased by a summarizing ὣς οἳ μὲν . . . | μνηστῆρες δὲ . . . (4.624–625). See the commentary in Heubeck et al. 1988: 231–232, and Heubeck and Hoekstra 1989: 231. Olson, however, takes a quite different view: "At the end of Book xiii both Athena and the poet make it clear that her journey to Sparta (μέν) is to balance Odysseus' visit to Eumaios (αὐτάρ) (xiii.439–40; cf. xiii.403–13), and there is accordingly no strong break in the narrative-line when she appears to Telemachos here (xv.1–5)" (Olson 1995: 234). Hellwig (1964: 100) found the break abrupt, grouping it with scene changes with a "hidden connection."

On the poet's apparent problems in handling simultaneous narratives, see also p. 51 below (on the Chryse voyage in *Iliad* 1).

[27] *Iliad* 8, 11, 19 (see note 24 above); *Odyssey* 2, 3, 5, 8, 16, 17.

[28] *Iliad* 2, 3, 4, 5, 6, 7, 9, 10, 12, 13, 14, 15, 16, 18, 20, 22, 23, 24; *Odyssey* 6, 7, 9, 11, 12, 13.

[29] *Iliad* 14, 17; *Odyssey* 14, 18, 19, 20, 22, 24.

[30] *Iliad* 21; *Odyssey* 4, 10, 21.

fall at scene changes, or do they interrupt the narrative? Are they bridged by the same kinds of link we noticed above at the book divisions?

First we must define the meaning of "scene." The basic facts about the articulation of narrative have been clarified by modern narratological studies, and applied to Homer in the excellent work of Scott Richardson (1990). From the narratological point of view, "The scene is the incorporation of the dramatic principle into narrative. Story and discourse here are of relatively equal duration."[31] In other words, in a "scene," the time taken to tell what is happening is roughly equivalent to the time that elapsed during the event. An example is, "Odysseus fell off the raft, and let the oar slip from his hands" (*Odyssey* 5.315–316). Another common example is dialogue, which of course takes about as long to read (or recite) as it would take to deliver in real life.

Besides "scenes" in this restricted sense, narrative consists of "summaries," where the narrator may (for instance) describe in a few words an action that lasted for a considerable period ("they feasted"); here the discourse time is shorter than the story time. This distinction means that the word "scene" now has two quite different senses: the ordinary sense, in which we would speak of the "scene" in which Chryses the priest supplicates Agamemnon to return his daughter for ransom (*Iliad* 1.12–33—and we might perhaps include his subsequent prayer for Apollo's intervention, 34–43); and the narratological sense, in which the priest's arrival is a "summary" (his approach to the assembly, which perhaps had to be summoned for the express purpose of his visit, and the preliminaries to his address to the throng, took far longer than it takes the narrator to describe it), which is followed by the "scene" proper, the real-time words spoken by him and by the displeased king. In this sense, this "scene" ends at the close of Agamemnon's speech (1.32), where the next "summary" begins, telling of the old man's departure for the seashore. His direct-speech prayer to his god will form the next "scene."

In a novel of the the usual kind, scene and summary regularly alternate. The Homeric practice, however, is different. Richardson says: "Notice that Homer does not make use of narrative's usual alternation between scene and summary. Scenes (including direct speech) comprise the bulk of the passage [*Odyssey* 5.315–443] and are interrupted primarily by descriptive pauses, commentary, and mind reading, rarely by summaries" (1990: 201). To demonstrate this, he gives a commentary on the passage (the wrecking of Odysseus' raft by Poseidon, the merciful interventions of Leucothea and Athena, and the hero's attempts to land on Phaeacia). The "scenes" and "summaries" he identifies are often short, and the listener is gently led from

---

[31] Chatman 1978: 72; cf. Bal 1985: 72–75; Rimmon-Kenan 1983: 53–55; S. Richardson 1990: 9–10. The following *Odyssey* example is taken from S. Richardson 1990: 201.

one to the next: over and over again Richardson observes the continuity of the narrative and the absence of sharp, sudden changes of location or character.

A few examples will show this. After the "scene" of Odysseus' shipwreck (*Odyssey* 5.315–320), a "summary" briefly describes the length of time he spent tossed about in the water, the long duration stressed by ἔνθα καὶ ἔνθα, "here and there," twice over, and ἄλλοτε μὲν . . . ἄλλοτε δ(ὲ) . . . , "at one time . . . at another time." Finally the sea-goddess Leucothea sees him, feels pity, and joins him on the wrecked raft. Sensibly, Richardson hesitates to call her arrival a new "scene": he comments, "Scene switch to Leukothea. In effect, however, we do not change scenes so much as we discover that our point of view has been shared with Leukothea, who, like us, is watching Odysseus battle the storm" (1990: 202–203). Similarly, after the next "summary" describing Odysseus' perplexity about whether to trust her and follow her advice, Richardson again hesitates to begin a new "scene," saying, "There is no actual scene switch to Poseidon, but more a broadening of our perspective" (ibid.: 204). A little later Poseidon sees Odysseus swimming, expresses his satisfaction with his own handiwork, and in a two-verse "new scene" (5.380–381) goes back home to Aegae; but Richardson points out that after the following "scene switch," the rescuing Athena sees not Poseidon's return but Odysseus's continuing hazards, and so 380–381 "are parenthetical to the ongoing scene" (ibid.: 205). Only after the narrator has told us of Athena's calming of the storm and of her intent that Odysseus find safety among the Phaeacians come two verses of unmistakable summary: "Then two nights and two days on the mighty surf | he was driven, many times foreseeing disaster," 5.388–389). When the "scene" resumes, the wind drops, and the hero sights land nearby. The remainder of the passage is diversified by descriptions of the shore, insights into the minds of Odysseus and Athena, similes, and another monologue, but Richardson wisely does not suggest further scene switches.

Despite the occasional changes from "scene" to "summary" and back, that is, in the relationship of story time and discourse time, it is obvious that to the listener, the whole passage, from shipwreck to landing, is effortlessly continuous. If an editor insists on dividing the narrative into paragraphs, the breaks will fall at some of the places where "scene" meets "summary." But they do not signal any break in the *action;* and in fact, there is no real change of location or time sequence until, after a summarizing ὡς ὁ μὲν ἔνθα καθεῦδε πολύτλας δῖος Ὀδυσσεὺς, "So there he slept, long-suffering Odysseus" (*Odyssey* 6.1), Athena (αὐτὰρ Ἀθήνη . . . , 6.2) begins to make her way to Nausicaa's bedroom. Then a new action begins, in a new location and with a new character.

Because of the ambiguity of the word "scene," we will in the future use the general term "episode" for a continuous action (including both "scenes"

and "summaries" in the narratological sense), usually taking place in one location and involving (mainly) the same character(s). Then it can be said that
the whole tale of Odysseus' difficult journey from Calypso's island to Phaeacia (*Odyssey* 5.269–6.2a) is a single episode, since from beginning to end the
hero is never out of our sight.[32] The episode might be thought to start with
the daybreak at which the hero began to build his raft (5.228), or when Calypso sought him out to tell him he might at last leave (5.149), or when Hermes left Olympus with the command that she should release him (5.43), or
even when the council of the gods met to discuss the issue (5.1)—for our
present purpose it is unnecessary to decide, since the very problem of de-
termining the boundaries of an episode makes it clear that the whole story
is all-but-indissolubly interconnected.

Let us experiment with dividing the narrative into "episodes" of this kind,
ignoring the paragraphs and the book divisions that our Greek and English
texts lay out before us. First, it must be noted that neither episodes nor
"scenes" (in the narratological sense) necessarily correspond to the type-
scenes, the recurrent, similarly structured descriptions of actions such as a
sacrifice, the launching of a ship, or the reception of a guest, of which
Homeric narrative is composed.[33] For instance, the voyage of Odysseus to
Chryse to restore the ransomed woman to her father (*Iliad* 1.430b-487) is
clearly one episode, but it is based upon six type-scenes, some of which are
narratologically mainly or wholly "scenes" (e.g., Odysseus' handing over of
Chryseis to her father, much of it in real-time dialogue), whereas others are
obviously "summaries" (e.g., the arrival and docking of the ship at 1.433–
436, which would surely be a fairly lengthy business but takes only four
verses to narrate).[34]

We can begin at the beginning. The actions of the story of *Iliad* 1 are
(after the proem, 1–12a): (1) Chryses' supplication, his prayer to Apollo,
and the resulting plague (12b–53); (2) the Greek council, including the
quarrel of Achilles and Agamemnon, Athena's advice to Achilles, and
Nestor's attempt at mediation (54–305); then, after quickly narrated summaries of subsequent actions (Achilles' return to his dwelling, the dispatch
of the ship bearing Chryseis, the purification of the army, and the ensuing
sacrifice, 306–318a), which might best be considered an interlude between
episodes, come (3) the dispatch of the heralds to Achilles' dwelling, the abduction of Briseis, and Achilles' appeal to Thetis (318b–430a); (4) the delivery of the ransomed woman to her father, the subsequent festivities, and

[32] With the possible but insignificant exception of Poseidon's return to Aegae, 381–382
(see above).

[33] For a fuller definition of type-scenes, see Edwards 1992a: 285–287; and for a brief account of their nature and use, Edwards 1991: 11–15.

[34] The type-scenes are described in Edwards 1980: 19–23, where I divide the book as a
whole into twenty-eight type-scenes.

the voyage home (430b–487); and, after a short summary of Achilles' misery (488–492), (5) the affairs on Olympus, including Thetis' supplication to Zeus, the quarrel between him and Hera, Hephaestus' mediation, and the retirement of the gods to rest; the action continues, through the uninterrupted focus on Zeus, on to his dispatch of the Dream to Agamemnon in the following book (1.493–2.35a). This looks like five episodes, plus two concise summaries.[35]

How does the poet pass from one of these episodes to the next? The first episode is linked to the proem, mid-verse, as a kind of exegesis: "Because he dishonored Chryses the priest, | Agamemnon did, when he came to the Greek ships . . ." (οὕνεκα τὸν Χρύσην ἠτίμασεν ἀρητῆρα | Ἀτρεΐδης· ὃ γὰρ ἦλθε θοὰς ἐπὶ νῆας Ἀχαιῶν . . . , 1.11–12)—the statement that Agamemnon blundered followed by the account of how he did so.[36] The plague with which it ends is coupled to the beginning of the second episode, the assembly: "*For nine days* among the army went the god's arrows, | and *on the tenth* to assembly he called the people, did Achilles" (1.53–54). When the assembly breaks up, the narrator tells us about the subsequent actions of both the main participants, joined by linked particles (Πηλεΐδης μὲν . . . , 1.306, Ἀτρεΐδης δ' ἄρα . . . , 1.308), and after Agamemnon has given orders to his men for the expiation and purification there comes a summarizing phrase of the type we have mentioned above, headed by ὣς οἱ μὲν . . . , "So *they* were working among the army. . . ." Then (mid-verse) the third episode begins, with οὐδ' Ἀγαμέμνων | λῆγ' ἔριδος, "But *Agamemnon* | did not forget his clash" (1.318–319), and it continues until Thetis leaves the sorrowing Achilles (430a).

At this point there *is* a break in continuity before the next episode (the fourth), because (mid-verse again) the narrator leaves Achilles on the shore and suddenly returns to the Chryse voyage: αὐτὰρ Ὀδυσσεὺς | ἐς Χρύσην ἵκανεν . . . , "And Odysseus | to Chryse came . . ." (1.430b–431). This voyage began at 308–311 and has been proceeding *simultaneously* with Briseis' abduction and Achilles' appeal to Thetis. The same kind of abruptness appears again at the end of this Chryse-voyage episode, as the returning ship crew scatters to their dwellings, and the narrator returns us once again to the still-grieving Achilles, who (it seems) has not moved in all this time: αὐτοὶ δ' ἐσκίδναντο κατὰ κλισίας τε νέας τε. | αὐτὰρ ὃ μήνιε νηυσὶ παρή-

---

[35] The table of "Scene-Distribution in the *Iliad*" in Latacz 1996: 108 divides *Iliad* 1 into fourteen sections, grouped into three parts separated by the nine-day period of the plague and the eleven-day absence of the gods with the Ethiopians; his sections are more numerous than mine because (for instance) he subdivides what I have above considered "the Greek council" into three parts, and "the affairs on Olympus" into another three. Nicolai (1973: 90–92 and 156) gives a complex analysis (on a different principle) into eight parts, and remarks that the return of Chryseis (430–487) is "in Form einer 'Enklave'" (92).

[36] For the grammatical reference of ὃ, see Appendix C, note 16.

μενος ὠκυπόροισι | διογενὴς Πηλῆος υἱὸς πόδας ὠκὺς Ἀχιλλεύς, "So *they* scattered to their shelters and ships. | But *he* nursed his anger by his swift ships, | he, the divinely born son of Peleus, the swift-footed Achilles" (1.487–489). The long, dignified name-formula (instead of just αὐτὰρ Ἀχιλλεὺς | . . .) confirms that the poet is intentionally producing a rather exceptional effect here, suggesting that Achilles' grief continues night and day, as he ignores assemblies and battles, sitting there eating his heart out in longing for the tumult of battle (1.490–492), all the time that the lengthy, much-amplified restoration of Chryseis has occupied our attention.[37] Since Odysseus' voyage and Achilles' brooding are concurrent—a rare thing in Homeric storytelling—the narrator cannot continue with the one-way passage of time as he usually does, and is obliged to make an abnormal jump from one location to the other at both beginning and end of the two contemporaneous narratives. (We noted a similar problem at the break between *Odyssey* 14 and 15, above, p. 46.)

After this brief reminder of Achilles' feelings, the final (fifth) episode of this book begins with a link through the passage of time: ἀλλ᾽ ὅτε δή ῥ᾽ ἐκ τοῖο δυωδεκάτη γένετ᾽ ἠώς, | καὶ τότε δὴ πρὸς Ὄλυμπον ἴσαν θεοί, "But when, *after this*, the twelfth dawn came, | then too to Olympus the gods returned" (1.493–494). First comes Thetis' supplication to Zeus and his response, then (further matching the type-scenes at the beginning of the book) the assembly of the gods, the quarrel of the two protagonists Zeus and Hera, the mediation of Hephaestus, and finally the feasting, entertainment, and retirement for the night. The episode can be considered to continue into the following book, because the connection to Zeus' next action, sending the Dream to Agamemnon, is very close: this "Now all the others . . . but not X . . ." motif (here ἄλλοι μέν ῥα . . . | Δία δ᾽ οὐκ . . . , 2.1–2) is often found with no break (see above, p. 45).

So not only do the "scenes" and "summaries" within each episode follow naturally upon each other: the episodes, too, are closely linked, the end of one and beginning of the next often falling in mid-verse; and even when two simultaneous actions must be narrated (an exceptional case), the switch from the first location to the second is made in mid-verse, bridging the transition, and the subsequent return to the first location is used as an opportunity to elaborate the portentous sight of Achilles brooding apart from the Greek host. Smoothly and almost uninterruptedly, action follows upon action, with continuity, not division, being always the poet's aim.

[37] See Edwards 1980: 24. S. Richardson 1990: 117 and 230 n. 17 includes 1.430 and 1.488 as two instances of "a clean break between scenes" (see below). It is worth noting that the content of the Chryse-voyage passage (1.430b–487), i.e., the restitution of the priest's daughter and the propitiatory sacrifice to Apollo, has already mostly been covered in 1.308–317, so the amplified version might be considered an afterthought or double recension.

JOINING EPISODE TO EPISODE

In the narrative of *Iliad* 1, as analyzed above, between the last two episodes came a change of location from the seashore near Troy to the gods' home on Olympus, which is managed by the narrator's summary of the passage of time. Such changes are common—in the *Iliad* from Greek camp to battle-field to Troy and to Olympus, in the *Odyssey* from Olympus to Ithaca to Pylos to Sparta to Calypso's island and so on; and in addition, Homer must change his focus from one character to another. How can this be contrived, while keeping the continuity and smoothness intact? Most of the answers can be found in Richardson (whose viewpoint is slightly different from mine); and as an additional check, we can examine the cases where an exchange between two new characters is suddenly introduced.[38]

The interconnections between one episode and the next are, of course, simply a more widespread exploitation of the same techniques we found linking one book to another, bridging the white space that unfortunately appears in our texts and translations. The retrospective and prospective summaries so often found between books, the familiar ὣς οἳ μὲν . . . δὲ (αὐτάρ) . . . , "So they . . . ; but [the others] . . . ," Richardson counts as "appositive summaries," and says, "Some appositive summaries look forward, but most refer to the immediately preceding scene and serve as a mark and a means of transition either to a new setting or to another action in the same scene. The backward-looking appositive summary is always a sign that the action just told is concluded, that we are to expect a change of some kind, and it is very often the harbinger of a scene-switch."[39] He lists the "appositive summaries" that lead to a change of location, finding thirty-six in the *Iliad* and ten in the *Odyssey*.[40]

A common and effective means of moving from one location to another,

---

[38] Basic work on the Homeric techniques of handling time and place was done in Hellwig 1964. Nicolai 1973 studied in particular the units of composition, the "Konstellationsein-heiten" (or "Absätze") and "Kapitel," which more or less correspond to what are here called "episodes" and "chapters" (he divides the *Iliad* into thirty-three "Kapitel," which roughly follow the book divisions, several of the books being divided into two parts). To a large extent, both these works have been superseded by S. Richardson 1990, which takes a modern narratological viewpoint but does not deal with the phraseology used at scene changes as fully as does Nicolai.

[39] S. Richardson 1990: 31.

[40] Ibid.: 213 n. 37. I have included in the totals the instances where he says, "The switch is not so abrupt because we follow a character to the next scene." He also lists (213 n. 39) many instances (fifteen in the *Iliad*, seventeen in the *Odyssey*) where the end of a speech is followed by a brief summary of its content before the next happening (e.g., ὣς φάτο νεικείων Ἀγαμέμ-νονα . . . | Θερσίτης· τῷ δ' ὦκα παρίστατο δῖος Ὀδυσσεύς . . . , "So he spoke, *abusing Agamem-non* . . . , | Thersites [did]; but quickly beside him stood Odysseus . . . ," *Iliad* 2.243–244). He also discusses some less frequent types of summary that I pass over here.

without allowing the listeners' attention to be diverted, is to have us led from place to place by a character—a deity, if Olympus is involved. "Homer retains the advantage of swift movement between scenes, but he lends the narrative the continuity that would be lost by an instantaneous change of scene" (S. Richardson 1990: 111). Or the scene we are leaving may be watched by a character whose reaction introduces the new episode. Homer generally uses standard phrases for this kind of transition, easily adaptable for different name-lengths and other metrical circumstances. For human observers, the most common phrases are, for example, τὸν δ᾽ ὡς οὖν ἐνόησε . . . , "When X saw him . . ."; Τρῶες δ᾽ ὡς εἴδοντο . . . , "When the Trojans saw . . ."; and οὐκ ἔλαθε . . . , "This was not unnoticed by . . . ," which begins *Iliad* 14 and 17.[41] In three instances the phrase begins in the middle of the verse, preventing modern editors from printing the paragraph division they would normally use in such circumstances.[42]

Often the character watching is a god, or the company of gods, looking down from Olympus. The same three phrases mentioned above recur,[43] and there are also four examples of a formula perhaps especially suited to the concerned deities, οὐδ᾽ ἀλαοσκοπιὴν εἶχε, "No 'blind-man's' lookout kept X" (*Iliad* 10.515, 13.10 = 14.135, *Odyssey* 8.285). Four times the location change is made in the middle of a verse.[44] Three times Zeus' pity for the sufferings of mortal men (and for the immortal horses who dwell among them) is used as a motive for the change, with expressions similar to τοῦ δὲ ἰδὼν ἐλέησε Κρόνου πάϊς ἀγκυλομήτεω, "Seeing them, pity filled Zeus" (*Iliad* 16.431 ≈ 17.441, 19.340).[45] Richardson also lists a number of cases

[41] References are taken from S. Richardson 1990: 229 n. 4. Versions of the phrases quoted are found at *Iliad* 5.95, 11.581, 11.599, 21.526–527 (elaborated), *Iliad* 15.484, 16.278, 16.419, 22.25 (elaborated), and *Iliad* 14.1, 17.1, 17.626, respectively.

[42] At least Allen's Oxford Classical Text, Lattimore, and Fagles. The phrases are: οἳ δὲ ἰδόντες | θάμβησαν . . . , *Iliad* 8.76–77; τὸν δὲ φράσατο προσιόντα | διογενὴς Ὀδυσεύς . . . , *Iliad* 10.339–340; νόησε δὲ φαίδιμος Ἕκτωρ, |, *Iliad* 17.483.

Richardson also lists four places in the *Iliad* and one in the *Odyssey* where "the watching is implied by the context, though not stated" (1990: 229 n. 4). As his words suggest, the "watcher" is already in our minds in the context, and has usually just been mentioned (*Iliad* 17.236–237, 17.497–498, *Odyssey* 13.164–165 [cf.160]) or is later said to be watching (*Iliad* 22.405–406, cf. 407). In the remaining case (a particularly interesting and impressive instance), Achilles has just ended his instructions to Patroclus to enter the battle, and after the summarizing phrase and switch to another character (*Iliad* 16.101–102, ὡς οἳ μὲν τοιαῦτα πρὸς ἀλλήλους ἀγόρευον, | Αἴας δ᾽ . . .), Ajax's defeat, and the firing of the Greek ships, all this is summarized, and in the same verse the narrative returns to Achilles' reaction to it: ὡς τὴν μὲν πρυμνὴν πῦρ ἄμφεπεν· αὐτὰρ Ἀχιλλεύς | . . . (16.124).

[43] Versions of them involving the gods are found at (respectively) *Iliad* 5.711 and 7.17; *Iliad* 8.397, 14.153, 17.198, *Odyssey* 5.282–283 (elaborated), 5.333, 5.375; *Iliad* 24.331. The references are taken from S. Richardson 1990: 229 n. 6.

[44] *Iliad* 15.4–6, 22.166, 24.331; *Odyssey* 5.375.

[45] Again Richardson lists cases where the gods' observation is only implied (229 n. 6). Here, too, they are sometimes said to be watching, either later (*Iliad* 4.1, cf. 4.4; 11.75, cf. 82) or previously (8.69, cf. 52).

where the connection between the episode that is ending and that which is to begin is made through hearing, not sight, with the hearer often being a deity (seven cases involve a break in mid-verse, with a phrase such as τοῦ δ᾽ ἔκλυε . . . , "He was heard by . . .").[46] There are also several instances where the link is that the newly entering character is *not* aware of the action we have just heard recounted; often this has pathetic effect, as when the movement is made from Hecuba's lament for Hector on the wall of Troy to Andromache's ignorance of his death as she sits weaving in her home (*Iliad* 22.437).[47]

In all these cases, which cover the majority of the episode transitions in the Homeric poems, the listener is carefully eased from one setting to the next with as little abruptness as possible. Even the examples where Richardson feels the scene changes "are effected in ways that break the chain and thereby call attention to our dependence on the narrator and his ability to travel from one location to another in an instant" often show a connection, as he points out.[48] Two parties may be performing the same action—and often in the same words, in phrases balanced by μὲν . . . δὲ . . . or by ἑτέρωθεν, "on the other side"; typical of many is:

> τοὶ δ᾽ ὁπλίζοντο μάλ᾽ ὦκα,
> ἀμφότερον <u>νέκυάς τ᾽ ἀγέμεν</u> ἕτεροι δὲ μεθ᾽ ὕλην·
> Ἀργεῖοι δ᾽ ἑτέρωθεν ἐϋσσέλμων ἀπὸ νηῶν
> ὀτρύνοντο <u>νέκυς τ᾽ ἀγέμεν</u>, ἕτεροι δὲ μεθ᾽ ὕλην.
>
> (*Iliad* 7.417–420)

"They prepared swiftly, | both *to collect the dead bodies and [others] to fetch firewood.* | The Greeks, on the other side, from their sturdy ships, | bestirred themselves *to collect the dead bodies and [the others] to fetch firewood.*"[49] The listeners would hardly feel this as a break in the action. Or the link may be that "the action in one scene has a great bearing on the other or is the topic of conversation of the other"[50]—Richardson's example is the switch from Paris and Helen in bed to the wronged husband Menelaus on the battlefield furiously searching for his vanished opponent (*Iliad* 3.448–449), which again would not be hard for a listener to follow (there is a μὲν . . . δὲ . . . link, too). Or a character may leave or arrive at a certain destination where the action continues, even when we do not accompany him/her on the journey: there are good examples where in one verse Athena leaves Olympus,

---

[46] These cases are *Iliad* 1.43 ≈ 16.527, 18.35, 21.388, 24.314, *Odyssey* 4.767, 6.328 (drawn from S. Richardson 1990: 229 n. 8).

[47] The references are in Richardson 1990: 229 n. 11. Often the phrase is a version of οὐδ᾽ ἄρα πώ τι πέπυστο . . . , "But he had not yet heard. . . ." In four cases in the *Iliad*, the location change is made mid-verse (11.497, 17.377, 17.401, 22.437).

[48] S. Richardson 1990: 115.

[49] Richardson lists many examples of this type of scene change (ibid.: 230 n. 13).

[50] Ibid.: 116; list at 230 n. 14.

heading for the plain before Troy, and in the next Achilles is continuing to pursue Hector there (*Iliad* 22.187–188); similarly, Hermes takes on his young man's disguise and sets off for the Trojan plain, and the next verse describes Priam and his companion driving past Ilus' tomb (*Iliad* 24.348–349). In such cases the link in our minds is of course close.[51]

Of special interest are the six cases in the *Iliad* and ten in the *Odyssey* where Richardson finds "a clean break between scenes," though he immediately adds, "Some of these might show a continuity I do not see," and further notes that "all but two seem to involve a continuation of the action from one scene to another but with a change of characters."[52] As an example he quotes *Iliad* 3.118–121, where in preparation for the portentous duel between Helen's two husbands, Agamemnon sends Talthybius the herald to the ships for two sacrificial lambs, and in the next verse Iris goes as a messenger to announce the impending action to Helen. In another instance (*Iliad* 20.42), the catalogue of the gods who are preparing to fight each other on the battlefield has just concluded, and as usual the narrator goes on to summarize the ongoing battle before the individual duels begin; the "break" is only unusual because of the unique switch from the catalogue of *deities* to the continuing fighting of *mortals*.[53] Something similar is the case at 21.520, where the gods quit and return to Olympus, and in the same verse the narrator begins to explain how Achilles continues the fighting. At 22.7 our attention has been engaged first (within a few lines) by the Trojans, rushing back into their city: then by the Greeks, moving unopposed towards the walls; then by Hector, standing alone before the gates; and finally to Achilles (22.7), sneered at by Apollo (who has lured him away from the pursuit of the Trojans). A movie camera would not find the transition difficult. In all these cases the action and the passage of time continue without interruption, and the break is minimal. (The remaining two "clean breaks" listed by Richardson in the *Iliad* occur before and after the voyage to Chryse [1.430, 1.488], and have been discussed above, pp. 51–52.)

Of the ten "clean breaks" Richardson identifies in the *Odyssey*, six are eased for the listener in the usual way by a preceding ὣς οἱ μὲν . . . summarizing phrase (followed by δέ or αὐτάρ).[54] In the remaining four, the two juxtaposed scenes are closely connected in the action as well as in time and place, and the break would hardly be obvious to a listener.[55]

[51] Ibid.: 117; list at 230 n. 15. In n. 16 he lists a few cases where there is a time lag (during which the action continues) between the character's departure from one scene and his arrival to begin another, as when Hector leaves the battlefield at *Iliad* 6.119 and arrives in Troy at 6.237.

[52] S. Richardson 1990: 117–118 and 230 n. 17.

[53] Cf. the similar switch between the end of the catalogue of Trojan allies at *Iliad* 2.877 and the onset of battle at 3.1; and Edwards 1991: 290.

[54] At *Odyssey* 4.624, 6.1, 7.1, 13.185, 24.203, 24.412.

[55] They are: *Odyssey* 3.464 (Nestor's people prepare the meal: then Polycaste bathes and dresses Telemachus to take his place at it), 7.14 (Nausicaa returns to her palace quarters: then

What about the instances where two new characters suddenly appear, where the verse introducing a direct speech, instead of containing the usual pronoun (for the continuing person, the Topic) and a single name (for the person newly introduced, the Focus), includes *two* names, those of both the speaker and the addressee? The use of both proper names might seem to indicate that neither of the characters is currently in the listener's mind, that is, there may be a break in the action. Speech introductions in Homer are both highly formulaic and very flexible, and most of the two-name verses can easily be found by checking the occurrences of the most common verbs meaning "he (she) spoke to": προσέφη, προσέειπε(ν), προσηύδα, προσεφώνεε(ν), and ἔειπε (εἶπε).[56]

Here again it is immediately noticeable that in almost all cases the two-name verse introduces no abrupt change, because in fact both the characters involved are already onstage and present in our minds. Simple examples are the verse where Odysseus, dining among the Phaeacians, asks Demodocus (who has just been escorted in by the herald) to sing about the Wooden Horse—δὴ τότε Δημόδοκον προσέφη πολύμητις Ὀδυσσεύς (*Odyssey* 8.486); and where Hector addresses Achilles in the middle of their duel after Athena has restored his spear to him—Ἕκτωρ δὲ προσέειπεν ἀμύμονα Πηλεΐωνα (*Iliad* 22.278). Usually at least one of the two characters has been mentioned recently, as when Zeus addresses Apollo (καὶ τότ᾽ Ἀπόλλωνα προσέφη νεφεληγερέτα Ζεύς, *Iliad* 16.666), asking him to remove Sarpedon's body, after a section in which his concern for his son has been the main issue. Occasionally one may even wonder if an earlier reference has intentionally prepared us for the introduction of the two characters, as when Sarpedon suddenly rebukes Hector (ἔνθ᾽ αὖ Σαρπηδὼν μάλα νείκεσεν Ἕκτορα δῖον, *Iliad* 5.471) after neither character has been in action for several hundred lines—except that four verses previously the disguised Ares has exhorted the Trojans to protect the fallen Aeneas, "whom equally we honor with great *Hector*" (κεῖται ἀνὴρ ὃν ἶσον ἐτίομεν Ἕκτορι δίῳ, 5.467).[57] Or there may be another kind of connection, as when Idomeneus addresses Nestor (αὐτίκα δ᾽ Ἰδομενεὺς προσεφώνεε Νέστορα δῖον, *Iliad* 11.510) when, though neither man has been mentioned for several hundred lines, he is requesting him to rescue Machaon, who has just been wounded (11.505–507), and this urgency serves to continue our line of thought. In some cases an apparent harshness is diminished if we realize (as does

---

Odysseus rises from where she left him and prepares to enter the city), 20.124 (the servingwomen light a fire in the hall: then Telemachus in his bedroom rises and dresses before entering it), and 24.1 (Athena leads Odysseus and his companions *from the hall* to the countryside: then Hermes summons the spirits of the suitors *from the hall* to Hades—see above, p. 46).

[56] These two-name speech introductions are discussed in Edwards 1968: 15–16 and 20–35. On the topic generally, see Riggsby 1992 and Beck 1999.

[57] There is a very similar instance at *Iliad* 17.582 (cf. 17.576–577).

Richardson) that the two characters who suddenly appear should be thought of as having been observing the scene all the time, as when Zeus, during the mourning of the Greeks for Patroclus, suddenly appears teasing Hera about her favoritism for their side (*Iliad* 18.356).[58] There are similar cases at *Iliad* 17.237 = 651 and *Odyssey* 24.472.[59]

It is now clear that in actuality *there are no narrative breaks within the* Iliad *and the* Odyssey. Each is a seamless whole. When the poet is obliged to change his focus from one character to another, or move the action from one location to another, a link is provided, or the completed action is summarized and mildly contrasted with the action to come (. . . μὲν . . . δὲ . . .). Often the change of focus happens in the middle of a verse, which obviously prevented any interruption in the discourse. The sequence of time, as has long been understood, proceeds continuously, one episode following smoothly after another.[60]

CONTINUITY AND ORAL POETICS

Listening to a Homeric epic must have been like watching a soccer match rather than a football game—play is continuous (except for the occasional penalty and infrequent goal) and the "ball" (the listener's attention) is always in movement, passing from one character to another from the beginning of the epic to its end. This uninterrupted continuity probably contributed to Matthew Arnold's repeated emphasis on Homer's "rapidity" or "flowing rapidity" in his famous essay *On Translating Homer*, though he was thinking primarily of the rhythm and movement of Homeric verse.[61] The word is picked up by a recent translator, Stanley Lombardo, who declares: "My primary concern as a poet has been, in producing text as in perform-

[58] See S. Richardson 1990: 229 n. 6; I had failed to observe this when I made my comments at Edwards 1968: 26 and 1991: 188.

[59] Other noteworthy two-name speech introductions occur when (twice) among the dueling divinities in *Iliad* 21 the next pair onstage is presented to us this way (21.435, 497); an action balancing a preceding one may be so introduced (*Iliad* 15.560, 15.568, 24.143). In two cases, a two-name verse follows the "would have . . . had not . . ." trope, bringing in two characters who are not in our minds (*Iliad* 6.75–76, 11.312: see S. Richardson 1990: 188 and 242 n. 53); this marks a very obvious narrator's intervention, bridging the change of characters. In the *Odyssey*, while we are waiting for Hermes and Calypso to begin their talk, the narrator reminds us that Odysseus is (concurrently) weeping on the shore, and has to mention both deities' names again to return us to their presence (*Odyssey* 5.85).

[60] The famous "Zielinski's Law" proving this is updated in Krischer 1971: 91–129. On the importance of maintaining the ordered sequence of episodes, see Finkelberg 1998: 121–130.

[61] For example, on pp. 9, 24, and 61–62 in a recent edition (Harold Bloom, gen. ed. [New York, 1983]). Bassett 1938: 119–128 has good remarks on Homer's economy of the listener's attention, and his unceasing care to keep it from straying.

ing, to represent as fully as possible the energy that comes from Homer's directness and rapidity" (1997: xi).

Occasionally this kind of unbroken continuity is found in modern works, though they do not approach the size of the Homeric epics. S. Richardson (1990: 118–119) compares the Alfred Hitchcock movie *Rope* (1948), in which there are no breaks in the filming and the camera follows the actors on the same set without interruption, "as though through the eyes of an on-looker." When a change of film reel is necessary, the camera passes behind something black, so that the viewer is not conscious of the interruption. As Richardson says, Homer, too, "fosters the illusion that his vision of the events and characters of the story is our vision" (ibid.: 119). Though the movie was (and is) highly regarded, the experiment was not repeated. An even closer parallel—likewise not repeated—occurs in Virginia Woolf's novel *Mrs. Dalloway*. Seymour Chatman (1978: 76–78) points out that in this 1925 work, "The elimination of summary contributes precisely to the abruptness and speed of the urban experience. The narrator need not sum-marize since the past so dominates the reminiscences of the major charac-ters. . . . A long period is covered, but discourse-time equals story-time: story-time is not the thirty years or so of elapsed life, but rather the time of [Mrs. Dalloway's] thinking about them" (ibid.: 77). Woolf's techniques for changing the focus from one character to another, or for moving the set-ting from Mrs. Dalloway's drawing-room to Whitehall to St. James's Park to Bond Street and so on, are often similar to Homer's.[62]

In Homer, this continuity is likely to be another surviving characteristic of oral poetry, arising because a sequential narrative without abrupt shifts of time, location, or characters was easier for the listeners to follow, or eas-ier for the composer-singer to keep track of, or (probably) both. Recently very significant progress in our understanding of the reasons for the devel-opment of certain Homeric techniques has been made in a series of articles by Elizabeth Minchin, who has applied to Homer the theories of cognitive discourse and recent studies of techniques of memorization.[63] Minchin has shown that certain characteristic Homeric structures (type-scenes or themes, ring-composition, lists, catalogues, invocations of the Muse, and descriptions of objects) are closely related to (or result from) the oral singer's art of storytelling and his need for help in memorizing and recall-ing his material and easing his audience's task of understanding and appre-ciating his song. They are an essential part of his oral art, including his re-lationship with his audience. To these oral techniques I think we must add the solicitous avoidance of sudden change in the narrative focus: a careful pursuit of continuity of narrative in maintaining the sequence of time, in

[62] See Appendix B.
[63] Minchin 1999, 1996, 1995a, 1995b, 1992; on ring-composition, see also Nimis 1999.

turning the focus from one character to another, and in moving the location of the scene of action.

For a fuller appreciation of the Homeric poems, we must observe and understand the function of techniques like these—this is the "oral poetics" called for by James Notopoulos fifty years ago, and more recently by J. B. Hainsworth.[64] Understanding Homer's desire for continuity is more significant than studying the positioning of the present book divisions. Whether the text is in Greek or English, a reader should attempt as far as possible to ignore both book divisions and paragraph markers. How the lack of designed break-points in the poems affected performances of the whole works, and of extracts from them, is discussed in Appendix C.

One final point. From the argument presented above, I think it follows that ideally the *Iliad* and the *Odyssey* should each be printed continuously, without breaks of any kind. In the final form in which we have received the epics, the narrative contains no positions for convenience breaks—not even the empty line-space that Woolf occasionally allows in *Mrs. Dalloway*. This would be practical in a Greek text intended primarily for professional scholars, such as the *Bibliotheca scriptorum graecorum et romanorum teubneriana* or the *Scriptorum classicorum bibliotheca Oxoniensis*, where a continuous text (with book numbers added to the marginal line numbers) would be manageable enough and the avoidance of inauthentic breaks would be well worthwhile.[65] For other versions, the practice would have to be accommodated to the purpose of the volume. In an annotated Greek text for students, in which a reader works on a relatively short section at a time and subheadings in English (like those in Benner's well-known 1903 edition of the *Iliad*) provide comfort for beginners struggling with the Greek, there might well be a break (mid-verse if necessary) after a retrospective summary, such as ὣς φάτο, "So he spoke." Where retrospective and prospective summaries are linked, for instance by μὲν . . . δὲ . . . , all or part of a verse might be repeated, appearing both at the close of one section and at the beginning of the next. For instance, in a passage like the following (*Iliad* 11.595–597), if a break must be made (and most translators make one[66]), it could best be done by repeating the middle verse of the three, as is done in the translation which follows:

[64] Notopoulos 1949; Hainsworth 1970. See also my section on the topic in Morris and Powell 1997: 282–283; and most recently the differing viewpoints of Janko 1998 (especially p. 11) and Foley 1999 (and the ongoing international conferences listed in Mackay 1999: vii).

[65] In the most recent Greek text of the *Iliad* (West 1998, in the Teubner series), the editor avoids white space at the book divisions (remarking that he thinks these divisions were first made for the Athenian Panathenaia festival, vi n. 3) but marks off paragraphs by insets as usual. Van Thiel (1991, 1996) follows the book divisions (and adds the book number to the line numbers) and marks the usual paragraph indents.

[66] E.g., Lattimore, Fitzgerald, and Fagles (all before 596, which Lattimore numbers 595).

στῆ δὲ μεταστρεφθείς, ἐπεὶ ἵκετο ἔθνος ἑταίρων.
ὣς οἳ μὲν μάρναντο δέμας πυρὸς αἰθομένοιο·
Νέστορα δ᾽ ἐκ πολέμοιο φέρον Νηλήϊαι ἵπποι.

He [Ajax] stood fast, turning around, when he had reached his
   companions.
So they fought on, looking like a fire blazing.

   So the others were fighting, looking like a fire blazing;
But Nestor was borne away from the battle by his Neleus-bred horses.

In a kind of compromise, Lombardo (1997: 216) places an empty line-space
both before and after 596 and begins his rendering of 597 (starting a new
episode) with an enlarged boldface capital, which seems an excellent solution. ("So he spoke," ὣς φάτο, he renders freely, in different ways.)
   Translations are commonly read in a different way than a Greek text,
more rapidly and in longer sections at a time; but continuous though
Homer's narrative is, printing without any breaks (except perhaps to distinguish the direct speech) would probably be unattractive to the modern
eye, and so far as I know, only one modern translation has adopted the practice.[67] In a modern translation it is probably desirable to mark off each
episode so that it can be detached from its context and read or recited aloud,
if necessary obliterating the retrospective and prospective links that Homer
has used to *prevent* such a break. On the whole, Lombardo's practice of
using very frequent empty line-spaces (thus reducing the impact of each),
avoiding paragraph divisions and indentation, and marking changes of
focus and breaks between episodes by enlarged boldface capitals, produces
both a pleasant-looking page and suggests—through the absence of paragraph breaks—the continuity that is Homer's characteristic. This is probably the best solution one can hope for.
   Of course, in these days we ought to be *listening* to Homer, using the cas-
sette tapes now available both in Greek and in English.[68] Until we reach
that level of emancipation from our traditional ways, however, our best aid
to a proper appreciation of Homer's meticulous care for the smoothness of
his narrative is an awareness of his techniques and his skill, and a disregard
(while we read) for the inauthentic divisions that our current texts and
translations impose upon us.

[67] *Homer: The Odyssey. A New Verse Translation*, by Albert Cook (New York, 1967). Cook
gives no explanation.
[68] Cassettes of the *Iliad* and *Odyssey* in Greek, read by Stephen G. Daitz, are available from
Audio-forum. The Fagles translation of the *Iliad* (with some cuts: nine hours) has been
recorded by Derek Jacobi, and the Fagles *Odyssey* (uncut: thirteen hours, ten minutes) by Ian
McKellen, both on Penguin Audiobooks.

Chapter Three

MUSIC AND MEANING
IN THREE SONGS OF AESCHYLUS

W E saw in chapter 1 how Homer's exploitation of the emphatic positions in the dactylic hexameter can give a more intense meaning to poetry in that meter. In addition to this, Homer sometimes evokes a special effect by using more spondees or dactyls (heavy or light syllables) than usual. Well-known examples are the six bounding dactyls (- ˘ ˘) describing Sisyphus' rock rolling back upon him, αὖτις ἔπειτα πέδονδε κυλίνδετο λᾶας ἀναιδής (*Odyssey* 11.598), and the six slow, dragging heavy spondees (- -) as Achilles calls on the shade of his beloved Patroclus, ψυχὴν κικλήσκων Πατροκλῆος δειλοῖο (*Iliad* 23.221).[1] Similar rhythmic variations occur in lyric meters, too, and are much less commonly observed and appreciated. Conspicuous examples of this can be found in the choral songs of Aeschylus' tragedies, and attention paid to them brings an enriched understanding of how he communicates to his audience the emotion he wants them to feel.

We shall never have all the information we would like about the songs and dances Aeschylus composed for the choruses of his plays. But many—probably most—of those who perform his plays or read them (in English or Greek) with students, and often, it seems, even many of those who translate the plays into English, are unaware of what we *do* know about the rhythms and meters Aeschylus used, how they contributed to the audience's pleasure and comprehension, and in particular how he manipulated the music and the dance to convey the sense he wanted. This he did, as we can still see, both by his choice of meter and by the significant variations he imposed on that meter, which, since (probably) both the sung words and the dance movements drew attention to the variations, both audibly and visually engaged the listeners' attention. This chapter will examine such techniques in the first three choral songs of the *Agamemnon* (with some reference to songs occurring later in the trilogy), and attempt to convey something of their effects by reproducing them (so far as possible) in an English translation.[2]

---

[1] Actually, we should probably read Πατροκλέεος, providing the usual dactyl in the fifth foot. The other five apparently all-spondee verses in Homer can also be regularized by similar resolution of vowel contractions (see West 1982: 37). For other such effects, see Edwards 1987: 118–119.

[2] This is also the topic of Scott 1984, which analyzes and comments on all the choral songs

First let me illustrate what I mean by the "significant variations [Aeschylus] imposed on that meter" by a few examples from poetry written in English. In "The Tuft of Flowers," a poem from his first published volume *A Boy's Will* (1913), Robert Frost uses rhymed couplets (printed as two-line stanzas) in one of the most common English meters, iambic pentameter (five feet, each normally an unstressed followed by a stressed syllable):

I went to turn the grass once after one
Who mowed it in the dew before the sun.

The dew was gone that made his blade so keen
Before I came to view the leveled scene.

I looked for him behind an isle of trees;   5
I listened for his whetstone on the breeze.

But he had gone his way, the grass all mown,
And I must be, as he had been—alone,

"As all must be," I said within my heart,
"Whether they work together or apart."   10

This is all very regular, with just (as is normal in this meter) the occasional substitution of a stressed for an unstressed syllable (e.g., "once," line 1), an unstressed syllable where we would expect a stress (e.g., "in," line 2), or an exchange of stresses at the beginning of a verse ("Whéthèr," line 10). But then comes:

But as I said it, swift there passed me by   11
On noiseless wing a bewildered butterfly,

Seeking with memories grown dim o'er night
Some resting flower of yesterday's delight.

---

in the *Oresteia*, discusses those in Aeschylus' other plays, and includes a full account of the meters (including bibliography to that date). I follow the same principles as Scott and agree with a great deal of what he says; however, I have gone further than he does in interpreting the changes in meter and the variations on the standard metrical shapes by relating them to the words and meaning.

Straightforward and up-to-date metrical analyses of the choral songs in the Agamemnon are also given in Denniston and Page 1957: 224–238; in Fraenkel's (1950) volumes of commentary ad loc.; and most recently in West 1991: 89–97. Parts of the choral songs discussed in this chapter are included in the analyses in Dale 1983. Specifically on Aeschylus' use of meter, see also Kitto 1942, 1955, 1964; Rash 1981; and Prins 1991. On Greek meter and dance generally (a huge field), the recent essential items are (in alphabetical order): Cole 1988; Dain 1965; Dale 1968, 1969, 1971, 1981, 1983; Herington 1985; Webster 1970; West 1982, 1992; Wiles 1997. On ancient Greek music, add Landels 1999 (with S. Goldhill's review on the *Bryn Mawr Classical Review* website) and Anderson 1994. On Sophocles' use of meter, see Scott 1996 (with J. Lidov's review in *Bryn Mawr Classical Review* 7.7 [1996]: 648–657); Burton 1980; van Nes Ditmars 1992; Pohlsander 1964.

And once I marked his flight go round and round,   15
As where some flower lay withering on the ground.

And then he flew as far as eye could see,
And then on tremulous wing came back to me.

The creature is "à bèwíldèred" butterfly—and in place of the regular duple unstressed-stressed-syllable beat, Frost gives us *three* syllables, using two unstressed syllables in the place of a stressed one: following classical precedent, we will call this "resolution." The three consecutive unstressed syllables suggest to an attentive, sympathetic ear (and internal eye) the fluttering wings of the creature. Four verses later there may be a reminiscence of this in "withering"—though we may well think of this as really only two syllables, "with'ring." But the next couplet indubitably repeats and intensifies the effect, for it is obvious that "on tremulous wing" is a rapid succession of no less than four unstressed syllables followed by one stressed one (the first syllable of "tremulous" might be stressed, but with its short vowel and the long vowel and diphthong in the two following syllables of the word, the stress is light and would hardly be apparent when the verse is read aloud).[3] By doing this kind of thing, Frost—who was interested in meter and even wrote a poem in Catullan hendecasyllabics—is using metrical effects to paint pictures.[4] In his summarizing final couplet he gives a twofold reprise: "'Mén wórk tògéthèr," Ì tóld hìm fròm thè heárt, | "Whéthèr thèy wórk tògéthèr òr àpárt.'"[5]

---

[3] Tennyson uses the same word, also for poetic effect, in his *Tithonus* (25–26):

> Close over us, the silver star, thy guide,
> Shínes ìn thòse trèmùloùs éyes that fill with tears. . . .

[4] See Appendix D, p. 171. Frost uses a great deal of this kind of resolution. T. Steele in Baker 1996: 221–47 marks this in his scansion of three verses from "The Road Not Taken" (226). In fact, in this poem there is resolution in every verse except "Though as for that the passing there . . ." and "I took the one less travelled by," both of which may be thought to have a slightly heavier sense than the others (and each stands as the fourth verse in the five-verse stanzas). In contrast, Frost's more somber masterpiece, "Stopping by Woods on a Snowy Evening," has not one resolution in its sixteen verses, though of course as usual it has occasional substitutions of stressed for unstressed syllables and vice versa.

[5] The lines are quoted from *The Poetry of Robert Frost*, edited by Edward Connery Lathem, copyright © 1969 by Henry Holt and Company. Reprinted by permission of Henry Holt.

Scholars often comment on the exchange or substitution of stressed and unstressed syllables in English verse, especially on the very common inverted first foot in iambic (D. Gioia in Baker 1996: 88 uses the example, "Cut is the branch . . ."), but less frequently on what is my interest here, the use of two syllables in place of one. In the fullest treatment of expressive variation that I have found, Fussell's chapter on the topic (Fussell 1979: 30–61), the author says, "In the eighteenth century the substitution of trisyllabic for dissyllabic feet is not good form," but "by the nineteenth century trisyllabic substitution had become a metrical convention" (49). He quotes only one example (from Browning). D. Gioia in Baker 1996: 91 mentions the substitution of a three-syllable foot in trochaic verse, saying it is "surprisingly rare" and quoting only Longfellow's "Funeral marches to the grave," where (as he says) "funeral" would usually

A more recent—and more moving—example of the same kind of resolution occurs in Thom Gunn's volume *The Man with Night Sweats.*[6] Gunn often uses the same meter as Frost in the poem quoted above (rhymed couplets in iambic pentameter). Here are the first few couplets of one of these poems, "The J Car":

Last year I used to ride the J CHURCH Line,
Climbing between small yards recessed with vine
—Their ordered privacy, their plots of flowers
Like blameless lives we might imagine ours.
Most trees were cut back, but some brushed the car
Before it swung round to the street once more
On which I rolled out almost to the end,
To 29th Street, calling for my friend.

(Gunn 1994: 480)

Generally the rhythm is very regular, with only the usual occasional inversion of stresses in the first two syllables ("Clímbìng bètweén . . .") or stresses on consecutive monosyllables ("Móst treés . . .")—in fact, it is perfectly "ordered" and "blameless," perhaps in intended contrast to the state of the sick man.[7] In only a few verses do two unstressed syllables stand in place of a stressed one, perhaps reflecting or drawing attention to the sense.[8]

But in "Lament," another poem in the same meter, Gunn very clearly breaks the smooth rhythm as he describes the slow, reluctant dying in hospital of a young victim of AIDS, drawing our attention to significant words. This occurs in the very first line, with the extra light syllable in "dífficùlt," and recurs especially in words with a disagreeable sense:

Your dying was a difficult enterprise.
First, petty things took up your energies,

---

be pronounced as two syllables. There is a very clear brief treatment of the phenomenon, from the linguistic point of view, in Hanson and Kiparsky 1997 (and more theoretical studies in Hanson and Kiparsky 1996: 295–301 and Kiparsky 1977: 236–239).

[6] Published in 1992 and reprinted in Gunn 1994: 403–488. Excerpts from "The J Car" and "Lament" are taken from *Collected Poems* by Thom Gunn, copyright © 1994 by Thom Gunn. Reprinted by permission of Farrar, Straus and Giroux, LLC, and Faber and Faber Ltd.

[7] "Qualities in [Gunn's] verse which once seemed to exist in an aesthetic vacuum now serve an urgent purpose: the scrupulous attention to detail brings his friends back to life; the formal elegance dignifies their dying; the restraint has something difficult to restrain—pity for them, fear for himself" (A. Alvarez, *The New Yorker*, 1 August 1994, p. 80); ". . . Poems of mortality, where metrical patterns help control elegiac emotions, like the steady drum tap accompanying a coffin to its cemetery" (H. Cole, *The Nation*, 31 August/7 September 1992, p. 223). Here and below, the markings of stressed and unstressed syllables are of course mine, not Gunn's.

[8] In the forty-six verses of this poem, I note only five that have resolution, about 11%. Possibly it is expressive in a line about childish thoughts ("Who think if they behave everything might . . ." [25]) and in the significant words "obvious" (22), "Finishing up" (28), "Catholic" (30), "feverish" (33).

The small but clustering duties of the sick,
Irritant as the cough's dry rhetoric.
Those hours of waiting for pills, shot, X-ray. . . .

(Ibid.: 465).

The extra syllables in "dífficùlt" and "clústèrìng," and the unexpected stresses in "Fírst," "Írrìtànt," "pílls, shót, X́-ray," make the words carry a heavier load of meaning. Later in the poem we hear other highly charged words including the same quick, short syllables: "Èmérgèncỳ Roóm"; "hóspìtàl roóm"; "Twó weéks òf àn àbómìnàblè cònstraínt."⁹ Then in the final line Gunn echoes the first, and reinforces what I have suggested about the expressive rhythm by adding to it a second rueful word with another resolution:

This dífficùlt, tédìoùs, painful enterprise.[10]

(Ibid.: 468)

I once heard a tape of Robert Frost reading "The Tuft of Flowers" and was immediately reminded of an effect I had long admired in Aeschylus' *Agamemnon.* In one of the lyric passages, the chorus sings of how Helen deserted her husband Menelaus to run off with their guest, the young prince Paris, to his home in Troy; and at that point Aeschylus for a moment does exactly what Frost and Gunn have done in the lines I've just discussed: he interrupts his slow, steady iambic rhythm for a sudden, much quicker, lighter verse, with a startling rush of short syllables:

ἄγουσά τ' ἀντίφερνον Ἰλίῳ φθορὰν
βεβάκει ῥίμφα διὰ πυλᾶν
ἄτλητα τλᾶσα. . . .[11]

(*Agamemnon* 406–408)

⁹ Tennyson uses the same word, with similar effect, for the visit of Strife to the wedding of Peleus and Thetis (*Œnone* 219–221):

> . . . I could meet with her
> Thè Àbómìnàblè, thàt únìnvítèd cáme
> Into the fair Peleïan banquet hall . . .

Cf. his use of "unprofitable" in *Morte d'Arthur* 96 (p. 138 below). I have noticed the same effect in Wordsworth's *The Prelude* (346–348):

> . . . oh, at that time
> While on the pérìloùs ridge I hung alone,
> With what strange úttèrànce did the loud dry wind
> Blow through my ears; . . .

¹⁰ There are resolutions in seventeen of the 116 verses of this poem, about 15 percent. Critics have paid attention to Gunn's syllabic verse but not, so far as I know, to this feature of his technique (see, for example, Attridge 1995: 98–99; Fussell 1979: 166–167; R. Hadas in Baker 1996: 99–101; and Gunn himself in an essay, Gunn 1993: 219–20).

¹¹ For the sake of the English I have slightly changed the usual colometry (the arrangement of the words into lines).

Marking the syllable-quantities in the usual way, this would run:

˘ – ˘ – ˘ – ˘ – ˘ –

˘ – – – ˘ ˘ ˘ ˘ –

˘ – ˘ – ˘

Imitating this in English:[12]

Tò bríng tò Tróy, ìn pláce òf dówrỳ, deáth,
  Shè stépped oút eásìlỳ fròm thè gátes
  À wróng ùnheárd-òf . . . .

It is almost certain that this abrupt speeding-up of the verbal rhythm, this ripple in the stream, was made even more vivid to the audience by a similar quickening in the movement of the music and dance.[13]

Later Greek playwrights do the same thing. When Oedipus enters blinded in Sophocles' *King Oedipus*, he utters a verse consisting of sixteen short syllables, and later matches it with a second (*Oedipus Rex* 1314, 1322; H.D.F. Kitto tries hard to match this in his translation, with something like "darkness abominable, | My enemy unspeakable, | In cruel onset insuperable"[14]). I have no doubt that Sophocles intended to produce a striking effect with this *tour de force*. Euripides, however, trumps it, Amphitryon uttering no less than twenty-two consecutive short syllables as he describes Heracles lying asleep after killing his wife and children (ὕπνον ὕπνον ὀλόμενον ὃς ἔκανεν ἄλοχον ἔκανε δὲ τέκεα, *Hercules Furens* 1062, quoted in Kitto 1942: 99—he doesn't try to put it into English). Pindar sometimes does the same thing: David Young has pointed out the "extraordinary sequence" of seven light syllables beginning the eighth verse of each strophe and antistrophe (eight matching stanzas) in his first Olympian Ode (hon-

---

[12] I mark the syllables I want to count as stressed (matching the heavy syllables of the Greek) with an acute accent, those I want as unstressed (the Greek light syllables) with a grave. The final syllable in a verse, which in Greek meters may always be heavy or light, I mark according either to what the Greek meter seems to require or (if this is indifferent) to what seems to be its natural stress (or lack of it) in English in its context.

Scholars of English verse differ in their usage for metrical markings (see, for instance, D. Baker in Baker 1996: xvi–xvii; Fussell 1979: 18–19). There is much to be said for the three levels of stress (instead of two) distinguished by Attridge (1995: 29–31) and used by D. S. Carne-Ross and K. Haynes in the introduction to their *Horace in English* (p. 46: stressed syllable; syllable carrying a lighter stress [e.g., the first of "nonplussed," the second of "backslash"]; syllable with no or minimal stress), but this is unnecessary for my purposes. Stress is, of course, only relative to that on other syllables, and infinitely variable (Pinsky 1998: 12; Winters 1957: 88).

Besides using stressed syllables to represent heavy syllables in the Greek, I have also tried to use in such cases syllables that are relatively slow to pronounce, because of either a long vowel or a following cluster of consonants (see Appendix D, p. 169). Of course, I have not always succeeded.

[13] On the association of song and dance, see most recently Wiles 1997: 87–113.

[14] Kitto 1962: 91.

oring the victor in a horse race), which "gives an unmistakable impression of rapidity" and indeed often includes the word *tachus*, "swift."[15] This kind of expressive variation in a meter is well known to classical scholars familiar with lyric meters, but normally unnoticed or at least ignored by translators.[16] But I think my Robert Frost and Thom Gunn examples show that the occasional use of two unstressed syllables when we are looking for one stressed one is perfectly natural in English, and may well be similar in effect to the ancient Greek practice.

Within a stanza, sometimes one metrical rhythm predominates, sometimes several different meters occur—every line may be in a different meter. Aeschylus uses many different meters, and there is a certain amount of controversy over whether, or rather to what extent, he and the other dramatists used a particular metrical rhythm for a particular emotional effect.[17] This use of a different rhythm in each verse of a stanza of course often occurs in English poetry; one example may be given from Ezra Pound's rendering of a stanza from a choral song of Sophocles, where (though he is not imitating Sophocles' meter) the rhythms are very like those of Greek tragedy:

Pardon if I reprove thee, Lady,
To save thee false hopes delayed.
Thinkst thou that man who dies,
Shall from King Chronos take
        unvaried happiness?
Nor yet's all pain.

(Pound 1957: 9)

These verses are much like Aeschylean iambic, the final verse (four stressed syllables, two spondees) being heavier to mark closure. In the same kind of Aeschylean rhythm, with resolution in the last verse, is:

Dark as the night falls
the winter falls darker

[15] David Young in *Ancient Writers*, vol. 1, ed. T. J. Luce (New York, 1982), 171; for J. F. Nims' use of Pindar's meter in English, see Appendix D, pp. 176–177. Scott 1984: 26–27 discusses the effect of resolutions, saying the rapid pace might have been reinforced in the dancing.

[16] On isometric translations, see Appendix D, p. 166.

[17] More on this below. Dochmiacs and ionics, at least, obviously convey a certain mood: Dale (1969: 248–58) says, "These dochmiac and kindred types are I think the only lyric rhythms which carry an inherent emotional expression—namely passionate feeling of some kind" (254), and, "In tragedy perhaps the only clear case is the ionic metres . . . sung in the orgiastic cults of Cybele and Dionysus introduced from Asia Minor" (256). See also Kitto 1955: 36–41 and 1964: 1–38. Van Nes Ditmars (1992: 16) is very dubious about meters being ethos-specific. Of English verse, Hanson and Kiparsky remark, "Particular settings may also be associated by convention with a particular style and hence subject to constraints from the tradition—the limerick form is a poor choice for an epitaph" (1996: 294).

still: yields stars
innumerable, fierce and clear.[18]

(C. O. Hartman in Baker 1996: 118)

In ancient Greek dramatic choral songs, both the meter and any metrical variations are made all the more obvious by the phenomenon known as "responsion" (or "corresponsion"—Dale uses the first, Scott the second). This is the fact that most of the time the stanzas are arranged in pairs, the members of each pair being metrically identical syllable-for-syllable. The matching pairs are known as strophe and antistrophe (something like "turn" and "counterturn"), terms probably referring to the dance movements that accompanied them, which are likely also to have been identical.[19] Occasionally this matching of markedly different rhythms and verse lengths is found in successive stanzas in English poetry, in recent times in particular by Marianne Moore and Dylan Thomas.[20] It is also noteworthy in musical comedy, where the rhythm is accentuated by ostentatious rhymes—and where it is often easy to see the difficulties the librettist struggles with in matching stanza to stanza, his success drawing a breath of relief from the audience: one thinks of Gilbert and Sullivan—

Our great Mikado, virtuous man,
When he to rule our land began,
   Resolved to try
   A plan whereby
  Young men might best be steadied.
So he decreed, in words succinct,
That all who flirted, leered or winked,
(Unless connubially linked),
  Should forthwith be beheaded.

This stern decree, you'll understand,
Caused great dismay throughout the land!
   For young and old
   And shy and bold
  Were equally affected.

[18] The stanza by Ezra Pound is from *Sophokles: Women of Trachis*, copyright © 1957 by Ezra Pound. Reprinted by permission of New Directions Publishing Corp. The lines by C.O. Hartman are reprinted by kind permission of the author.

I have marked the scansion of these stanzas in Appendix D, pp. 167–169. M. Holley in Baker 1996: 161–162 scans passages from T. S. Eliot's *Four Quartets*, showing that every verse has a different rhythm and remarking that "unpredictability and echo intertwine." As an example of English poetry "directly patterned on a classical, Greek, form," Carne-Ross (1990: 125) quotes a stanza of Shelley's "Hymn of Pan."

[19] So Wiles 1997: 103; Scott 1984: 24–26.

[20] See Baker 1996: 13, 153–157, 257. On J. F. Nims' "Water Music," written in metrically matching strophe-antistrophe-epode form, see Appendix D, pp. 176–177.

> The youth who winked a roving eye,
> Or breathed a non-connubial sigh,
> Was thereupon condemned to die—
>> He usually objected.

(The Mikado, Act I)

Another great lyricist, Ira Gershwin, sometimes faced even greater problems than Gilbert: in a review article,[21] Brad Leithauser notes George Gershwin's musical sequence of ten, seven, and again ten notes, followed by one single note; Ira obediently followed him—

> They all laughed at Christopher Columbus
>> When he said the world was round.
> They all laughed when Edison recorded
>> Sound.
>
> They all laughed at Rockefeller Center—
>> Now they're fighting to get in;
> They all laughed at Whitney and his cotton
>> Gin![22]

Accordingly, the rules of responsion insist that when, in the passage I have mentioned, Aeschylus uses a rush of light syllables to describe Helen's flight from her husband's home with her lover Paris—

> Tò bríng tò Tróy,   ìn pláce òf dówrỳ, deáth,
>> Shè stépped oút   eásìlỳ fròm thè gátes
> À wróng ùnheárd-òf . . . .

(Agamemnon 406–408)

—like W. S. Gilbert and Ira Gershwin he must repeat the effect in the following stanza—and he does so with equally significant effect. The deserted Menelaus dreams of his absent wife, stretches out his arms to embrace the phantom—

> μάταν γάρ, εὖτ᾽ ἂν ἐσθλά τις δοκῶν ὁρᾶν,[23]
> παραλλάξασα διὰ χερῶν
> βέβακεν ὄψις . . .

(Ibid.: 423–425)

[21] *The New York Review of Books*, 17 October 1996, 35–38.

[22] Quoted by Leithauser (in ibid.: 37; reprinted with permission from *The New York Review of Books*, copyright © 1996 NYREV, Inc.). I have ventured to emend Leithauser's colometry in the last two lines. I don't think Aeschylus ever tried a monosyllabic line, but Marianne Moore did, in "The Fish" (see Baker 1996: 157). Ira Gershwin was very clever indeed at playing with line length as well as rhyme, and even wrote a book about the difficulties of tailoring words to music (saying, "Filling in the seventy-three syllables of the refrain wasn't as simple as it sounds") and about the mechanics of rhyme (he insisted that the work of the lyricist "depends a good deal on perfect rhyme's jingle"; both quotes from Leithauser in *The New York Review of Books*, 36).

[23] Text of West 1991; see note 55 below.

Or in English:

> Fòr vaínlỳ, whén   òne seéms tò seé   hìs heárt's dèsíre,
> Thèn glídíng   eásìlỳ fròm hìs árms
> Thè dreám hàs vánìshed.

I find it hard not to believe that the chorus' movements, as well as the rhythm, imitate the swift, light motions they are describing as Helen slips away from Menelaus' palace, and later as her husband's dream of her slips through his arms.

Now, bearing in mind these three characteristics of Aeschylus' song—occasional resolution (two light syllables for a heavy one), significant change in meter, and responsion, the syllable-for-syllable matching of the meter in successive stanzas—we can examine the first three choral songs in his mightest surviving work, the *Oresteia*.

The First Choral Song (*Agamemnon* 104–257)

The *Agamemnon* begins with an eloquent Watchman on the roof of Agamemnon's palace telling us about the loneliness of his endless nighttime vigils during his master Agamemnon's long absence, then suddenly shouting in excitement that he has seen the flaming beacon that proclaims the fall of Troy. But before he dashes off to rouse Queen Clytemnestra, he warns us that things have happened in the household that he ominously prefers to say nothing about to those who don't know. (We, the audience, of course, must already know all about Clytemnestra's infidelity and treachery.) The chorus of old men marches into the orchestra, chanting in the anapaestic meter; the rhythm is *DE DE DUM, DE DE DUM*, with occasional substitution of a heavy syllable for two light ones and vice versa (for English anapaests, M. Holley quotes, "'Twas the night before Christmas when all through the house . . ."[24]). The old men's words tell of the departure of the

---

[24] In Baker 1996: 167. The powerfully marked marching rhythm of anapaests in English, together with the easy substitution of one stressed for two unstressed syllables and vice versa, can be seen in R. L. Stevenson's "From a Railway Carriage":

> And charg | ing along | like troops | in a batt | le,
> All | through the mead | ows the hor | ses and catt | le:
> All | of the sights | of the hill | and the plain
> Fly as | thick as | driving | rain;
> And ev | er again, | in the wink | of an eye,
> Painted | stations | whistle | by.

(Quoted by A. Finch in Baker 1996: 67–68, taking a different approach to the scansion.) Tennyson used anapaests (often substituting an iambus for a spondee) in "The Voyage of Maeldune" and elsewhere (see Hanson 1992: 159). To show that anapaests occur naturally in every-

72 CHAPTER THREE

thousand ships to Troy ten years ago with the two royal leaders Agamemnon and Menelaus, sent by Zeus against the wrongdoers to avenge the loss of Helen, "the woman with too many husbands," as they call her (πολυάνορος ἀμφὶ γυναικός, 62), and of the sufferings of both attackers and defenders around Troy. They explain that they themselves had to remain at home in Argos because of their old age; and they address Clytemnestra their queen, who is now performing sacrifices all over the city (quite possibly right in our view onstage), and ask what news has caused such a sudden eruption of burnt offerings to the gods.

They don't wait for an answer. Instead, they begin to sing,[25] and enter upon the movements of a dance. They sing a twelve-line stanza telling of an omen of two eagles that pounced upon and ate a pregnant hare, seen ten years ago as the expedition left for Troy. Almost all the lines are in long rolling dactyls (*DUM DE DE DUM DE DE*, as in Longfellow's, "This is the forest primeval. The murmuring pines and the hemlocks . . ."), with occasionally a heavy syllable replacing two light ones (forming a spondee: *DUM DUM*). In two verses Aeschylus varies the meter by beginning with a iambic metron (*DE DUM DE DUM*), which is always tied to the dactyls by an overlapping word ("ȯf hȯw thȅ twȋn-" in 109, and "ȁppeȃrȋng neȃr" in 116),[26] and these iambs are picked up in a single iambic line (120; two iambic metra) before the final dactylic refrain (121), which will be twice repeated. Using stressed and unstressed English syllables to correspond to the heavy and light syllables in the Greek, the stanza may be rendered:[27]

---

day English, Finch (in Baker 1996: 63) quotes, "Please return | to your seats | and make sure | that your seat | belts are fas | tened secure | ly." On the meter here, see further Scott 1984: 33–34; and on anapaests in Greek generally, Rosenmeyer 1982: 33–34, and C. J. Ruijgh, "Les anapestes de marche dans la versification grecque et le rythme du mot grec," *Mnemosyne* 42 (1989): 308–330.

[25] Scott 1984: 30–32 gives a more detailed technical analysis of this ode.

[26] On such word overlap between rhythmic units, see Rash 1981: 6, 14–16; he points out (16) that "words which bridge this reversal of rhythm [from rising to falling, as here] stand out." West (1982: 128–129) notes that most of Aeschylus' dactylic strophes include iambics, and analyzes this passage, pointing out the frequent coincidence of word-end in strophe and antistrophe.

[27] For the accentual markings, see note 12 above; and on attempts to match ancient Greek and Latin quantitative meters in English rhythms based on syllable stress, see Appendix D.

I am assuming that readers who wish to follow the meter closely in the Greek will have access to a text (e.g., Denniston and Page 1957; the Oxford Classical Texts of Page 1972 or Murray 1955; or the Teubner edition of West 1991), and, if necessary, to a metrical scheme as given in Denniston and Page 1957: 224–238; West 1991: 89–97; and Scott 1984 and Fraenkel 1950 ad loc. To include text and metrical scheme here would overload my pages and be less convenient than referring a separate volume. Where editors vary significantly in their colometry (the division into lines) or metrical analysis, I usually follow Murray 1955, and add a comment in the notes. (It is Murray's text that appears on CD-ROM D of the *Thesaurus linguae Graecae*.)

Stróng àm Ì stíll fòr thè tále òf thè ómèn òf goód òn thè joúrnèy
Sént fòr thè kíngs; fòr thère stíll fròm thè góds ìs àn ínspíred   105
Proóf tóld, sóng's stréngth, meét fòr thè ágéd;
Òf hów thè twín-thróned sìnglè-heárted còmmánd òf thè Greék yoúth,
Leádèrs ùnítéd,   110
Sét fórth, speárs ìn theìr hánds fòr thè pénàltỳ,
Sént bỳ thè fiérce bírd—strífe fòr thè Trójáns—
Bírd-kíngs seén bỳ thè kíngs òf thè shíps, thè òne dárkèr, thè óthèr
      wìth whíte taíl,   115
Àppeárìng neárbý tò thè pálàce, thè síde òf thè speár-thrúst,
Márked oút plaín òn theìr pérchès,
Teárìng, dèvoúrìng thè flésh òf thè háre-mòthèr, heávỳ wìth
      óffsprìng,
Àrréstèd fróm hèr fínàl coúrse.   120
Waílìng, lèt waílìng bè chántéd; bùt máy goód wín throúgh.

The insistent dactyls remind us of Homer's *Iliad*, which is in the same meter,
and carry us back to the ancient epic tales of Troy we Athenians know so
well. In addition, the dactyls recall Delphic oracles, also traditionally in this
meter, and prepare us for omens and prophecies.[28] The final portentous
dactylic line (emphasized by contrast with the all-iambic line that precedes
it) reminds us of yet another association of this meter: the repeated dactyl
αἴλινον (*aílìnòn*), an unintelligible cry from the ritual of mourning.[29] The
stanza is carefully shaped, the rhythms matching the words in invoking leg-
end and prophecy and anticipating what is to come.

Then follows the antistrophe (122–139), a stanza matching the first, syllable for syllable. Now the kings' seer speaks out directly, interpreting this
omen and predicting both the fall of Troy and the anger of the goddess
Artemis. Again the stanza ends with the ambiguous dactylic refrain. A further independent stanza (140–159), without metrical response and almost entirely in the same prophetic dactyls,[30] amplifies the sinister side of
this prediction, setting it in ambiguous but impressive language against the
terrible, murderous wrongdoing in the House of Atreus in the past. Then

---

[28] For instance, in the fourth choral song, the chorus sings one line of five dactyls (in the
middle of an otherwise trochaic stanza), when the dreadful foreboding that it is feeling is depicted as singing an unwanted prophecy (979): "Próphècìès síng ìn mỳ bósòm ùnásked-fòr,
ùnpaíd-fór" (μαντιπολεῖ δ' ἀκέλευστος ἄμισθος ἀοιδά). Add this to Scott's other examples of
Aeschylus' use of dactylic rhythm (1984: 34–36). Denniston and Page's comment on the meter
of 979 (1957: 232–233) seems to me very curious.

[29] On *ailinon* (which recurs in a lament in Sophocles' *Ajax* 627), see Fraenkel 1950 ad loc.
On single-verse refrains in Aeschylus, see Moritz 1979.

[30] The first line (140) is two iambic metra; the second (141) is three iambic metra, the second taking the form of a choriamb (- ˘ ˘ -) and the third a bacchiac (˘ - -). Line 145 is also basically iambic.

once more the repeated refrain, "Waíllìng, lèt waíllìng bè chántèd; bùt máy goód wín throúgh," concludes these themes—for the moment.

The next stanza (160–167) introduces both a striking change of meter—all the more striking in that we may well be expecting a further dactylic stanza in responsion to the previous one[31]—and a weighty new idea. The chorus, from its very first word, calls upon the almighty power of Zeus, the incomparable lord of all, a very present help in trouble. The seven-line stanza is almost entirely in the trochaic meter, mainly the form very common in Aeschylean songs, known as the lecythion: *DUM DE DUM DE DUM DE DUM.* It is a heavy, solemn movement, the rhythm William Blake turned to when he meant to be at his most impressive:

> Tyger! Tyger! burning bright
> In the forests of the night,
> What immortal hand or eye
> Could frame thy fearful symmetry?

The meter (in English) has been said to be "traditionally the measure for magic spells and visions."[32] In Aeschylus' stanza, after the first verse, which has a spondee (two heavy syllables) before the lecythion begins, the regular lecythia are broken only by a run of five dactyls in the last verse but one (165).

> Zeús—wé knów nòt whó—ìf só ìt bést   160
> Pleásès hím tò bé àddréssed,
> Só shàll hé bè námed bỳ mé.
> Weíghìng áll bỳ bálànce-árm,
> Í hàve naúght tò sét bèsíde
> Zeús, ìf ìndeéd sìllỳ búrdèn òf cáre fròm mỳ reásòn   165
> Múst bè súrelỳ cást àwáy.

This change of meter in the last line but one of the stanza is like the iambic line inserted amid the dactyls in the three preceding stanzas, and is common in Aeschylus. The technique seems to lay emphasis upon the final verse as it returns to the earlier rhythm, and perhaps helps to mark the end of the stanza. The matching trochaic antistrophe (168–175) emphasizes Zeus' conquest of his predecessors to become supreme deity, and the dactylic line (174)—again beginning "Zeus!"—this time raises the cry of celebration that greeted his victory.

The following strophe (176–183) continues mainly in the same trochaic

---

[31] A good suggestion made by Scott (1982: 189).

[32] By D. Gioia in Baker 1996: 90. Longfellow's "Hiawatha" changes the feeling of the meter entirely by adding a extra unstressed syllable to the end of each line, thus drastically diminishing the retarding effect of line-end. Poe's "The Raven" is like "Hiawatha," but it doubles the length of the verse. Scott (1984: xvi–xvii) gives a detailed analysis of this and the following stanza.

meter as the last pair, its eight verses asserting four times in different words the great change that Zeus's rule has brought about in human life: that now suffering brings about wisdom, and humankind must *learn*—whether it wants to or not. The rhythm is modified slightly, and significantly, in some verses. Here is a version in English:

Hé hàs guídèd mán tò thínk,   176
Màkìng hís èstáblìshed láw:
"Leárnìng cómes fròm súffèríng."
Oózíng   throúgh thè heárt   ìn pláce òf sleép[33]
Ánguìsh dríps,   tórtùríng;   thoúgh ùnsoúght,   180
Fór mànkínd còmes témpèránce.
Góds gìve fávòr sómehòw víòléntlý
Thróned ìn áwe às steérsmèn thére.

After three lecythia (176–178: *DUM DE DUM DE DUM DE DUM*), the fourth verse (179) begins with a spondee (like 160), then puts in a cretic (*DUM DE DUM*) before the final iambic metron; the next (180) consists simply of three cretics, replacing the steady pace of the lecythia with this rocking, less progressive movement. The metrical changes seem to slow the words even further, emphasizing the human suffering that precedes the divine favor of wisdom. After another regular lecythion (181), mentioning "temperance," the penultimate verse adds to the lecythion the additional three syllables of a bacchiac (*DE DUM DUM*)—an unexpected metrical extension and sense, the word βιαίως,[34] "by force" or "violently," again emphasizing that we do not have a choice.

Then again something surprising happens, this time not in the meter but in the content. In the matching antistrophe (184–191), instead of elaborating or repeating this highly significant message about Zeus' reign, Aeschylus suddenly begins his great *example* of learning through suffering, one that will not be concluded until the end—the end not of this play, but of the trilogy. Replicating the meter of the strophe closely connects the narrative example given in this antistrophe back to the moralizing statement that it exemplifies, since it is presented with the same music and dance movements:

Thén thè éldèr sóvèreígn,
Leádìng Greéks ìn návàl fórce,   185
Blámed nò fórtùne-téllèr's wórds,
Fáte's stróke   tákìng—nó   rèsístìng breáth—
Whén dèláy,   hárbòr-lócked,   fámìshíng,

---

[33] Aeschylus sometimes emphasizes the rhythm by ending each metrical unit at the end of a word; in my renderings I have (where appropriate and possible, as here) indicated this by extra spacing. On this effect, see Korzeniewski 1968: 196 §1; Rash 1981: 13; West 1982: 6.

[34] Or βίαιος. The sense and meter are not affected.

Hárd òppréssed thè hóst òf Greéks
Fácìng Cálchìs, whére thè súrgìng tídes flów 190
Báck ànd fórth bỳ Aúlìs lánd.

The song leaps back to the expedition to Troy and the dangerous prophecy
of Calchas mentioned a few minutes ago in the first three stanzas, and tells
us that Agamemnon, not finding fault with the prophet (as he did later at
Troy, *Iliad* 1.106–108), consenting . . . —but there is no verb yet to specify
what he did. This time, the slower verses in the middle of the stanza (187–
188) correspond to the suffering described in the strophe (179–180), describing the god-willed delay of the Greek fleet at the harbor of Aulis. Then
the unexpected extra syllables (*DE DUM DUM*) at the end of the penulti-
mate line (190) represent the powerful reversing (παλιρρόχ- | θοις) tides in
the narrows between Aulis and the island of Euboea.

So, after the prophet's sinister proclamation (104–159), Agamemnon
does *what?* We all wait for action, for movement, for someone to *do something*, for a VERB. No verb comes: the delay, the lack of any forward motion,
the heaping-up of participles and long compound adjectives continue in the
next strophe (192–204), again reinforced by word-end after each metrical
unit. The meter changes to a very slow type of iambic that Aeschylus often
uses: *DE DUM DE DUM   DUM DE DUM   DE DUM DUM* (technically
an iambic metron, a cretic, and a bacchiac; cretics and bacchiacs often occur
in iambic verses). Ezra Pound's line "Tò sáve theè fálse hópes dèlàyed" is
similar, without the final bacchiac.[35] Aexchylus' lines run:

Ànd stíll thè gáles   blówìng fróm   thè cóld nórth, 192
Wìth íll dèláy,   fámìne-fraúght,   ìll-ánchóred,
Thè créws àstráy,
Òf véssèl's húlls,   moórìng-rópes,   ùnspáríng, 195
Pròlónged tíme,   doúblèd tíme,   ìmpósíng,
Hád wórn àwáy,   stríppìng báre,   thè Greéks' bloóm . . . .

Then suddenly, after this interminable, long-drawn-out misery, midway
through the stanza, comes the remedy, the prophet's explanation and demand, more bitter even than the delay.

Thén tò stíll thè bítìng stórm,
Rémèdỳ néw ànd griévoús,
Fállìng ùpón thè leádérs, 200
Criéd ìn à loúd   voíce bỳ thè príest
"*Ártèmìs!*"   Só   stríkìng thè eárth

---

[35] See Appendix D, p. 167. Note that cretics (- � -) occur in conjunction with both trochaic
(- ˅ - ˣ) and iambic (ˣ - ˅ -) metra. On the relationship of iambic and trochaic meters, see Scott
1984: 193 n. 30; and more recently, M. Haslam in *Classical Philology* 86 (1991): 229–239 (especially 232), and J. Lidov in *Bryn Mawr Classical Review* 7.7 (1996): 653–654.

Hárd wìth theìr stáffs   Átrèùs' sóns
Bróke ìntò teárs   ànd weépíng.

After one lecythion (198),[36] the words of relief (if that is what they are!) are couched in a striking succession of long choriambic verses (DUM DE DE DUM), the sequence often ending in a bacchiac (DE DUM DUM). It is Artemis (the seer claims), demanding the sacrifice of Agamemnon's daughter so that the fleet may be released. This choriambic meter[37] is associated with prophecy elsewhere, too; Aeschylus has used it for this purpose in an earlier play, where the words say, "Ányòne hére   skílled tò èxplaín   criés òf thè bírds. . ." (*Suppliants* 58), and Sophocles will use it after him for the same purpose in the *Oedipus Rex*, after the seer Teiresias has prophesied, where the meaning is, "Fearful indeed,   fear to our hearts   now has the wise   prophet proclaimed.   Can I believe?   How can I not?   I do not know   what I can say" (*Oedipus Rex* 483–486).

The antistrophe, matching the slow, heavy iambics of the delay at Aulis, brings a matching heaviness of heart—Agamemnon says slowly, dragging out the words:[38]

Ànd thén àt lást   thís thè éldèr kíng saíd: 205
"À heávỳ fáte   súrelỳ, nót   tò heárkén;
Ànd heávỳ toó
Tò sláy mỳ ówn   chíld, thè hoúsè's jéwél,
Dèfílíng   hánds wìth maídèn-slaúghtèr's
Bloód-streáms, à fáthér's, bèsíde   thè áltár.   210
Whích, wìthoút càlámìtý?"

Then the choriambs of the bitter prophecy break out again (212–217), giving Agamemnon's reaction to it, telling of his anguish at the thought of "jumping ship" and deserting his fleet (the Greek word *liponaus*, "ship-deserter"—here translated "traitor"—invokes an act considered criminal in Athens as well as cowardly). And, horribly, he declares that it must be *themis*, "lawful, right," to desire this human sacrifice:

"Hów càn Ì bé à traítór   212
Faílìng mỳ shíps' àllíánce?

[36] So printed by most editors; West 1991 attaches the last three syllables of the previous verse to the head of 198, dividing the lines . . . κατέξαινον ἄν- | θος . . . , adding an iambic metron before the lecythion.

[37] West (1991) and Murray (1955) agree here in dividing 201–204 as ionics (so scanned by West 1991: 90). I prefer to take the lines as choriambic, following Dale 1983: 266; Denniston and Page 1957: 227; Fraenkel 1950, 2: 59; and the text of Page 1972; and my version follows the line division of these latter editors. When the metra run on continuously, as here, ionics (◡◡– –) and choriambs (–◡◡–) have to be distinguished mainly by the metrical context, and differences of opinion are possible.

[38] On the interpretation of this perplexing passage, see especially Winnington-Ingram 1983: 81–88, 95–96.

Stórms càn bè stópped   ónlỳ bỳ bloód
—bloód òf à chíld!—sácrìfìce cráved   215
Nów bỳ thèm áll   eágèrlỳ ánd
Láwfùllỳ. Goód   bèfáll ús!"

After this long run of choriambs, the next strophe begins with two more
verses (218–219) of the same slow, dragging iambics as in the first lines of
the preceding stanzas, relating how Agamemnon yielded to what he saw as
necessity and made up his mind for the dreadful act. (His situation is like
that of Abraham preparing to sacrifice Isaac.)

Bùt whén hè shoúldéred còmpúlsiòn's yóke-stráp,
Hìs púrpòse veéred   líke ùngódlỳ wínd-shíft.

Then, after this metaphorical allusion to the change of wind he longs for,[39]
quite unexpectedly in the next verse (220) there comes a sudden resolution,
two light syllables in place of a heavy one producing a rush of four light syllables, a kind of metrical shudder;[40] his decision is ἄναγνον, ἀνίερον, "ùnhólỳ, rècklèsslỳ wróng." Afterward, the slow iambics resume (221–222):

Ùnhólỳ, rècklèsslỳ wróng; ànd thén   220
Tò dángèroús   dárk ìntént   hìs mínd chánged
Fòr mán ìs máde   bóld wìth báse-còntríving,

And after these slow, generalizing lines comes another with a resolution
(223),[41] a shiver of light syllables in the word *parakopā*, "criminal folly, de-
rangement":

À foólìsh wìckèdnèss, díre soúrce òf évíl.

Then back once more to the solemn iambics (224):

Hè dáred thén   tò bé thè sláyér   224

At this point Aeschylus gives his audience the biggest shock yet. For as
the chorus' words go on (225–227) to contrast Agamemnon's innocent
young daughter with the war to recover the adulterous wife Helen, the
meter (and the song and dancing) suddenly switches to a meter we have not
seen before in this play, called "ionic."[42] The rhythm of ionics is basically

---

[39] I have explained why I term this "metaphorical" in Edwards 1977: 26.

[40] Line 220 consists of two iambic metra, scanning ⌣ – ⌣ ⌣ ⌣   ⌣ – ⌣ –.

[41] Scanning ⌣ – ⌣ ⌣ ⌣   ⌣ – –   ⌣ – –.

[42] Fraenkel (1950; 2: 59) considers the lines iambic (with some choriambs), and so do Dale
(1983: 267, choriambic dimeters), Denniston and Page (1957: 11, 227), and Page (1972).
Against all this authority, however, I have preferred to follow the colometry of Murray 1955
(West 1991 and Thomson 1938 are much the same), treating the lines as ionic, which involves

DE DE DUM DUM   DE DE DUM DUM (sometimes the last syllable is omitted), with a very common syncopated form *DE DE DUM DE DUM DE DUM DUM*, known as the anacreontic. Edward Fitzgerald used anacreontics and ionics like this in English (accents added):

Lìke à dreám throùgh sleép shè glídéd
      Throùgh thè sílént cìtỳ gáte,
Bỳ à guíltỳ Hérmès guídéd
Òn thè feáthèr'd feét òf Théft.[43]

Aeschylus presents:

Hè dáred thén   tò bé thè sláyér
      Òf hìs daúghtèr, wìfe-àvéngér,   225
      Tò sùppórt hìs wárfáre;
      Lìtùrgỳ laúnchìng vésséls

—an iambic (224: a bacchiac—*DE DUM DUM*—an iambic metron, and an extra syllable), an anacreontic (225), a short ionic[44] with a bacchiac (226), and a choriamb with a bacchiac (227).[45] Later, anacreontics and ionics will reappear when the chorus tells more about the wife-to-be-avenged, the adulteress who fled to Troy—Helen (below, p. 86). They invoke, as most scholars agree, an Asian or oriental tone, usually rather passionate:[46] in his play *The Persians*, Aeschylus used them very extensively in the first song of the worried Persian nobles who form the chorus, and they are also much used by the excited Asian women of the chorus in Euripides' *Bacchae*. In

---

less word overlap between cola and makes Aeschylus anticipate here some of his later effects. West (1991: 90) also calls the lines ionic. Cf. note 37 above. Murray prints:

ἔτλα δ' οὖν θυτὴρ γενέσθαι
   θυγατρός, γυναικοποίνων
      πολέμων ἀρωγὰν
   καὶ προτέλεια ναῶν.

[43] Quoted in Poole and Maule 1996: 129. To improve the example I have marked the second verse as an ionic (lacking the final syllable), but it might well be taken as an anacreontic like the others (though it is inset in Poole and Maule). This is from Fitzgerald's translation of the *Agamemnon* (1865), though this passage is not close to Aeschylus' text. For further examples of ionics and anacreontics in modern English poetry, see Appendix D, pp. 172 (by Bunting) and 177 (by Nims).
[44] Cf. West 1982: 125 on short ionic forms in drama (though he does not mention this verse).
[45] The Greek is καὶ προτέλεια ναῶν, something like "preliminary marriage rites on behalf of the ships" (cf. Denniston and Page 1957: 89 and Fraenkel 1950, 2: 40–41), and the rhythm may suggest marriage—Helen's adulterous one and Iphigeneia's never-to-be-fulfilled one.
[46] E.g., West 1982: 124; Dale 1969: 256; Dain 1965: 232. Herington 1985: 217–219 compares the use of ionics and anacreontics in Anacreon and Aeschylus.

Latin, they appear (in the form of galliambics) in Catullus' "Attis," the lament of the self-castrated young priest of the Asiatic goddess Cybele.[47] The change in rhythm is rather like that in Hardy's "Beyond the Last Lamp" (1914), where he similarly switches suddenly from an iambic movement to something like an ionic (I have added markings to suggest this), then returns (via a choriamb) to iambic:

> The pair seemed lovers, yet absorbed
> In mental scenes no longer orbed
> By love's young rays. Each countenance
> 　　Às ìt slówlý, às ìt sádlý
> 　　Caùght thè lámplíght's yèllòw glánce,
> Héld ìn sùspénse à mísèrý
> At things which had been or might be.

So Aeschylus has switched to three different versions of the ionic to describe Agamemnon's murder of his daughter for the sake of recovering the adulterous wife who has fled to Asian Troy. But what about the antistrophe still to come, which must match syllable for syllable? The effects are hardly less striking. First the two verses of slow iambics (228–229: iambic metron, cretic, bacchiac) tell us of the maiden's vain cries to her father:

> Hèr pleás ànd thóse　plaíntìve criés　òf "Fáthér!"　228
> Wère nóthìng—thát maídènhoód　às wórthléss . . . .

Then the strophe's shuddering "Ùnhólỳ, rècklèsslỳ wróng; ànd thén . . ." (220) is matched by

> Thèy coúntèd—lòvèrs-òf-wár,　thè chiéfs.　230

The iambics resume (231–232):

> Hèr fáthèr tóld　aídes thèn áftèr práyìng　231
> Tò líft hèr goát-líke àbóve　thè áltár;

and the sudden rush of short syllables in "À foólìsh wìckèdnèss, díre soúrce òf évíl " (223) is repeated as the young girl is held high like a sacrificial animal (233):

> Hèr róbes dròp dòwn tò thè groúnd;[48] thén wìth stróng wíll . . .　233

Finally, after another slow iambic (234),

> Thèy hóld hígh　hèr fórm rècúmbént;　234

come the ionics again:

---

[47] Catullus 63. See Appendix D, p. 177.
[48] The meaning is disputed (see most recently Ferrari 1997, and Hooker 1968), and my rendering is meant to be ambiguous.

Òn hèr líps, sò sweétlỳ mólded,   235
Wàs à gág, tò chéck hér
Crý thàt coùld cúrse thè househóld.

By this use of his art, the sudden appearance of resolved metrical feet to
express the most horrific parts of the description of the king's terrible sacrifice of his virgin daughter, and the introduction of ionics to suggest his
unlucky motivation (to recover a faithless wife from a foreign city), Aeschylus brings in rhythm, music, and dance to develop his effect. The final strophe and antistrophe (238–257) are almost entirely quiet iambics, the strophe continuing to paint a poignant picture of the gagged girl trying to
speak, trying with her eyes to win compassion from her killers, who had
often heard her holy voice as she sang a hymn of thanksgiving for her
beloved father's guests; one change, a choriamb in that last verse, perhaps
suggests the hymn. The antistrophe returns us to the thoughts of the chorus, repeating its maxim that justice leads sufferers to learn, and saying it
must wait and watch the outcome. The matching choriamb in its final verse,
perhaps slighting her gender, hails Clytemnestra as the only bulwark of the
land.[49]

So in this mighty choral song—far longer than the first song in other
Greek tragedies—the chorusmen have told us of the departure of the naval
force to recover the adulterous wife Helen and bring retribution to Troy;
of the sinister omens; and of the appalling sacrifice made by Agamemnon
in order that the fleet might depart. They have told us of the only light they
can see in all this darkness, their faith that Zeus will somehow bring good
from all this suffering. And they have introduced us to dactylic meter (the
meter of Homer's Trojan tale and of the Delphic oracles) for the tale of the
omen, to the solemn trochaics for their call upon Zeus, and to the slow, un-
dulating rhythm of their iambics, interspersed with special effects of sudden swift runs of light syllables. Choriambs we have seen for prophecy, and
ionics for the theme of the adultery-tolerating Asian city of Troy and the
agony its misdeeds have caused Agamemnon.

THE SECOND CHORAL SONG (*AGAMEMNON* 367–488)

In the scene that follows (258–354), Clytemnestra makes a powerful speech
describing the relay of beacon fires she has set up to give her advance warning of her husband Agamemnon's return, and a second in which she pictures the scenes at the sack of Troy and the dangers that may be incurred

---

[49] Most editors take the reference to be to Clytemnestra, though actually I would prefer
Denniston and Page's interpretation (1957: 93), which understands the chorus to refer to itself.

by the rampaging of the victorious Greek army if it violates the holy things there.

Then again the chorus begin to sing. As usual, this second choral song is introduced by a passage of "marching" anapaests (355–366), in which the chorus again hails Zeus, Zeus who presides over the host-guest relationship and who in anger at its violation by Paris has now destroyed the city of Troy. Then the lyric stanzas begin. First (367–380), more of the same slow iambics that described the Greek fleet stalled at Aulis by Artemis' anger (iambic/bacchiac, cretic, bacchiac). But this time the words proclaim the anger of Zeus himself directed against the guilty Trojans and the punishment he has inflicted upon them:

Bỳ Zeús whípped;   thís thèy háve   tò téll óf;   367
Thè fóotprínt   plaín ànd cleár   tò tráck dówn.

In various combinations of iambic metra, the slow rhythm continues to the end of the stanza, telling in sonorous style how the arrogance of wrongdoing, by those who think the gods do not notice trespassers and grow presumptuous from their wealth, has brought ruin upon Troy. Only the short final line (380) lightens the rhythm a little with a choriamb (*DUM DE DE DUM*): may there be wealth enough to satisfy (they say) "sénsìblè mén's òpínión."

This choriamb serves as a bridge.[50] Unexpectedly, there follows a four-line tailpiece (381–384), a coda, which will be repeated in identical metrical shape but with different words after each stanza of this song. And this little coda is not in iambic, but in aeolo-choriambic. This meter can be thought of as a choriamb (or more than one) preceded and followed by a group of two syllables, or in some rhythms by only one; common forms are the glyconic (usually *DUM DE DUM DE DE DUM DE DUM*, though the first two syllables may be varied), the pherecratean (the same, lacking the final syllable), and the lesser asclepiad (like a glyconic but with a second choriamb following the first). John Frederick Nims' line, "'Nothing noble as water, no, | and there's gold with its glamor . . . ,'" is a glyconic followed by a pherecratean, and Basil Bunting's "Please stop gushing about his pink | neck smooth arms and so forth, Dulcie, it makes me sick" is a glyconic followed by a lesser asclepiad.[51] Aeolo-choriambic is very common in Greek

[50] Dale (1968: 83) speaks of the verse as "forming a transition to the four-lined choriambic ephymnion which follows." Editors usually print the coda as four verses, though the third and fourth might well be combined (as a priapean, like Catullus 17: *O Colonia quae cupis ponte ludere longo*); Thomson prints it as two verses. West (1982: 115) describes the coda as "a metrically and syntactically independent tailpiece . . . which has the effect of a separate little stanza such as might be found in a popular song," and scans the third and fourth lines as a unit (so, too, in West 1991: 91; in the latter text he prints the pherecrateans with an extra-large indent).

[51] See Appendix D, p. 173. Lee (1998: xix) suggests the mnemonic lines, "Here's how ev'ry Glycónic goes," "Here's your Phérecratéan," and, "One more | chóriamb makes | Lesser Asclé | piad."

solo lyric songs and poems, as well as in the choral songs of drama. It always seems to be a light, cheerful meter, and in fact it is often used for epithalamia, marriage hymns; we find it in some of Sappho's songs, in the marriage hymns at the end of Aristophanes' *Peace* and *Birds*, and in Latin in one of Catullus' marriage songs (61).[52]

Here the group (381–384) consists of two pherecrateans, a glyconic, and a final pherecratean. But the sense of the words is very solemn: wealth, they say, is no defense for one who has dishonored the great altar of Justice:

> Thére's nò sáfeguàrd ìn weálth, whén   381
> Mán, ìn súrfeìt òf príde, hás
> Spúrned thè áltàr òf Ríghteoùsnéss,
> Thrúst ìt dówn ìntò dárknéss.

There seems to be a contradiction between the light meter and the ominous meaning, a hint that we shall come to understand later on.

The slow tones of the antistrophe (385–398) tell how the wrongdoer is overcome by the irresistible force of Temptation, and with the futile folly of a child chasing a flying bird brings doom on his city. Then again come the lightly tripping verses of the aeolo-choriambic coda:

> Súch wàs Párìs, àrrívíng
> Guést òf hóst Mènèláùs,   400
> Cástìng sháme òn hìs róyàl hóst's
> Boárd bỳ théft òf hìs cónsórt.

Now we understand why Aeschylus used this meter in this and the preceding coda! Paris came to Menelaus' house and dishonored the hospitality offered him by stealing and seducing his host's wife—*that's* why we had that metrical (and probably musical) reminder of a marriage hymn! One imagines wedding music playing against the grim warning of doom, like a Wagnerian leitmotif, or the recurring theme "One fine day . . ." in *Madama Butterfly* as the heroine dies.

Slow iambics (with many cretics) begin the following strophe (403–415), telling how Helen, leaving her compatriots to mobilize for war and man their avenging fleet, bore off to Troy her dowry of disaster;

---

[52] In a study of marriage songs, Contiades-Tsitsoni (1990: 90) says, "Glykoneen als volkstümliches Versmaß sind geläufig in den Hymenäen . . . Glykoneen (in erweiterter Form) und Choriamben sind die typischen äolischen Versmaße für Hochzeitslieder." Many of Sappho's songs are in glyconics or pherecrateans with dactylic expansion. D. Page (in *Sappho and Alcaeus* [Oxford, 1955], 73–74) is noncommittal ("None of our questions can be answered so long as we possess no specimens of any of the different types of hymeneal song, and no reliable external evidence about their themes and metres"), and Herington in his brief study of the history of the glyconic-pherecratean combination (1985: 219–222) does not connect it with marriage.

Shè léft hèr tównsfólk tò seíze   speár ànd shiéld,
wìth bústlè troóps   móbìlízed,
shíps wère ármed,   màrínes saíled   405

With unprecedented outrageousness she left her husband's home—and the
meter, music, and dance change to portray her light frivolity (406–408).
This is the verse with the resolution I referred to at the beginning of this
chapter (above, p. 67):[53]

Tò bríng tò Tróy,   ìn pláce òf dówrỳ, deáth,   406
Shè stépped oút   eásìlỳ fròm thè gátes
À wróng ùnheárd-òf.

Then the iambics return, reporting the lamentations of the palace counsel-
lors:

À wróng ùnheárd-òf. Mánỳ tímes làméntèd thén   408
Thè pálàce seérs;   groánìng loúd,   thèy spóke thús:
"Àlás! Àlás!   Woé tò hoúse!   Tò hoúse ànd kíngs!   410
Àlás fòr páths   whích shè tród   ìn márrièd lóve!"

After a few words more (412–415) about the phantom of his beloved wife
that Menelaus will imagine still rules in his house—a thought to be amplified in the next stanza—the pherecrateans and glyconic of the four-verse
"marriage hymn" coda tell of the flight of Love from Menelaus' empty eyes,
unresponsive now to the beautiful images of his wife in his palace (416–
419):

Chárm òf rádìant líkenéss   416
Hátefùl nów tò hèr húsbánd;
Ábsènce, émptìnèss meét hìs éyes;
Vánìshed áll Àphròdíté.

The corresponding antistrophe (420–432) must of course again show the
swift-footed rush of syllables that depicted Helen's unthinking, irresponsi-
ble flight from Argos with her young lover and her ill-omened entry into
Troy's gates; and Aeschylus is of course equal to the challenge. As it begins,
first the continuing iambics drive home again Menelaus' loss, his delusive
dreams of his missing wife (420–422)—

Thè dreám-dìscérned   fántàsiés   stíll pèrsuáde;[54]   420
Ìmáginíngs   cóme—bùt théy
Ónlỳ bríng   à vaín jóy;

[53] The resolution here is commented upon by Kitto 1955: 40; similar techniques elsewhere
by van Nes Ditmars 1992: 20 and Rash 1981: 16. Scott 1984 does not comment.

[54] Reading Housman's conjecture πειθήμονες, with Murray and many older editors (but
not Denniston and Page, Fraenkel, or West). The manuscripts' πενθήμονες might be rendered
in my translation "stíll tòrmént."

—delusive, for as he reaches out his yearning arms to embrace the dream, the phantom vanishes, in the same resolved syllables that impressed upon us Helen's slipping out through the gates (423–426):

> Fòr vaínlỳ, whén   hè thínks hè seés   ànd seéks tò clásp,[55]
> Thèn glídíng   eásìlỳ fròm hìs árms
> Thè dreám hàs fádèd, névèrmóre tò bé   425
> Òn wíngs, àlóng   páths òf sleép,   còmpánión.

After describing at such length Menelaus' sorrowful loss, the chorus broadens its vision and goes on to tell of the similar bereavement in so many other households throughout the land of Greece; all those who have lost the men who left for Troy. *This* is the theme of the next lilting little coda (433–436):

> Eách thè mén thàt thèy sént fórth
> Knóws; bùt nów, ìn theìr ábsénce,
> Úrns ànd áshès ìn pláce òf mén   435
> Cóme àgaín tò thè hoúsehólds.

In place of the beloved menfolk the families sent to the war, back to their homes come—the body bags (the Greek equivalent was a clay pot filled with ashes from the pyre). The rhythm, and probably the melody too, insistently reminds us of the impious, ill-fated marriage that caused so many Greek soldiers never to come home again to their wives.

The stanza that follows (437–451) is the most poignant and moving in Aeschylus—and especially so for his Athenian audience, for many of their compatriots had recently died fighting abroad, defending or expanding the Athenian empire. It is a funeral elegy for all those who have died in battle, equal to the best of the poems produced during the First World War. It begins, in Aeschylus' way, with poetic metaphors: Ares the War God, holding up his balance beam like a money-changer, weighs out in return for the bodies of fighting men not a banker's heavy gold dust, but a handful of ashes from the funeral pyre, heavy only with the tears of mourners. It begins with four lines (437–441) of the same slow iambics (including cretics) as the other stanzas of this song:

> Thè Gód òf Wár,   hóldìng úp   báttlè-scáles,
> Weíghìng oút   bánkèr-líke   dúst fòr flésh,
> Fròm blázìng pýres   hóme fròm Tróy   440
> Tò kínsmèn sénds   heávỳ dúst . . . .

[55] Reading Housman's conjecture ἐς θιγὰς, with Murray. Few editors accept this, but I find the indefinite pronoun in the manuscripts' ἐσθλά τις hard to understand here—I think Aeschylus specifically means Menelaus, not "someone." The usual text here (Denniston and Page's) is rendered above (p. 71) as "Fòr vaínlỳ, whén òne seéms tò seé hìs heárt's dèsíre. . . ."

Then three lines (442–444) of equally solemn lecythia (*DUM DE DUM DE DUM DE DUM):*

> Áshès lóng-tò-bé-bèwaíled,   442
> Eásỳ-stówed   ìn úrns òf cláy,
> Loádìng dúst   ìn pláce òf mén.

Three more lines of iambics (445–447):

> Wìth eúlògiés   thèy moúrn thèm, hów   445
> À mán wàs skílled   ìn deéds òf wár,
> Ànóthèr diéd   à nóblè deáth . . .

Then comes another of Aeschylus' abrupt metrical changes. He is telling how the grieving relatives praise one man for his skill in fighting, another for dying nobly amid the slaughter—and suddenly he gives us their actual bitter words, in direct speech. And the meter of their four verses is anacreontic (*DE DE DUM DE DUM DE DUM DUM*), the Asian-type meter (see above, p. 79). The abduction of Helen again!—the cause of all this suffering (447–451):

> Ànóthèr diéd   à nóblè deáth—"Áll   447
>   Fòr à wífe òf sómeòne élsé's!"
>   Ìn à whíspèr sómeòne múttérs;
>   Ànd rèséntmènt òvèrcómes thém   450
>   Fòr thè kíng-àvéngérs.[56]

The following "marriage-hymn" coda is more reflective, full of pathos and irony: the beautiful young men now lie in their graves around the walls of Troy, holding on to the land, which in turn holds them. The marriage— if that is what it is—of Helen has brought them to their death (452–455).

>   Neár Tróy's wáll thèy àre lýíng;   452
>   Gráves thèy óccùpỳ; áll thát

---

[56] My version follows the line division of Murray 1955, which reads (447–451):

> τὸν δ᾽ ἐν φοναῖς καλῶς πεσόντ᾽ —"ἀλ-
>   λοτρίας διαὶ γυναικός"·
>   τάδε σῖγά τις βαΰζει·
>   φθονερὸν δ᾽ ὑπ᾽ ἄλγος ἕρπει
>   προδίκοις Ἀτρείδαις.

West (1991), Dale (1983: 179), and Fraenkel (1950) print the lines similarly, except that they all place the syllable ἀλ- at the beginning of 448 (prefixed to the anacreontic) instead of at the end of 447 (in the antistrophe, by Murray's colometry there is no mid-word division here). They all scan the lines as anacreontic (West 1991: 92; Fraenkel 1950, 2: 184–186—a full discussion). Page (1972) and Denniston and Page (1957: 229–230) break the lines differently (dividing words at the end of each) and scan each as a choriamb + iambic metron, which to me is less effective. As Fraenkel (ad loc.) says, "I leave it to the reader to make his choice." Aeschylus, of course, trained his chorus himself, so his intentions were not in doubt.

Gráce, thàt cómelìnèss úndèr eárth;
Tróy hèr cónquèròrs cóvérs.

With the people's grief comes the people's resentment. The first half of the antistrophe (456–466)—slow iambics again—speaks even more openly of the dangerous anger among the citizens, and among the gods, too: those responsible for many deaths, say the old men of Argos as they await their returning king, are not unobserved by the gods or by the Furies. And in the second part of the stanza, the repeated light anacreontics (467–470) recall the fatal abduction referred to in the strophe, and reaffirm the principles at work here: no hope for the unjust, the overly proud, for they are blasted by Zeus' thunderbolt—his anger matches that which the voices of the citizens expressed in the strophe. Him who is prosperous without justice the black Furies . . .

. . . Tò dárknèss thrów dówn; thére, thè únseén   466
    Hàve nò hópe òf hélp oò cómfórt.
    Tò bè praísed bèyónd thè meásúre—
    Pèrìl! Whén thè éye òf Zeús seés,
    Còmes thè stróke òf líghtníng.[57]   470

After this, the last "marriage-song" coda summarizes the chorusmen's re-flections on the whole Trojan War, in which (they have just heard) their king has been victorious and has mightily avenged the abduction of his brother's wife. They want no part of it (471–474):

Í choóse ríchès ùnénvíed;   471
    Nót tò bé cìtỳ-sáckér,
Nór ènsláved bỳ ànóthèr máy
    Í seé lífe às à cáptíve.[58]

Finally, the chorusmen add a short lyric epode (475–488), a stanza not matched with another.[59] Perhaps they divide their group into two parts, or even three, the better to convey that they are no longer ruminating on the lessons of Troy's offense and fall, but discussing the immediate situation in their own city. Can the good news brought by the beacon fire be true (this in iambics)? But who can be so foolish as to allow his belief to be fired up,

[57] Murray's text (see last note) runs (446–470):

τιθεῖσ' ἀμαυρόν, ἐν δ' ἀίστοις
τελέθοντος οὔτις ἀλκά·
τὸ δ' ὑπερκόπως κλύειν εὖ
βαρύ· βάλλεται γὰρ ὄσσοις
Διόθεν κεραυνός.

[58] Reading ὑπ' ἄλλῳ (473–474) with Page 1972 and Denniston and Page 1957.
[59] Scott (1982: 184) suggests, "This song [475–488] does not come to an obvious conclu-sion but seems interrupted by the announcement of the Herald's approach."

only to be distressed when the news is changed? It fits a *woman's* mind (a jibe at Clytemnestra) to offer thanks before the facts are clear! Then, adding further proof that Aeschylus likes to divert us with song, music, and dance, there follow two lines (485–486) rushing headlong with multiple resolutions, twenty light syllables interspersed with only five heavy ones, including three sequences of four light syllables and one of no less than seven. With these scurrying syllables, Aeschylus seems to be mimicking the frivolousness of feminine credulity,[60] before the final steadying iambic line:

> À wómàn's heárt   évèr thús—
> Èmbrácìng jóy   whén nò jóy   hàs yét àppeáred.
> Crèdùloùs toò fár, thère círcùlàtes thè fèmìnìne bèliéf   485
> Tràvèlìng sò fást!   Bùt pèrìshìng fást
> À wómàn-voíced   rúmòr diés   wìthoút à tráce.

(Of course, we know how mistaken the old men of Argos are in disbelieving their queen!) Then the chorus ends its singing, and its leader resumes the spoken dialogue, announcing the appearance of the army's herald coming up from the harbor, bringing the hope of confirmation of this incredible "woman-voiced rumor."

THE THIRD CHORAL SONG (*AGAMEMNON* 681–781)

The third choral song introduces the third constituent of the pattern Aeschylus is developing: wrongdoing—suffering—punishment. The first choral song told of Agamemnon's departure for Troy and the wrong he did in killing his daughter. The second has described Paris' wrongful abduction of Helen, and the suffering this caused both Menelaus and the other Greeks who likewise lost their loved ones. The following scene presents Agamemnon's herald, returned from Troy with his lord, who delivers the news of the fall of Troy, including more wrongdoing—the destruction of the city's altars by the Greeks; he goes on to tell of the suffering of the Greeks during the siege, and finally of the punishment the gods have laid upon them, the loss of many more Greek lives in a storm on the homeward voyage, and the uncertainty of even Menelaus' return. Aeschylus is arranging the presentation of his thought in a structure very familiar in ancient Greek, ring form (A: B: C: B′: A′). He reports (through the herald) the Greeks' wrongdoing, and immediately afterward their divine punishment (item C); Paris' wrong-

---

[60] Scott (1984: 48) says: "Up to this point in the *Oresteia*, lyric meters have been largely unresolved. . . . Resolution shows that anxiety has begun to work its way into the previously uniform and simple meter as the chorus reveals its concern that the message from Troy may be true."

doing (item B) was told in the second choral song, and his punishment (item B') will be the subject of this coming song; Agamemnon's wrongdoing (item A) was the subject of the chorus' first massive song—and at the end of this present song, Aeschylus will immediately bring him onstage before us, ripe for his own punishment (item A') at the hands of his unfaithful wife Clytemnestra.

Afer the herald's shocking report, one would expect real old men of Argos to wonder with agonized uncertainty whether their own kinsfolk lie dead in Troy, were lost at sea, or will soon be here again behind their leader Agamemnon. But instead Aeschylus continues to use his chorus to work out his thought before us, and it moves on to the punishment of Paris and the Trojans for their wrongdoing. It begins by telling of Helen, the *means* as well as the cause of Troy's doom, driving home her responsibility for the suffering by a fateful play on her name (681–685). The verses are trochaic (mainly lecythia: *DUM DE DUM DE DUM DE DUM*), which we have not heard since the invocation of Zeus in the chorus' first song:[61]

> Whó wàs hé thàt námed hèr thús,   681
> Fíttìnglý, wìth pérfèct trúth?
> Súrelỳ óne wè máy nòt seé,
> Préscìént,
> Knówìng déstìný's dèsígn,
> Guídìng tóngue tò ríghtfùl námíng. . . .   685

And just as in the chorus' second song, where the meter changed as Helen slipped out of her chamber in Argos (407), now again Aeschylus evokes a different emotion with his meter as he tells us in greater detail how she left the luxury of her palace to sail off to Asia, many soldier-hunters following the trail of her oar blades to land on the beaches of Troy (684–698):

> . . . Knówìng déstìný's dèsígn,
> Guídìng tóngue tò ríghtfùl námíng: 685
>   Wìth thè speár shè wéd, wìth wárfáre,
>   Hèlèn—héll ìndeéd shè cárriéd!

---

[61] Murray prints the lines as:

> τίς ποτ' ὠνόμαξεν ὧδ'   681
> ἐς τὸ πᾶν ἐτητύμως—
> μή τις ὄντιν' οὐχ ὁρω-
> μεν προνοι-
> αισι τοῦ πεπρωμένου
> γλῶσσαν ἐν τύχᾳ νέμων;— τὰν   685

Fraenkel, Page, and especially West group the cola into longer lines but make no significant change except for the final syllable (on which see below). Dale (1983: 182) takes 683 differently. Denniston and Page (1957: 230) call the stanza "iambic, ionic, glyconic"; the first word must be a slip.

Tò thè shíps, tò mén, tò à proúd
Cìtỳ, troússeaú⁶² sòftlỳ-wóvén   690
Ìn hèr chámbèr léft, ànd saílíng
Òn thè breáth òf míghtỳ Zéphýr.
    Mànỳ thoúsánds
Òf pùrsúèrs, sóldìèr-húntsmén
Òn thè fádìng traíl òf oárbládes   695
Soúght préy beáched bỳ thè Trójàn streám's
Leáf-shìvèred shóres, fòr sáke óf
Hìdèoùs strífe, wrètchèd bloódshéd.

The shift is to anacreontics (*DE DE DUM DE DUM DE DUM DUM*),⁶³
which we have seen used to describe Agamemnon's sacrifice of his daughter to free his warships to sail to Troy (225–227), her piteous appeal (235–
237), and the resentment of bereaved Greeks toward Helen (448–451).
Here the meter suggests her Asian destination, and her un-Greek behavior.
One line (690) is composed of two ionic metra (each *DE DE DUM DUM*),
and another (693) of one metron, among the anacreontics; 696 is probably
a glyconic beginning with three heavy syllables; the next line (697) is a cho-

---

⁶² Editors take προκαλυμμάτων to mean something like "bed- (or bed-chamber-) curtains,"
but Seaford (1987: 124) argues cogently that it means "bridal veil," which is so apt here that I
have tried to suggest it in my rendering.

⁶³ Murray prints:

             [τὰν]
δορίγαμβρον ἀμφινεικῆ   686
 θ᾽ Ἑλέναν; ἐπεὶ πρεπόντως
ἐλένας, ἔλανδρος, ἐλέ-
πτολις, ἐκ τῶν ἀβροπήνων   690
προκαλυμμάτων ἔπλευσε
Ζεφύρου γίγαντος αὔρᾳ,
πολύανδροί
τε φεράσπιδες κυναγοὶ
κατ᾽ ἴχνος πλατᾶν ἄφαντον   695
κελσάντων Σιμόεντος
ἀκτὰς ἐπ᾽ ἀεξιφύλλους
δι᾽ ἔριν αἱματόεσσαν.   698

Denniston and Page and Fraenkel scan the first line after the trochaics (686) as choriambic,
but in view of the succession of anacreontics that follow, I prefer Murray's colometry, which
takes this as anacreontic, too. West (1991: 92, where it is numbered 687) calls it ionic. On 689,
where the penultimate syllable is light instead of heavy, see West 1982: 125 ("a freak form").

I have to disagree here with Scott, who says, "The old men contentedly sing of the crime
of Helen and Paris. . . . They take their time in this comfortable and safe reminiscence of the
past. . . . Such enjoyment of the past is an indulgence for this serious chorus; they are escap-
ing from their worrisome thoughts about the return of their threatened king, and the meter
framing this escapism appropriately has no thematic import" (1984: 53–54).

riamb plus a bacchiac,[64] and the last verse (a pherecratean) Aeschylus begins with three light syllables, very rare in aeolo-choriambic and marking (as such streams of light syllables did in the first choral song) a horrified shudder.

As always, the antistrophe (699–716) repeats the metrical pattern of the strophe, and (as so often) also its other striking features:

Wéddìng-bónd ànd bónds òf woé
Plán-fùlfíllìng Ángèr dróve   700
Ón tò Tróy, èxáctìng fór
Táblè shámed,
Zeús dìshónòred, gód òf guésts,
Púnìshmént ìn àftèrtíme, fróm
     Thè dèlíghtèd célèbrátórs   705
     Òf thè loúdlỳ-chántèd bríde-sóng,
     Wèddìng hýmn, whìch thén wàs thè lót[65]
     Òf thè kínsfólk òf thè brídegroóm.
     Hàvìng chángèd tò díff'rènt músìc,
     Ìn thè àncìènt tówn òf Príám   710
         Mànỳ dírgés
     Thèy nòw úttèr, lámèntátións,
     Càllìng Párìs "bloódỳ-béddéd"—
     Áll nów lóst ìn hèr peóplè's líves,
     Mánỳ à dírge tò síng nów,   715
     Pìtèoùs bloódshèd èndúrìng.[66]

First comes another word play: there came to Troy κῆδος ὀρθώνυμον, "a well-named *kēdos*" (699–700), the noun meaning both "marriage-bond" and "affliction." Then the trochaics (701–704) tell us the reason—this is the punishment for Paris' dishonoring of the host-guest relationship, the anger of Zeus who presides over it. The chorus' song then *changes* (as in the strophe) to anacreontics (705–716), and at the same time Priam's ancient city has "chángèd tò díff'rènt músìc"—from the loudly celebrated wedding hymn to a lamentation for the awful bloodshed this disastrous marriage caused. Once again wedding music is counterpointed by a dirge, and the strophe's "Many thousands . . ." (*poluandroi*, 693) of warriors who set off in pursuit of the elopers are balanced by the "Many dirges . . ." (*poluthrēnon*, 711) to be sung by the offenders.

[64] There are slight uncertainties in text and colometry here (see Denniston and Page and Fraenkel ad loc.), but the general rhythm and sense are clear enough.
[65] On the scansion of this line (like that of 689), see note 63 above.
[66] Text and meter of the first two of the last three lines are uncertain. I have followed the meaning suggested by Denniston and Page ad loc., adapted to the meter of the strophe.

The concluding lines of this pair of stanzas (696–698, 714–716) modulate from ionics to aeolo-choriambic, the meter I have suggested might be associated with wedding songs when it was used for the little coda in the previous choral song (p. 82 above). Now this aeolo-choriambic rhythm continues in the second strophe and antistrophe (717–726, 727–736), which illustrate further the reversal of fortune at Troy after Helen's arrival. Here the chorus presents an extended metaphor; it tells of a pet lion cub, fawning on and beloved by young and old alike when it was young, but then (in the antistrophe) as time went on, revealing its inborn nature by slaughtering domestic animals and drenching the house with blood, fulfilling its god-given task of destruction.[67]

In the third strophe (737–749), the chorus explains the application of this metaphor. Helen came to Troy (solemn iambics again, including some cretics and bacchiacs; cf. lines 192–197 above). She came like something lovable—a calm sea, the alluring display of wealth, the heart-stirring flower of love:

> Àt fírst thère cáme, seémìnglý, tò Ílìúm   737
> À dáy-dreám, às Í woùld sáy,
> Wíndlèss cálm, sèréne, stíll,   740
> Thè tránquíl lóvelìnéss òf rích góld. . . .

Then, as the thought turns towards love (and Helen), the next verse (742) begins with a choriamb, and the following one (743) holds a choriamb in the middle, that is, it has fallen into the aeolo-choriambic rhythm previously associated with marriage:[68]

> Ténderlỳ dártìng glánce òf éye,   742
> Heárt-còródìng dèsíre ìn fúll bloóm.

But then, "veering aside" (παρακλίνασ')—and here the meter itself *veers aside* again to the exotic ionics and anacreontics—she brought about, by Zeus' will, a bitter end of her "marriage" for Priam's people (744–749):

> Bùt à veéríng lèd hèr brídáls
> Tò à bíttèr cońsùmmátión;   745
> Hòrrìd neíghbór, hòrrìd cómráde
> Tò bè loósed òn kín òf Príám.

---

[67] It may well be another example of Aeschylus' technique of using several light syllables to emphasize disaster that lines 723–724 in the strophe, where the initial light syllables (both lines scan ˘ ˘ ˘ ˘ – ˘ ˘ –) help to express the pleasure of cuddling the little cub, like a newborn child, are matched by 733–734 in the antistrophe, where the corresponding syllables mean "irresistible [agony]" (ἄμαχον [ἄλγος]) and "great disaster" (μέγα σίνος).

[68] Actually, 743 is a hipponactean (= a glyconic with an additional syllable at the end).

Zeús Lórd òf Guésts sènt hèr thére,[69]
Bríde-bèwaíled sìn-àvéngér!

The antistrophe (750–763) begins the chorusmen's reflections upon all this. There is an old saying, they tell us in these slow, measured iambics, that from prosperity and good fortune in a family arises inevitable ruin. This is a very common idea in ancient Greek literature:

Fòr lóng àmóng   húmànkínd   thè áncìent sáw   750
Còntínúes: thàt "Whén à mán's
Weálth hàs grówn   tò rípe áge
Ìt gíves bírth—doés nòt wíthèr chíldléss."

Then the choriambs begin:

"Próspèroùs fórtùne prógèný   755
Beárs fòr kíndrèd à wóe ùnéndíng."

But, the chorusmen go on, they themselves—or Aeschylus?—have a *different* opinion, and here of course comes again the *different* meter, the "veering" we noted in the strophe, the ionics/anacreontics heralding the new viewpoint. *They* hold that it is not prosperity that begets ruin, but impious actions—a household that practices justice, they tell us, need suffer no misfortune:

Ùnlìke óthérs mỳ òpínión.
Ìt ìs ónlỳ deéds ùnhólý
Thàt bègét móre—wìckèd óffspríng
Òf thè sáme breéd as̄ their fáthérs.   760
Whén júst ànd straíght ìs thè hoúse,
Álwàys blést àre hèr chíldrén.

In the short final pair of stanzas of this song (763–772, 773–782), the chorusmen sum up the philosophical and theological underpinnings of their moral beliefs. They talk of *hubris,* "impious arrogance," with the additional significant meaning "improper violent action." Agamemnon has been guilty of both. (No English word comes close to the always-negative connotations of *hubris;* in my rendering I have used "Pride," to be taken in all its pejorative associations as the first of the Seven Deadly Sins, and worse.) The first slow iambics (763–765) tell how *hubris* in the past gives birth to new *hubris* in the present, in the miserable history of human affairs:

---

[69] Denniston and Page (1957: 231) call 748 "a form of anacreontic, with - ◡ ◡ - for - ◡ ◡ - - in the second half." Fraenkel (1950, 2: 328) and Scott (1984: 52) call it a choriambic dimeter, West (1991: 93) a telesillean with anaclasis. The final verse is aeolo-choriambic (a pherecratean).

Bùt Príde ìs wónt   broód tò beár,
Áncìent Príde—Príde thè néw;
Oút òf húmàn évìl soón   765
Òr láte àppeárs—whènèvèr thè tíme àppoíntèd cóme. . . .

And as the "new *hubris*" appears, the regular iambics give way to a line (766) with a heavy syllable resolved into two light ones, giving a surprising sequence of four lights.[70] Then comes a further description—and even more remarkable effects of resolution:

Thè dáy òf bírth—díre dèvìl òf háte,
Spìrìt ìrrèsìstìblè, ìmpìoùs, bóld,
Dèfíant bláck wréck òf thè hoúse, Dìsástér   770
Trúe tò hèr párènt's nátúre.

The first iambic metron is followed by an irregular sequence including three light syllables (- ⌣ ⌣ ⌣ -), and the next verse (769) is resolved into a clattering cacophony of light syllables—ten of them in succession. This striking effect—the most violent use of resolutions so far—must mark the disastrous perpetuation of overweening presumption and of violent act after violent act. The two remaining lines each includes a choriamb in its iambic structure.[71]

Finally, the antistrophe (773–781)[72] paints the contrasting picture: Justice shines brightly in the dark homes of the righteous poor (this in the

---

[70] As usual I follow the colometry of Murray, which runs:

φιλεῖ δὲ τίκτειν Ὕβρις   763
μὲν παλαιὰ νεά-
ζουσαν ἐν κακοῖς βροτῶν   765
Ὕβριν τότ᾽ ἢ τόθ᾽, ὅτε τὸ κύριον μόλῃ
φάος τόκου, δαίμονά τ᾽ ἔταν,
ἄμαχον ἀπόλεμον ἀνίερον,
Θράσος, μελαίνα μελάθροισιν Ἄτα,   770
εἰδομένα τοκεῦσιν.

Dale (1983: 185) agrees with this; other editors vary. Because all modern editors combine some of the cola separated by earlier editors, but keep the traditional line numbers, a line number is occasionally omitted in my translation (as in Murray's text).

[71] Line 770 is iambic metron + choriamb + bacchiac; 771 is choriamb + bacchiac.

[72] Printed by Murray:

Δίκα δὲ λάμπει μὲν ἐν   773
δυσκάπνοις δώμασιν,
τόν τ᾽ ἐναίσιμον τίει [βίον].   775
τὰ χρυσόπαστα δ᾽ ἔδεθλα σὺν πίνῳ χερῶν
παλιντρόποις ὄμμασι λιποῦσ᾽,
ὅσια προσέβατο δύναμιν οὐ
σέβουσα πλούτου παράσημον αἴνῳ·   780
πᾶν δ᾽ ἐπὶ τέρμα νωμᾷ.

matching slow iambics); but she abhors (here the rattle of the resolved forms begins again: 776) the gilded mansions of the filthy rich:

> Bùt Jústìce shínes⠀⠀bríght ìn hómes
> Poór ànd dím,⠀⠀dárk wìth smóke;
> Hónòrs júst ànd ríghteoùs mén.⠀⠀⠀⠀⠀⠀⠀⠀⠀⠀⠀775
> Fròm góld-bèspánglèd pàlàcès soíled bỳ fílthỳ hánds. . . .

As the number of light syllables increases (in 778–779), she scurries quickly to the homes of the pious, shuddering away from counterfeit imprints. And *she* directs everything to its fulfillment:

> Wìth túrned-àsíde éyes quìcklỳ shè goés
> Tò thè dèdìcàtèd tò pìetỳ, nót
> Rèvérìng weálth stámped wìth à fálse ìmpréssió́n.⠀⠀⠀780
> Áll tò ìts énd shè guídéth.

At last, having concluded all this declamation and illustration of the inevitable victory of Disaster, Punishment, and Justice on the evildoers who ignore what is right and holy and follow self-willed pride and ungodly violence, the chorusmen turn to greet their returning King Agamemnon, the inheritor of the still-unexpiated guilt of Atreus' murder of his brother Thyestes' children, the slayer of his own daughter, the destroyer of Troy, the ultimate killer of the hosts of Trojans and Greeks who fought there—and accompanied as he rides in his chariot into the orchestra by Cassandra, the violated princess of Troy and now his concubine, still robed in the insignia of a virgin priestess (a nun's habit). For a dramatic entrance, this is hard to equal. Agamemnon will speak of Justice three times in his first four verses, as he faces the one who will execute it upon him, his wife Clytemnestra.

THE REST OF THE *AGAMEMNON*, AND OF THE TRILOGY

After the entrance of the returning king in the *Agamemnon*, the crimes of the recent past (the abduction of Helen, the murder of Agamemnon's daughter, the destruction of the temples of Troy) are augmented by the seer Cassandra's visions of the more remote but still unexpiated crimes to which Agamemnon inherits the guilt—Atreus' murder of his brother Thyestes' children and his serving up their flesh as a meal for their father. Then the rest of the play and the rest of the trilogy move on to the horrific actions happening, or likely to happen, presently onstage. The same techniques of sudden conglomerations of light syllables to draw attention to something especially agitating continue in evidence, as well as the use of dactyls and choriambs to invoke the solemnity of prophecy, anacreontics and ionics for

foreign (and hence suspicious, dangerous) habits and influences, and aeolo-
choriambic for wedding rituals.

However, in the remaining portion of the *Agamemnon*, conglomerations
of light syllables usually occur in the two wildest rhythms in Greek drama,
in paeonic and as resolved forms of dochmiac—neither used in the first
three choral songs. Paeonics (*DE DE DE DUM, DE DE DE DUM*), which include three successive light syllables, begin the second strophe (1001–1002)
of the fourth choral song, as the chorus speaks of man's arrogance and fall,[73]
and in the antistrophe (1118–1119) proclaims the irrevocability of blood
spilled on the ground—a closer allusion to the play's action than they yet
know. The terrifying qualities of this meter[74] are shown by its use for a repeated refrain in the "Binding Song" of the Furies around Orestes in the
Eumenides, which seems to have inspired Lattimore to imitation (*Eumenides*
328–330 = 341–343; see p. 167 below).

Of dochmiacs, Dale says, "These dochmiac and kindred types are I think
the only lyric rhythms which carry an inherent emotional expression—
namely passionate feeling of some kind" (1969: 254).[75] The basic rhythm
is *DE DUM DUM DE DUM* ("Rebel, serfs, rebel!"[76]), often with one or
more of the heavy syllables resolved into two light ones (and other changes
are possible); Oedipus' sixteen successive light syllables (after he has blinded
himself: see above) are technically two fully resolved dochmiacs (*Oedipus
Rex* 1314, 1322). In the *Agamemnon*, dochmiacs are common in Cassandra's
frenzied outcries (beginning ἀπόλλων ἐμός, "dèstróyér tò mé!" 1081), and
as the chorus becomes more and more worried by her visions of past and
future bloodshed in the palace, it adopts them, too, interspersing them in
its iambics (first in 1121; see Scott 1984: 8–9). Later, the chorus' first lyric
reaction to the sight of Clytemnestra standing over the bodies of Agamemnon and Cassandra falls into dochmiacs (1407–1411 and 1426–1430). In
the *Choephoroe*, the chorus sings in dochmiacs in its song of triumphant
vengeance after the murders, *Choephoroe* 935–972 (concluding πάρα τὸ φῶς
ἰδεῖν, "Hère ìs thè líght tò seé!" 972), and in the *Eumenides*, the first two
utterances of the chorus of Furies are in dochmiacs mixed with iambics
(143–178, 254–275). The Furies resort to dochmiacs again in their frus-
trated confrontation with Athena after the vote has gone against them (*Eumenides* 777–792 = 808–822, 837–846 = 870–880).

The meters analyzed in the first three songs of the *Agamemnon* are also
widely used in the remainder of the trilogy. The most striking resolutions
in iambic come at the entry of the chorus—terrified foreign slave-women,

[73] The text is mangled.

[74] See Prins 1991: 186–192: "Paeons are in fact associated with ἄτη throughout the
Oresteia" (189).

[75] See also Rosenmeyer 1982: 34–35.

[76] Attributed by F. S. Edwards to the late Lionel Pearson.

beating their breasts—at the beginning of the *Choephoroe*, where some verses are almost entirely light syllables (e.g., 25 = 35); once such a verse is juxtaposed with another made up almost entirely of heavy syllables (29–30 = 39–40), which must have been a striking effect.[77] A little later, their short song (without responsion) as Electra performs the libations at the tomb of her father is in heavily resolved iambics (152–155) leading on to dochmiacs.[78]

The dactyls of epic poetry and the Delphic oracle were prominent in Calchas' prophecy at the beginning of the first choral song of the *Agamemnon*, and the association is repeated in the first stanzas of the fourth, where slow trochaics are interrupted by a single dactylic line when the words of the strophe speak of prophecy (979; see above, note 28), and those of the antistrophe of a song of the Furies (992). This latter association is confirmed in the "Binding Song" sung by the Furies as they dance around Orestes in the *Eumenides*; there are in fact two strophe-antistrophe pairs formed of dactylic verses (four and three respectively) finished off with a trochaic line (349–353 = 360–366, 367–371 = 377–380). And the final song of the trilogy, sung as the Furies, now reconciled and calling down blessings on the land of Athens, leave the orchestra at the end of the trilogy, is again in dactyls; Scott well remarks (1984: 135) that "at the end of the trilogy the recurrence of dactyls recalls the dactylic prophecy of Calchas in the first part of the parodos of the *Agamemnon*."

Ionic/anacreontic and aeolo-choriambic rhythms are not used so dramatically after Helen has dropped out of sight, but they predominate in the complex mixture of meters in the mighty song of chorus and actors together in the *Choephoroe*, the invocation of the spirit of the dead Agamemnon by Orestes, Electra, and the chorus (315–475: analyzed in Scott 1984: 85–87). In the same play, the first and last of the nonresponsive refrains in the choral song celebrating the coming revenge on Aegisthus are in ionics (790–793, 827–830; Page's colometry), the middle one in paeons and ionics (807–811). Perhaps their use is partly at least because the chorus-women are slaves captured abroad (*Choephoroe* 75–78), likely to be thought of as from Asia Minor.

The above analysis of the meters of the first three choral songs of the *Agamemnon* has shown that we can still discern, however distantly and imprecisely, something of how Aeschylus, γλῶσσαν ἐν τύχᾳ νέμων, "guiding tongue to rightful naming" (*Agamemnon* 685), exploits metrical techniques to reinforce the emotional significance of his descriptions of past events for

---

[77] Contra, Scott 1984: 82: "Because they are a dour, gloomy chorus, the lack of any variation in their meter is quite consistent with their characterization."

[78] Analysis in ibid.: 83.

his listeners (and watchers). Later in the play, as violence becomes imminent, he increases the excitement with the introduction of dochmiacs, and also by exchanges in the meters of dialogue.[79] Then, in the rest of this great trilogy, he will go on to present further scenes of the agonies caused by an apparently unstoppable succession of wrongdoing and the punishment of it involving further wrongdoing (as we saw Agamemnon's punishment of Paris and the Trojans drive him to the crime of murdering his daughter, for which he will in turn be punished by being murdered by his wife, who in turn will be punished by being murdered by their son, who will be driven mad by the horror and pollution of this murder . . .)—he will go on to celebrate the eventual replacement of this hereditary blood-feud system by the institution of a democratic judicial procedure organized by the state and executed by a jury of representative citizens. Though we can never hope to understand the full experience of the Athenian populace who attended the presentation of Aeschylus' drama—the music they heard, the dancing they saw—our attention to the meters he chooses and the ways in which he adapts them to convey changes of mood will be amply repaid.[80]

---

[79] In the dialogue portions of the *Agamemnon*, there is a dramatic metrical effect as the king's death cries from within the palace interrupt the chorus, which is chanting anapaests and (we think) preparing for another lyric song. In this passage (mercilessly parodied in Housman's *Fragment of a Greek Tragedy*, though he ignores the change in meter) Agamemnon utters a verse in the usual iambics of dialogue (1343); the astounded chorus (or perhaps just the chorus leader) responds in the other meter of dialogue, the swifter and livelier trochaic tetrameter; Agamemnon cries out again; and the chorus (or its leader) speaks a further two tetrameters, before splitting up and speaking individually in twelve separate iambic couplets as the chorusmen express (visually as well as in speech) their disunity and perplexity (1348–1371). Later, as the discourse between Aegisthus and the chorus threatens to become violent (1649ff.), both parties switch from iambics to trochaic tetrameters until the end of the play. Aeschylus elsewhere uses such tetrameters only in his *Persians*, in dialogues between Atossa and the chorus and Atossa and the ghost of Darius. In Euripides' *Bacchae*, tetrameters are used when the disguised Dionysus describes to the chorus what happened when he was imprisoned inside the palace (*Bacchae* 604–641; see E. R. Dodds' note ad loc. in his commentary [Oxford, 1944]).

[80] Some familiarity with recent poems in English, by well-known poets, that have made use of ancient models should make it easier to comprehend the rhythms of the originals in both choral and solo lyrics, and accordingly some examples are discussed in Appendix D.

Chapter Four

POETRY IN THE LATIN LANGUAGE

Although in their historical development the Greek and Latin languages are closely connected, in the classical period they have differences that are vitally important for appreciating the nature of the poetry that we read or listen to in each of them. Unlike Greek, Latin has no definite or indefinite articles, and this allows a greater freedom in word order and juxtaposition of words. This characteristic imprecision also provides Latin with a much greater capacity for ambiguity, which is further increased by its habit of omitting possessive pronouns. These qualities give the language a potential richness of allusion and suggestion that can be exploited by a poet—and that greatly complicates the task of a translator. We have already examined, in the first chapter of this book, the effects of the positioning of words in the Homeric hexameter. Now we shall consider such effects in Latin verse, and in particular how the possibilities of the language are exploited by one Augustan poet, Propertius.

Latin Word Order

Surprisingly, the importance of word order in Latin is all too often neglected. One of the best modern translators of Horace's *Odes* prints this rendering of one of my favorite stanzas, expressing a theme to which many poets, ancient and modern, have given voice:[1]

> Many brave men lived before Agamemnon,
> But all went down unmourned, unhonoured into the smothering
>   darkness
> For lack of a minstrel to be their glory-giver.

Horace had written (*Odes* 4.9.25–28):

> vixere fortes ante Agamemnona
> multi; sed omnes illacrimabiles
>   urgentur ignotique longa
>   nocte, carent quia vate sacro.

[1] Michie 1965: 235.

The translator (perhaps not at his best) has obscured—or perhaps not noticed—what I consider one of Horace's most effective exploitations of word order here. Of the two renderings of this poem in the new Penguin volume *Horace in English*,[2] Pope's version (1751), expansive and florid though it is, *omits* the word I weigh most heavily:

> Sages and Chiefs long since had birth
>> E're Caesar was, or Newton nam'd,
> These rais'd new Empires o'er the Earth,
>> And Those new Heav'ns and Systems fram'd;
>
> Vain was the chief's and sage's pride
>> They had no Poet and they dyd!
> In vain they schem'd, in vain they bled
>> They had no Poet and are dead!

Philip Francis' version (1746), a rather good one, omits it too:

> Before great Agamemnon reign'd,
>> Reign'd Kings as great as He, and brave,
> Whose huge Ambition's now contained
>> In the small Compass of a Grave;
> In endless Night they sleep, unwept, unknown,
> No Bard had They to make all Time their own.[3]

In modern commentaries on Horace (and probably in most classrooms), the first line of the stanza is usually translated, "Many heroes lived before Agamemnon"; even in one of the most valuable contemporary scholarly appreciations of Horace's *Odes*, the stanza is given as, "There were many brave men who lived before Agamemnon; but all of them, unwept and unknown are compassed by long night for lack of a sacred bard."[4]

But if we look carefully at the stanza (or better still, listen attentively), we observe that Horace arranges his sequence of words so that we receive the main idea early, complete in the first verse, with a solemn dignity: *vixere fortes ante Agamemnona* "There lived brave men before Agamemnon." Incontrovertible, we feel; but what's the point? What's *Agamemnon* doing here in Rome? Horace continues, in the emphatic position at the beginning of the next verse placing an adjective that holds and focuses our attention on these warriors of the past: *multi*, "many [they were]"—and we reflect a moment upon the innumerable dead. Then Horace confronts us with his contrasting idea: "*many* [they were]—*but they all*, unlamented"—and without

---

[2] Carne-Ross and Haynes 1996: 161.
[3] Ibid.: 185.
[4] Davis 1991: 158.

pause he runs over to the next verse, beginning with another emphatic word—"[are] overwhelmed, unknown, in endless . . ." (new verse again) ". . . night." We think of the sadness of mortality, of human transience, of Gray's "The paths of glory lead but to the grave." Finally in the last part of the final verse of the stanza Horace comes to his climactic point: *carent quia vate sacro;* "because they have no sacred poet." *Now* we see: Horace, like Homer before him and most poets since, is proclaiming the necessity of poetry for ensuring fame amongst later generations—and by referring to Agamemnon, he is (as elsewhere), in his quiet, unemphatic way, taking his stand alongside the almighty Homer. And his simple adjective *multi,* "many [they were]," for a moment postponed and emphatically and unexpectedly placed at the beginning of a verse, contributes much to the solemn effect, both by slowing the rhythm and by encouraging us to reflect more seriously on the incomprehensible number of the unknown dead, as worthy in their time as those we hear so much about, but now nameless, uncommemorated—a fate from which Horace's genius will preserve those he glorifies. But if a translation omits *multi,* or places it too early in the verse, this aspect is greatly weakened, and Horace's deliberative slowness lost.[5]

There is, of course, nothing new in remarking the significance of word order in Horace in particular. Nietzsche's comment is often quoted:[6]

> Up to this day I have not had an artistic delight in any poet similar to that which from the beginning an *Ode* of Horace gave me. What is here achieved is in certain languages not even to be hoped for. This mosaic of words, in which every word, by sound, by placing, and by meaning, spreads its influence to the right, to the left, and over the whole; this minimum in extent and number of symbols, this maximum thereby achieved in the effectiveness of the symbols, all this is Roman, and believe me, elegant par excellence.

It is noteworthy that Nietzsche includes the importance of the influence words have on others adjacent to them. In his interesting book on translating Horace, J. B. Leishman claims that Horace was the first to use the device of separating nouns from their dependent adjectives "extensively and elaborately in lyric," and writes that when used like this, "each temporarily

---

[5] Despite F. Stack's careful examination and appreciation of Horace's word order ("these lyrics use extremely complex and intricate patterns in word order: Latin, being an inflected language, allows much greater freedom in the 'placing,' or rather 'displacing,' of words in poetry than is possible in English . . ."), he, too, translates, "There lived many heroes before Agamemnon . . ." (Stack 1985: 101, 113). However, Guy Lee (using Horace's meter) retains the word order and emphasis very well indeed: "Brave men there were before Agamemnon's time, | A multitude, but buried in endless night . . ." (Lee 1998: 181). Another recent translation, that of David Ferry (New York, 1997), like Pope, omits *multi* altogether.

[6] E.g., by Commager 1962: 50; D. West 1967: 88; Stack 1985: 101; translated slightly differently in Tomlinson 1993: 244. All these writers give examples of Horace's complex manipulations of word order.

isolated and suspended word was, as it were, washed and brightened till it shone like a cleaned picture, acquired, or re-acquired, a new meaningful-ness, and became an end as well as a means."[7] Basil Bunting, a poet whose work includes translations from Latin, also praised the language: "The del-icate alterations brought about by the arrangement of the words in a latin [sic] poem, where they are free to an extent unknown in any other european [sic] language, is inconceivable to anyone unacquainted with the classics."[8]

What *is* fairly new is reader-response criticism. Some years ago one of the leaders of the movement, Stanley Fish, stressed in particular the *tempo-ral* nature of the reader's experience: "The concept is simply the rigorous and disinterested asking of the question, what does this word, phrase, sen-tence, paragraph, chapter, novel, play, poem, *do?*; and the execution involves *an analysis of the developing responses of the reader in relation to the words as they succeed one another in time.*"[9] Fish referred to the expression of a similar prin-ciple in a famous 1966 article by Michael Riffaterre.[10] In reference to the same article, the editor who reprints it writes:

> Riffaterre believes he can isolate those linguistic features that are poetically sig-nificant. His description of those features of the text is notable for its emphasis on the emotional and intellectual activities of the reader moving through the son-net line by line. His key terms, predictability and unpredictability, are derived from a temporal model of the reading process that views the text as arousing cer-tain expectations which it then either satisfies or frustrates. The frustration of ex-pectation, i.e., the unpredictability of a given locution, is synonymous, for him, with poetic significance.[11]

Again, Wolfgang Iser, in his well-known *The Implied Reader*, published in English in 1974, says, "As a starting point for a phenomenological analysis we might examine the way in which sequent sentences act upon one an-other," and speaks of "the process of trial and error" by which "we organize and reorganize the various data offered us by the text. These are the given factors, the fixed points on which we base our 'interpretation,' trying to fit them together in the way we think the author meant them to be fitted."[12]

I think that this theoretical approach, by which reading (or listening) is regarded as an experience in time, and due regard is paid to the possibility of temporary misunderstanding of the succession of words, is particularly important for the appreciation of Latin poetry. In fact, a viewpoint similar

[7] Leishman 1956: 80, 82.
[8] In his essay "Some Limitations of English," printed in Caddel 1994: 23.
[9] Fish 1980: 73 (first published 1970); Fish's italics.
[10] Riffaterre 1980 (first published 1966).
[11] J. P. Tompkins, in Tompkins 1980: xiii.
[12] Reprinted in Tompkins 1980: 50–69 (the quotations are from pp. 52 and 62).

to that of Fish and others, with reference to Latin poetry, was expressed years ago by T. F. Higham:

> The mind of the reader forms tentative conclusions about the grammatical relationships of the words as they meet his eye. They keep him guessing; and the pleasure which he gains, for example, from an elegiac couplet, lies partly in the relief from suspense, and partly in satisfaction of his own and the poet's achievement when the sense and the sound, after their complex interplay, are completed together. But besides all this, the temporary isolation of each word makes its own peculiar imagery the more vivid.[13]

This reminds us of Nietzsche's remark about Horace's style, already quoted: "This mosaic of words, in which *every word, by sound, by placing, and by meaning, spreads its influence to the right, to the left, and over the whole*" (my emphasis). He seems to be suggesting that juxtaposed words have an effect upon each other—or rather, upon us as we read or hear them in sequence—even when they are not grammatically connected. We shall note several possible examples of this in Propertius. More familiar are the effects of this phenomenon in the rhetorical trope known as *hypallage*, the transference of an adjective between two closely associated nouns. A well-known example occurs in Virgil's description of the descent of Aeneas and his companion the Sibyl to the underworld, *ibant obscuri sola sub nocte per umbram* (*Aeneid* 6.268), "They go on, the dark figures, in the lonely night through the shadow." Logically it is the night that is dark and the live human figures who feel alone, but Virgil's reversal of the expected arrangement sheds darkness and isolation over both the travelers and the night itself—and the juxtaposition of *obscuri* and *sola* intensifies the effect. A good deal has been written about this kind of effect in Latin: one scholar, Adelaide Hahn, wrote of "Vergil, who in order to distribute epithets beween two different nouns without overloading either, or occasionally to suit the exigencies of the meter, and above all for the sake of variety, vividness or vigor, frequently violates the prosaic precision demanded by rigorous logic."[14] Near the end of Horace's well-known ode on the coming of spring, which as usual reminds him of death, comes the couplet: *infernis neque enim tenebris Diana pudicum | liberat Hippolytum* (*Odes* 4.7.25–26), "Nor from death's darkness may Diana chaste Hippolytus release." We expect *Diana pudica*, giving the

---

[13] Quoted by Leishman 1956: 84–85, from an unpublished paper of Higham's. Leishman also quotes (86) Higham's word-by-word description of how our minds operate as we read Horace's famously intricate *nunc et latentis proditor intimo | gratus puellae risus ab angulo* (*Odes* 1.9.21–22).

[14] E. A. Hahn, "A Source of Vergilian Hypallage," *Transactions of the American Philological Association* 87 (1956): 147–189 (the quotation is from p. 147). C. M. Bowra's comments on Latin word order are mentioned below.

goddess her conventional attribute; but we hear *pudicum,* and are startled and confused until the end of the following line brings *Hippolytum;* then at last we understand why Diana wanted to restore him to life—she loved him for his chastity because she was chaste herself, and the juxtaposition *Diana pudicum* sums this up.[15] From Propertius, where this trope is very common, I will quote only *furta pudica tori* (2.23.22), "chaste robbery of a marriage-bed" for "robbery of a chaste marriage-bed," and the more commonplace *feros serpentis hiatus* (3.11.11), "the fierce jaws of the snake" for "the jaws of the fierce snake."

Research into classical Latin word order using the Functional Grammar approach mentioned in the first chapter[16] has shown that in normal circumstances, the same word order obtains as in Greek: the Topic comes first, then the Focus (the new information), then the Verb. However, in highly stressed or emotive sentences, the Focus may come first and then the Topic, the verb still coming at the end. This initial placement of the Focus (for emphasis) sometimes occurs in English, too, but the characteristically Latin terminal position for the verb is hard to find there.[17] So Latin word order often causes the same problems as Greek for translators into English, where normally the Focus, the new information, is placed at the end of the sentence or clause.

Besides highlighting translators' problems, the Functional Grammar approach can sometimes clarify nuances in the text that might otherwise be passed over. The eminent classicist C. M. Bowra, in an essay that has been described as "one of the best short essays ever written on the *Odes* as pure poetry,"[18] speaks of Horace's skill in exploiting to the utmost the possibilities of variety in word order allowed by the highly inflected forms of Latin, and quotes three short verses as examples of Horace at his best; translations, presumably Bowra's own or at least acceptable to him, are given in a footnote. The first is *fortes creantur fortibus et bonis* (*Odes* 4.4.29), where the con-

---

[15] Part of this comment I owe to John Heath. The point is well conveyed in Leishman's translation of the lines (1956: 177): "Chaste Diana has failed from encompassing darkness to carry | chaster Hippolytus back."

I have not been convinced by J. P. Sullivan's rejection of this kind of influence of adjacent words: "In the instance just mentioned [he has quoted Propertius' *Coi sacra Philetae*] the belief seems implicit that the close association by position of an adjective, say, with a noun grammatically not connected with it, infects that noun with certain associations of the adjective. But it would require the reading of but a few lines of Milton or any other poet whose technique allows abnormal adjectival position to show the falsity of this" (Sullivan 1964: 99).

[16] See above, pp. 9–10.

[17] See Panhuis 1982: 148–149; Pinkster 1990; and Bolkestein 1996. Hannay's example of initial Focus position in English is "London I hadn't considered actually" (Hannay 1991: 134–135, 147).

[18] Bowra, "The Odes of Horace," in *The Golden Horizon,* ed. C. Connolly (London, 1953), 438–454 (quoted passages, 450), so described by D. Armstrong, *Horace* (New Haven, 1989), 115.

text makes it clear that the sense (amplified) is, "Strong men like these young Neros are born from *strong and noble* fathers, and therefore we pick good sires when we breed bulls and horses; but it is *upbringing* [or *training—doctrina*] that brings out the inborn talent." So it is clear that *fortes* is the Topic, *creantur* is the Verb, and *fortibus et bonis* carries the emphasis as the Focus, the new information; and I think one can see that Bowra's translation, "From the strong and noble strong sons are born," does not fully convey this emphasis, which in his version tends to fall on "strong sons." The English might better read "Strong sons [= Topic] are born from *strong and noble* fathers [= Focus]," or even (using the initial position, after the dummy subject "it," for the Focus), "It is from strong and noble fathers that strong sons are born."

Bowra's second example is *dulce et decorum est pro patria mori* (*Odes* 3.2.13), where the context may be paraphrased as, "The young Roman should become an attacking lion—he may get killed, but death comes anyway"—*mori* is immediately picked up and amplified in the next verse *mors et fugacem persequitur virum*, "Death pursues even the deserter." So *dulce et decorum* is the Topic, implicit in the preceding paradigm of what *robustus acri militia puer | condiscat* ("the young man hardened by strict army service should learn well," 2–3), and the Focus is (*pro patria*) *mori;* the normal English, reserving the Focus for the end, might be, "Sweet and fitting it is indeed, for one's country [even] to *die*." Bowra's "It is sweet and fitting to die for fatherland" leaves the emphasis indeterminate. In his third example, *nutrit rura Ceres almaque Faustitas* (*Odes* 4.5.17), *rura* is repeated from the previous verse *tutus bos etenim rura perambulat*, and it is clear that *nutrit rura* is the Topic and the deities' names the Focus, or in the usual English sequence, "The fields are nursed by Ceres and kindly Favor." Bowra gives "Ceres and kindly Plenty nurse the fields," which is accurate, the Focus being given the initial position, as English allows.

AMBIGUITY IN LATIN VERSE

I have already quoted Iser's remark about "the process of trial and error" by which "we organize and reorganize the various data offered us by the text. These are the given factors, the fixed points on which we base our 'interpretation,' trying to fit them together in the way we think the author meant them to be fitted." And I have mentioned the potential richness of meaning allowed in Latin by the absence of definite and indefinite articles and its frequent omission of possessive pronouns.

This can be illustrated by two familiar examples. At the very beginning of the *Aeneid* a translator is forced to decide if in *arma virumque cano, Troiae qui primus ab oris,* it is "Arms and the hero I sing, from Troy's shores the first . . . ," or "Arms and *a* hero"—a significant difference, because the first phrase implies that the hero is already known to us, the second that the tale is new. Virgil's Latin makes no such distinction. Perhaps the significance is not here very great, but it is significant that in English a choice must be made—and that popular translators choose differently: Dryden, C. S. Lewis, and Rolfe Humphries plumped for "the man," Fitzgerald and Mandelbaum for "a man."

The importance of personal pronouns—or rather, of their omission—emerges clearly in the scene where the distraught Dido, in tears, sends her sister Anna to Aeneas to try to change his mind about leaving. Virgil says Aeneas stands firm as an oak tree buffeted by gales. But he is moved: *magno persentit pectore curas* (*Aeneid* 4.448) "In his great heart he feels . . ."—*his* pain, or *Dido's* pain, or *their* pain? A further ambiguity arises from the word *curas*, which (like "care" in English) can mean both "trouble" and "love"—but is it *his* love, or *her* love? Virgil, of course, intends *all* these meanings, and the translator *must not limit the options*. Most do—among them Dryden ("Sighs, groans, and tears proclaim his inward pains") and C. S. Lewis ("His great heart thrilled through and through with the pain of it"):[19] Mandelbaum retains one ambiguity and drops the other (". . . he feels care in his mighty chest").

Virgil continues: *mens immota manet*, "His will remains unchanged," and finally *lacrimae volvuntur inanes*, "Tears roll down in vain," where (in Virgil's way) I think he means not only Aeneas' tears, not only Dido's and Anna's, but the useless tears of humankind in the most general sense. He is paraphrasing the famous words of Homer's Achilles to Priam long before: οὐ γάρ τις πρῆξις πέλεται κρυεροῖο γόοιο, "Nothing is gained by sorrowful lamentations" (*Iliad* 24.524). Here most modern translators do well and keep the typically Virgilian universalizing note: Mandelbaum's "the tears fall, useless" is fairly representative. But Dryden's "tears proclaim his inward pains" and C. S. Lewis' "unavailingly rolled her tears" again reveal a restricted vision and lose something of Virgil's poetry.

Among the several kinds of ambiguity, the nearest type to Iser's meaning is "transient ambiguity," which refers to what happens when, as we read or listen to a succession of words, we misinterpret the sense or association of a word, and only later realize how it must properly be understood.[20] In a work on English grammar and usage, this has been termed a "false scent," with the example, "Behind each part of the story I shall tell lies an untold and often unsuspected story of hard work. . . ."[21] In poetry in English, it has recently been observed that in Emily Dickinson's stanza

[19] Fitzgerald and Humphries use very general wording.

[20] On ambiguity in Latin poetry (especially in Propertius), see Quinn 1960; Edwards 1961; Levin 1969; Stahl 1985.

[21] E. Gowers, *The Complete Plain Words* (revised by S. Greenbaum and J. Whitcut [Boston,

A Charm invests a face
Imperfectly beheld—
the Lady dare not lift her Veil
for fear it be dispelled—

"the only moment of syntactical uncertainty comes in the fourth line with the unremarkable *it*. Normal parsing connects it to *Veil*; then the reader must revise the rules and look all the way back to *Charm* for an adequate antecedent."[22] This momentary misunderstanding and subsequent "revision" is common in Propertius. One particular example is prominent not so much for specially significant poetic effect, but because Ezra Pound drew attention to it in his *Homage to Sextus Propertius*. Reading Propertius' *nocturnaeque canes ebria signa fugae* (3.3.48, "You will sing of . . . the tipsy tokens of midnight vigil"),[23] Pound wrote, "Night dogs, the marks of a drunken scurry" (taking *canes* as noun instead of verb); but Virgil's line *obscenaeque canes* (*Georgics* 1.470, "ominous howling dogs"[24]), in which the words are adjective and noun (as Pound read Propertius), shows that a momentary misunderstanding is very possible here—and Pound's version leaves it uncorrected.[25]

Sometimes, instead of our later understanding of the meaning being substituted for an initial incorrect one, we should remain conscious of *both* the alternatives: this is "simultaneous ambiguity." The critic Edmund White has drawn attention to a fascinatingly convoluted couplet in James Merrill's "The Book of Ephraim" (published in 1976), where he is juxtaposing memories of a performance of Wagner with thoughts of a nuclear-warfare holocaust.[26] Merrill writes:

Götterdämmerung: From a long ago
Matinee—the flooded Rhine, Valhalla

1988]), 125. I am afraid I was unable to find a good example in William Empson's old but excellent *Seven Types of Ambiguity* (1930, often reprinted).

[22] Roger Shattuck in *The New York Review of Books*, 20 June 1996, p. 56. The poem, dated c. 1862, is no. 421 in T. H. Johnson's edition (1890, etc.).

[23] Translation of Goold 1990, reading *morae* for *fugae*.

[24] Translation of L. P. Wilkinson in the Penguin Classics edition (Harmondsworth, 1982).

[25] I pointed this out in Edwards 1961: 133 n. 14. J. P. Sullivan disagreed: "Similarly there seems implicit in certain of Pound's practices a theory that homophones in a language (for example, *canes*—'you will sing' and *canes*—'dogs') somehow infect each other and thus each meaning carries the contagion of the other . . . but in general such automatic infection does not happen. . . . Pound translates '*nocturnaeque canes ebria signa fugae*' . . . by 'Night dogs, the marks of a drunken scurry.' But . . . the Latin simply does not admit of any ambiguity here . . ." (Sullivan 1964: 99–100).

[26] Edmund White, "On James Merrill," in *The Burning Library*, ed. David Bergman (New York, 1994), 43–55 (first published in *American Poetry Review*, Sept.–Oct. 1979). The extract is from p. 56 of "The Book of Ephraim," in *The Changing Light at Sandover* by James Merrill, copyright © 1980, 1982 by James Merrill. Reprinted by permission of Alfred A. Knopf, a Division of Random House Inc.

In flames, my thirteenth birthday—one spark floating
Through the darkened house had come to rest
Upon a mind so pitifully green
As only now, years later, to ignite
(While heavy-water nymphs, fettered in chain
Reaction, sang their soft refrain *Refrain*).

Hearing the last two lines, with our minds on Wagner, we shall understand "heavy water-nymphs" and think of a chorus line of plump Rhine maidens "in chain"; but if atom bombs are closer to our thoughts—a little earlier in the poem, Merrill has mentioned helium, plutonium, and Hiroshima—we shall hear "heavy-water nymphs," and "chain reaction"; and of course, "soft refrain" suggests the nymphs' chorus, while the imperative "*Refrain*" enjoins us to stop the use of nuclear weapons.

A similar (though less complex) effect can be seen when Virgil's widowed Dido, admitting her new interest in Aeneas, tells her sister, *huic uni forsan potui succumbere culpae*" (*Aeneid* 4.19), which we first understand (in the context) as "(If I were not sick to death at the thought of remarriage), *to this one man* perhaps I could yield"—and then we hear the final word *culpae* and must rearrange the grammar and finish with a kind of double sense, "to this one man perhaps I could yield—to this *wrongdoing*." Aeneas, recognizing the meaning of the thunder, lightning, and vision of arms in the sky, says *hoc signum cecinit*— which we understand as, "This battle-call sounds—" following the usual idiom;[27] but when he continues —*missuram diva creatrix*, the sense must be corrected to, "My goddess mother foretold that she would send this sign"—but to some extent the two meanings both overlap and contrast (*creatrix* and instigator of battle). Propertius, entering Cynthia's bedroom late at night, finds her *consertis nixa caput manibus*, "pillowing her head on her linked hands" (1.3.8); but the next verse begins *ebria*, "drunk," and we inevitably attach this reproach to the poor woman until, as the verse continues, *ebria cum multo traherem vestigia Baccho*, "When I dragged in my feet, heavy with much wine," we find that it is *the poet's feet* that are drunken, not the sleepy Cynthia—*ebria* turns out to be not feminine singular but neuter plural. I have little doubt that Propertius intended this humorous effect here, switching the imputation of drunkenness from Cynthia to himself, but leaving her a little smeared by the passing imputation.

There are two further major kinds of ambiguity, which are not as dependent on the sequence of words as the others. These are "syntactical" and "lexical" ambiguity. Syntactical ambiguity occurs in cases where a word may be connected with more than one other word, either alternatively or (often) simultaneously. Good examples of this are Virgil's *clipeum super intonat ingens* (*Aeneid* 9.709), where Virgil has emphasized both Bitias' size and the

---

[27] Cf. *cano* §6d in *The Oxford Latin Dictionary*, and for the context, Edwards 1960: 164.

thickness of his shield, and here *ingens*, "mighty," may qualify either or both—as he falls, "his great shield thunders above him" or "his great body thunders on top of his shield"; and Horace's *sunt quos . . . meta . . . terrarum dominos evehit ad deos* (*Odes* 1.1.3–6), where either the triumphant victor or the gods—or better, both—may be honored as "lords of the earth."[28] There is something similar to this early in Gray's *Elegy*, where in the line "And all the air a solemn stillness holds," it is not clear if the air holds the stillness or the stillness holds the air; and probably also in the first line, which is normally taken as "The curfew tolls the knell of parting day," but which can be punctuated to give the more stately movement "The curfew tolls, the knell of parting day."

Lexical ambiguities, or puns, occur where a word can have either or both of two senses. In Horace's first ode again, the *pulverem Olympicum* (1.1.3), "Olympic dust," that the victorious chariot collects may be "Olympic" from the games at Olympia or "Olympian" from the gods' home on Olympus— or, rather, *both*. There are many examples in Propertius: the Muses, he says, sing of Jupiter's love affairs, and *ut Semela est combustus* (2.30.29), "how he was inflamed by Semele," the Theban princess who was herself "inflamed," that is, *incinerated*, when (at her request) Jupiter appeared to her without mortal disguise; and in another poem, his friend's passion, Propertius tells him, was greater than the *flagrans amor* (1.13.23–24), the "fiery love" of Hercules himself, when he first enjoyed the divine Hebe on the peaks of Mt. Oeta—that is, after his body had been *burnt* on his funeral pyre.

Such is the richness of ambiguity in Latin poetry—a challenge for translators, not only in attempting to transfer the different meanings to English, but in properly identifying such instances in the first place. "Ambiguity" is perhaps a misnomer: it may sound pejorative, whereas the contrary is true—it is a positive characteristic of Latin poetry in particular, a way to suggest more than one meaning through the same words. And in many cases it is not that we have to deal with a second meaning that must be substituted for the first, or choose between possible alternative meanings, but we must welcome them *all*. Instead of "ambiguous," perhaps one should often prefer the more contemporary terms "polysemic" or "multivalent." Let us now see how careful attention to word order and ambiguity can enrich a reading of a Latin poem.

PROPERTIUS 1.19

Following are comments upon a short poem by Propertius (1.19), with special stress on word positioning, word sequence, ambiguity (of various

---

[28] Noted by Quinn 1960: 38.

types), and significant juxtaposition of words.[29] Propertius does not have the brilliant verbal facility of Horace, but he too has deeply felt things to say, usually of a more personal nature; and he says them not with the lapidary brilliance of Horace's immortal aphoristic sound bites, but often with a suggestive imprecision that is poetical in a different way. He often exploits as effectively as Horace does the potentialities of the Latin language. Propertius has been praised (by Gordon Williams) for "the capacity to select a word which will create, by itself, a maximum appropriate effect in a given context," for "the use of a word with just that degree of imprecision that . . . permits the widest interaction of its semantic and associative components," and for "his power to combine widely disparate semantic fields in his imagery."[30] One might well apply to him T. S. Eliot's comment about "that perpetual slight alteration of language, words perpetually juxtaposed in new and sudden combinations," that occurs in poetry.[31]

Below I print the text of Propertius 1.19 line by line,[32] together with a fairly literal translation and a commentary. Since the sequence of words in the Latin is often important, but is sometimes unavoidably obscured in my translation, I have tried to help any readers not quite comfortable with Latin by translating every word at some point in the commentary.

Non ego nunc tristis vereor, mea Cynthia, Manes,   1
No more do I, unhappy lover, fear the gloomy ghosts,

Ego, "I," is both emphatic (the Focus) and subjective; Propertius is going to be talking about his own emotions—his *immediately present* and presumably new emotions (*nunc*). *Tristis*, "sad," tells us (by its conventional meaning in Roman erotic elegy) that Propertius is in love, and that his theme will include the melancholy that can accompany the erotic state: in another poem in this first book Propertius declares *seu tristis veniam seu contra laetus amicis | quicquid ero, dicam "Cynthia causa fuit,"* "Whether I am *downcast* or joyful when I meet my friends, I shall tell them, whatever my mood, 'Cynthia was the cause'" (1.11.25–26, trans. Goold). But already the reader—whether one is reading aloud to an audience or to oneself—has a problem: reading the line for the first time, one naturally connects *non ego nunc tristis* and understands "*I* am not now unhappy," expecting some word con-

---

[29] A number of my comments originate in observations made by the late Craig A. Manning in class discussions and an unpublished paper in a course I taught at Brown University about forty years ago. There are recent studies of this poem in Boyle 1974; Flaschenriem 1997; Hodge and Buttimore 1977: 194–201; Lyne 1980: 140–148; Papanghelis 1987: 10–19; and Williams 1968: 766–774.

[30] Williams 1968: 781.

[31] Quoted by Cleanth Brooks, *The Well Wrought Urn* (New York, 1947), 9.

[32] I have followed the text and punctuation of Goold 1990 except where noted, omitting his division into groups of six verses.

trasting with *ego*, and then (at *vereor,* "I fear") modifies the sense to "*I* do not now, miserable, fear. . . ." But as the sequence of words continues—remember Stanley Fish's "We have to analyze the developing responses of the reader in relation to the words as they succeed one another in time"[33]—we reach *Manes*, "the ghosts," and realize in an instant that *tristis* is more likely to qualify *them* (as an accusative plural), and we should have understood (and pronounced) the word *tristīs*, not *tristĭs*. Technically, the adjective must be pronounced either *tristīs* or *tristĭs*, and therefore cannot qualify both "I" and "the ghosts"; but the word as written on the page allows both pronunciations, and to a Roman reader (reading silently or aloud, to himself or to an audience[34]) the inevitable transient ambiguity will draw attention to the word and attach its meaning both to the poet, "wretched" because he is in love, and to the ghosts, "gloomy" because they are dead.[35] (Therefore I have translated the word twice.) Propertius uses the same double sense again in *i quaeso et tristis istos compone*[36] *libellos*, "Go, I tell you, now you are *in love*, and compose those *lovesick* books" (1.9.13).

So Propertius tells his beloved Cynthia that *he* (unlike others), though in love (and consequently miserable), doesn't fear the gloom of death—

[33] See above, p. 102.

[34] On whether silent reading was known in the ancient world, see Knox 1968 and (with an even more forcefully positive answer) Burnyeat 1997. Quinn 1982: 140–164 gives an excellent account of the recitation of poems by their author to a group of friends (Ovid says *saepe suos solitus recitare Propertius ignes,* | *iure sodalicii, quo mihi iunctus erat, Tristia* 4.10.44–45) and of other more public performances (a contest of poets, usually in a temple; a public performance by the poet; and a performance by a professional in a theater: Quinn 1982: 154). There is a briefer but very sound account, stressing the demands made on the performer, in Gamel 1998.

[35] Could—or would—Propertius have made it clear in his text whether he intended *tristīs* or *tristĭs*? The *apex*, shaped like the modern acute accent, had long been used in inscriptions and papyri to indicate long vowels: Oliver (1966: 131) writes, "The apex is found in thousands of inscriptions, and also in the few surviving papyri and wax tablets, of the last six decades of the Republic and the first two centuries of the Principate, after which it becomes increasingly rare. The innumerable occurrences of it make it obvious that its function was to distinguish long vowels." Quintilian (1.7.2) says it is *ineptissimum* to put the *apex* on *all* long syllables, but says it should be used from time to time (*interim necessarium*) when the same letter can give a different sense according to whether it is long or short. His examples, however, are *mălus/ mālus, pălus/pālus*, and the final *-ă* or *-ā* of nominative or ablative, and he says nothing of the *-ĭs/-īs* that is our concern. The *I-longa* (a extra-tall *I*) was also used to represent *ī* from 111 B.C.E. and is found in the papyrus of the *Carmen de Bello Actiaco* (which must be dated between 31 B.C.E. and 79 C.E.: see Oliver 1966: 158–70, and Edwards 1961: 143–144). So we can only say that Propertius *might* have indicated how *tristis* should be pronounced, for the convenience of his readers: "For this is the use of letters, to preserve our words and to restore them (like a deposit) to readers; and so they must express what we want to say" (Quintilian 1.7.31). (On the stages a text underwent from the author's draft to commercial publication, see Quinn 1982: 169–171.)

[36] The manuscripts' reading, not Goold's.

nec moror extremo debita fata rogo;   2
nor care about the last debt I owe the funeral pyre;

The repeated initial negative *nec* gives further preparation for the strong affirmatives to come in lines 3 and 4. In some part this line reiterates the previous statement: *nec moror,* "nor do I mind," or even "nor do I defer, put off," *fata,* "the fate, end," *extremo debita . . . rogo* "owed to the final funeral pyre"; and perhaps the juxtaposition of *extremo,* "final," and *debita,* "owed," includes some connotation of the "final debt" we all owe. The last four words all heavily and repeatedly invoke death.

sed ne forte tuo careat mihi funus amore,   3
but that perhaps there might be wanting, at my funeral, your love

Now comes the contrasting, positive idea: *sed ne forte tuo,* "but that perhaps your . . ." (contrasting with *ego*), *careat,* "might be lacking, fail in," and then *mihi,* "my"; *funus,* a repetition of "funeral"; and beside it this time, reinforcing the idea already implicit in *tristis,* comes *amore,* "love" (grammatically marked to be taken with *tuo* and *careat*). The three previous lines have all ended with a word meaning "death"; now, again at the verse-end, Propertius puts the word "love." *Funus* is a vague, general word, and we wonder if he means essentially that he fears dying unloved, or that Cynthia's love for him will not survive his death.[37]

hic timor est ipsis durior exsequiis.   4
this fear is harsher than my actual obsequies.

Repetition and reinforcement come from the positive statement this time, but again it includes fear (*timor*) and erotic unhappiness (*durus,* "harsh," is very often used of someone who rejects love or entreaties—Propertius once suggests his epitaph will read *Huic misero fatum dura puella fuit,* "An unrelenting girl was the death of this poor man"[38]). *Durior,* "harsher," is locked in between *ipsis . . . exsequiis,* "than my actual death"—and "death" once again concludes the verse.

non adeo leviter nostris puer haesit ocellis,   5
Not so lightly has the boy-god clung to my eyes

"Not so lightly has the boy [i.e., the love-god Cupid] clung to our eyes"— or is it "*my* eyes"? The possessive pronoun *nostris,* literally meaning "our" but often used by a poet of himself, might refer to Propertius and Cynthia, or just to Propertius himself; and manuscripts offer us both *nostris,* "our eyes," and *noster,* "our boy-god Love."[39] The ambiguity remains until clar-

---

[37] This point is made in Boyle 1974: 899.

[38] Propertius 2.1.78, translated by Goold.

[39] Hodge and Buttimore (1977: 196) prefer *noster,* on the grounds that this reading makes

ified in the next line. "Eyes" and "clinging" of course occur frequently in love poetry, and suggest intensity, long duration, and a measure of duress; and again a word meaning "love" ends the verse.

> ut meus oblito pulvis amore vacet. 6
> *that* my *forgetful dust could be free from love forgotten.*

Meus, "my," is emphatic (at the beginning of verse and clause), suggesting the meaning is close to the implied contrast in "on *my* part," and confirming that *nostris* (or even *noster*) in the previous verse really means "my," the temporary ambiguity drawing our notice to the distinction being made between Propertius' passion (which he knows is true) and Cynthia's (of which he is always rather unsure).[40] *Oblitus* is normally active in sense, "having forgotten,"[41] and though grammatically it cannot be taken here with *meus . . . pulvis,* its position between these two words juxtaposes the senses "my dust" and "forgetful" (as my translation rather too strongly suggests); this holds our attention to some extent until we see *amore* and reconfigure the sense to take *oblitus* passively[42] and the construction as ablative absolute, "love having been forgotten." The final verb *vacet,* "be free," may stand alone; or it may be used (like *careat* in verse 3) with *amore,* thus slightly altering the sense we had understood—"that my dust be free from a love forgotten" instead of "that my dust, love forgotten, be at peace."[43]

> illic Phylacides iucundae coniugis heros 7
> *There Protesilaus, the hero with the lovely wife,*

Illic, "there"—and we understand easily enough, in this funereal context, that he means "in the underworld." *Phylacides,* "Phylacus' scion"—and Propertius knows his audience is well educated enough to understand that by the old-fashioned, conventional, self-consciously poetic Greek patronymic he means Protesilaus, heroically famous on two accounts: he was the first Greek to leap from their thousand ships onto the Trojan beach, being immediately killed (as an oracle had foretold) by Hector or Aeneas (depending on which authority one reads—Homer doesn't specify); and his wife Laodamia loved him so much that she preferred to die rather than to live without him. Here we know at once what Propertius has in mind, for he continues *iucundae coniugis heros,* "the lovely-wived hero," using what we take as a "genitive of quality," as in *vir summae virtutis,* "a man of the high-

---

the love mutual, whereas *nostris* would refer to Propertius' eyes only. I am not sure this is correct.

[40] This aspect is heavily stressed by Boyle 1974: 900.

[41] As in *totam causam oblitus est,* "He forgot the whole case" (Cicero *Brutus* 217).

[42] As in Virgil's *oblita mihi tot carmina* (*Eclogues* 9.53).

[43] "Be at peace" is Camps' rendering (1966: 91). Fedeli very properly takes *amore* in a double construction, *ut meus pulvis, oblito amore, amore vacet* (1980: 443).

est character."[44] So we register: the high-pedigreed hero, and his lovely wife—her epithet *iucundus* conveying a slight erotic charge,[45] but of itself nothing more than the charm normally expected of a big man's wife.

To us, the change from Propertius' apparently real personal emotion to the affairs of the traditional mythical characters of long ago may well seem frigid. It has been well said by J. H. Gaisser that

> [Propertius'] use of mythology is uncongenial to modern sensibilities and has frequently proved an embarrassment even to his most sympathetic interpreters. Part of the difficulty results from the Alexandrian qualities of erudition and artificiality displayed in the mythological *exempla*. More important, however, is the fact that in many cases the *exempla* are not clearly relevant to the situation they ostensibly illustrate; indeed, sometimes they appear inappropriate or even at variance with their contexts.

But as Gaisser goes on to say, "This very incongruity or irrelevance is in fact a deliberate part of Propertius' poetic technique. . . . By the use of apparently incongruous *exempla* the poet creates a tension between myth and context that runs as a kind of counterpoint to the apparent meaning of the elegy."[46] In this particular instance, we must not write off the mythology as a learned irrelevance—in a few moments we shall see what is in the poet's mind.

> non potuit caecis immemor esse locis,   8
> *could not, even in the sightless lands, forget her;*

Two highly significant changes in meaning should strike us here. First, the grammar: we read *non potuit caecis . . .* , "He could not, in the blind . . ."— and then we reach *immemor* (once again, remember Stanley Fish on the importance of observing sequential aspect of reading—and of listening!), and we have to go back and reconfigure the sentence and the sense, realizing that the genitive phrase in the previous verse, which we had taken as qualifying Protesilaus, is also, and primarily, dependent on *non . . . immemor esse*, "not . . . be unmindful of." Protesilaus, though still remaining in our minds "lovely-wived," now "could not forget his lovely wife in the sightless lands." The transient ambiguity, this temporary misunderstanding, attracts our attention forcefully to Protesilaus' love for his wife, which endured beyond his death.[47]

---

[44] For some reason the five occurrences of forms of *iucundus* do not appear in B. Schmeisser, *A Concordance to the Elegies of Propertius* (Hildesheim, 1972), and one must resort to the computer or to J. S. Phillimore, *Index verborum Propertianus* (Darmstadt, 1905; reprinted Oxford, 1966). The context is always erotic.

[45] Cf. 1.10.1–3 *O iucunda quies, primo cum testis amori | affueram vestris conscius in lacrimis! | O noctem meminisse mihi iucunda voluptas*, where Propertius twice uses the adjective in a context where he portrays himself witnessing the lovemaking of his friend Gallus and his mistress.

[46] Gaisser 1977: 381.

[47] The ambiguity is noted in Edwards 1961: 133 and Boyle 1974: 901.

The thought is all the more striking because, well-read Romans that we are, we know that until now it has always been *Laodamia's* love for her husband that has characterized the story, not his love for her. Homer mentioned her, noting that her husband left her ἀμφιδρυφής, "cheeks torn in mourning" (*Iliad* 2.700). As Catullus told the story, Laodamia came to Protesilaus' house *flagrans . . . amore*, "aflame with love" for him, and lost him before the long nights of two winters *avidum saturasset amorem*, "had sated her fervent passion" (68.73, 83: other accounts said that he left for Troy the day after their wedding); Catullus says Protesilaus was dearer to her than her life (*vita dulcius atque anima | coniugium*, 68.106–107). Ovid composed a loving letter from her to him while he was delayed at Aulis, describing her misery at his absence, her concern for his safety rather than his prowess (*bella gerant alii, Protesilaus amet!* "Others can wage war—let Protesilaus be a lover!"), and how she has fashioned a lifelike waxen image of him that she embraces and lavishes endearments upon.[48] This image is a regular feature of the tale: some said that after Protesilaus' death Laodamia's father saw her with the statue in her bed and hurled it into a fire to destroy it, and Laodamia threw herself into the fire too, so that she might rejoin her husband in Hades; others said that the gods saw her with the statue, took pity on her, and allowed Protesilaus to return from the underworld for a few hours, after which she returned there with him. Some versions tell of Protesilaus' brief return and Laodamia's joining him in Hades but omit the statue tale.[49] The focus always seems to be on Laodamia's love for her husband, not his for her. So Propertius has chosen to alter the design of the myth, to stress Protesilaus' love instead of Laodamia's, because he is certain of his own undying love for Cynthia; and the poem is obviously going on to consider whether her love for him will be as strong.

Finally, the juxtaposition of *caecis* and *immemor* should be noted: *caecus*, "blind, unseeing," not only conjures up the darkness of Hades, but (next to *immemor*) gives something of the sense "though he could no longer see her, he could not forget her."

sed cupidus falsis attingere gaudia palmis   9
but longing with deceiving hands to feel his joy

[48] Ovid *Heroides* 13.150–156 (the verse quoted is 82). The theme is at least as old as the Gilgamesh epic, where the hero has a statue fashioned of his dead friend Enkidu (M. G. Kovacs, *The Epic of Gilgamesh* [Stanford, 1985], 71), and is suggested in Aeschylus' *Agamemnon* 416ff. (above, p. 84). A modern parallel is attested, too: the *San Francisco Chronicle* of 5 January 1998 (p. E8) announced, "*New York* magazine reports that 'Doll,' a play about the love affair between artist Oskar Kokoschka and Alma Mahler, the composer Gustav's widow, is in the works. Mrs. Mahler was a colorful figure who numbered among her lovers architect Walter Gropius and painter Paul Klee. When Mahler left Kokoschka, he had a doll made in her image, which he carried with him everywhere, hence the name of the play."

[49] This is the version in Servius on *Aeneid* 6.447. The various accounts may be found in J. G. Frazer's notes to Apollodorus 3.30 (Loeb Classical Library [London and New York, 1921, etc.], vol. 2); Jacobson 1974: 195–212; Fedeli 1980: 443–445; Palmer 1898: 400–402.

Every word in the line (after *sed*) has powerful erotic connotations. *Cupidus*, "desiring," needs no comment (though the phrase "something of an erectile shade" has been used).[50] The immediate sense of *falsis*—especially juxtaposed to *cupidus*—might seem to be "faithless," as is usual in an erotic context; but this does not fit Protesilaus, and we remain mystified until at verse-end we hear *palmis*, "palms." So the final sense is the frustratingly insubstantial nature of a ghost's hands (cf. Romeo's "unsubstantial Death is amorous"); but the idea of a lover's deception remains, for Protesilaus, faithful though he still is in one sense, is unfaithful in another, for he is no longer in the full sense her husband—and also perhaps there is the idea that his insubstantial hands *betray*, that is, refuse to satisfy, their owner's passion. The verb *attingo* means primarily "to touch," as well as "to gain possession of," and more generally "to achieve"; and *gaudium* means both "joy" and "source of joy," here of course referring both to the pleasure of sex and to his beloved Laodamia.[51] These multifarious meanings of *falsis* in particular are stressed by the arrangement of the words, juxtaposing and contrasting *cupidus, falsis,* and *attingere*.[52]

> Thessalus[53] antiquam venerat umbra domum.   10
> *the Thessalian to his former home came as a shade.*

Antiquam here means both "former" (with emotional implications—he never returned from the war to his home except now, as a ghost: so Virgil has a soldier at Troy say *nec mihi iam patriam antiquam spes ulla videndi*, "nor have I now any hope of seeing my old fatherland," *Aeneid* 2.137), and "ancient," referring to the antiquity of the story for Propertius and his listeners. At the end of the line, *venerat umbra domum*, "he came as a shade to his home," there may perhaps be an allusion to the main Homeric reference to Protesilaus, where it is said that on his departure he had left his house half-built (*Iliad* 2.701).

> illic quidquid ero, semper tua dicar imago: 11
> *There, whatever I shall be, forever I shall be famed as* your *idol;*

This is a climactic line. The first word, *illic*, "there," links Propertius' case with Protesilaus', and *quidquid ero*, "whatever I shall be," returns us to Propertius' own personal perspective. *Semper*, "forever" (like verse 6), allows of no time limit for his love; *tua*, "your," directs his address emphatically to Cynthia; and *dicar*, "I shall be spoken of, I shall be known," may well remind

[50] Papanghelis 1987: 11.

[51] Cf. 2.14.9–10: *quanta ego praeterita collegi gaudia nocte*, "All their joys were as nothing to those I garnered this past night" (translated by Goold).

[52] Boyle (1974: 902) points out the "startling juxtaposition" of *falsis* and *attingere*, and Lyne (1980: 101) notes that *falsis* means "cheated, deceived" as well as "false."

[53] Reading *Thessalus*, with Camps 1966 and many editors.

Latinists—and Propertius' readers, too—of the poet Horace's famous statement in the concluding ode of his third book, where he claims he has built in his poems a monument more lasting than bronze: *dicar*, he says— "I shall be renowned . . . as the one who first fitted Greek rhythms to Latin verse" (*Odes* 3.30.10–14). Propertius claims that forever in the underworld he will be known—perhaps we might better say "he will be famed"—as "your *imago*"—and with the Horatian parallel in mind, this is close to "Future generations shall know me as yours."

Translators render *imago* as "shade," "ghost," even "lover."[54] Commentators suggest "image." Everyone understands *imago* to refer to Propertius' ghost in the underworld. But Propertius' meaning is more intricate than this—and it is not usually appreciated, although *this* is the reason he chose to include this superficially rather unsuitable myth: he also has in mind the "image," the εἴδωλον, the *statue* of her dead husband made and loved by Laodamia.[55] *This* is why Propertius chose this myth to illustrate his passion and his poem; but most present-day readers of the poem (in Latin or English) will not be made aware of it.[56]

The mighty *Oxford Latin Dictionary* of 1982 divides the meanings of *imago* into thirteen sections, of which only one ("an illusory apparition, ghost, phantom") refers specifically to a shade in the underworld; most of the others (for instance, "a representation in art of a person or thing," "a duplicate, copy, reflection, likeness, image," "visible form, shape, appearance") more strongly suggest the statue than the ghost. Propertius intends *imago* to have at least three senses: "shade in the underworld," "phantom returning from the dead, as Protesilaus did, *to visit you*," and "statue of the lost lover, like Laodamia's," and the second and third bring with them all the suggestions of the legendary couple's eternal love and their reunion after death. "Image" is too weak to render all this; perhaps one might try— at least to attract a reader's attention—something like "your idol," or "your icon."

> traicit et fati litora magnus amor.   12
> *it crosses even death's boundaries, does a great love.*

The most emphatic words (the Focus) are *et fati litora*, "even death's shores," the next the initial *traicit*, "[it] crosses over." At first there is another transient ambiguity, for it makes good sense to think that *imago* is the subject of

---

[54] So Constance Carrier (*The Poems of Propertius* [Bloomington, 1963]).

[55] See Edwards 1961: 137 and n. 29.

[56] Lyne (1980: 143) says merely, "The word used for 'shade' or 'spirit' there is *imago*, the significance of which can extend to the figment of a diseased imagination." Fedeli 1980 makes no remark on the special appropriateness of *imago*. Hodge and Buttimore (1977) translate as "spectre," and remark, "Its use is jocular"(!). Richardson 1977 and Camps 1966 make no comment. Only Boyle 1974 makes the right point.

traicit, bearing in mind the return of Protesilaus' shade. As we reach the verse-end it becomes clear that not the *imago* but what is here identified with it, *magnus amor*, "a great love," is what crosses death's boundary: Protesilaus crossed the river between life and death when he died, his love and Laodamia's counted it no barrier, the hero's shade had recrossed it to visit her, and then she herself crossed it at her own death, following his shade. Propertius has already told us more than once (lines 6, 11) that his own love for Cynthia will not end with his death, but will pass over to the underworld with him and from there extend back to Cynthia. This is what a great love can do—and already we are wondering if Cynthia's love for him can be, and will be, powerful enough for this. (In a later poem Propertius repeats the same idea: even if a lover is already sitting on Charon's boat, *si modo cla-mantis revocaverit aura puellae,* | *concessum nulla lege redibit iter,* "if only the voice of his calling mistress summon him, he will return on the journey no law allows," 2.27.15–16.)

> illic formosae veniant chorus hērōīnae,   13
> *There the beauties will come, a chorus line of fabled figures*

Still imagining himself in the lower world, Propertius goes on, "There [*illic* reminds us of *illic Phylacides* . . . in line 7] beautiful women will come up, a chorus line, figures-of-fable"—three nouns in apposition,[57] a depersonalized bunch of beauty queens from the old Homeric stories, their utter conventionality emphasized by the mock-Greek word (found in Latin only in Propertius) and spondaic rhythm of *hērōīnae*.[58] What a contrast with the intensely personal feelings of the poet! And he continues,

> quas dedit Argivis Dardana praeda viris: 14
> *given to the Greek warriors of old as Trojan plunder.*

"whom Troy's plunder bestowed upon the Greek warriors of old"—women as unindividualized, undifferentiated, and unidentifiable to the eyes of Propertius, besotted by Cynthia, as the bronze tripods or shambling oxen also given as prizes in the contests in Homer (suggested by the Homeric word for the Greeks at Troy, *Dardana*). Homer comes off badly here—the plot of his *Iliad* depends entirely upon the allurements of the prize captive women Chryseis (Agamemnon's) and Briseis (Achilles')—but this is nothing new: long before Propertius' time Sappho had sung of the preeminence of love poetry over epic song (fragment 16).

---

[57] I think it would be natural to take *formosae* at first as a noun. Postgate (1881: xcvi) comments on Propertius' unusually free use of apposition, quoting another triple example: *non oculi, geminae, sidera nostra, faces* (2.3.14).

[58] Papanghelis (1987: 12 n. 9) notes that this word occurs three times in Propertius and quotes his four other spondaic lines. Boyle (1974: 906) feels that the Trojan women "were famed not so much for beauty (though like all *heroinae* they were beautiful) as for chastity, loyalty, and faithfulness," but I find it hard to stress those aspects here.

quarum nullā tuā fuerit mihi, Cynthia, formā   15
    gratior   16
None of them, more than you, *for* me, *Cynthia, will have charms*
    more pleasing;

But Cynthia was a cultivated, even learned young woman (several times
Propertius compliments her as *docta*, "learned"), and she knows how the
shades of dead heroines clustered about Homer's Odysseus when *he* visited
the underworld in *Odyssey* 11. So Propertius swiftly reassures her, the Latin
emphatically juxtaposing "not one of them—than *you*, to *me*, Cynthia, in
beauty."

          et (Tellus hoc ita iusta sinat)   16
          and (may Earth be just and permit this)

The parenthesis, "May Mother Earth, being just, permit this so," can be
pronounced in several different tones; one scholar has considered it a de-
cline from high formality, suggesting impromptu composition,[59] but it
could equally well be taken as an especially formal initial build-up for the
measured assertion Propertius will make in line 18. That Earth is "just"
must mean "claiming her due only at the proper time," recalling *debita fata*,
"the fate owed" of line 2.[60] The poet prays to Mother Earth, it seems, not
so much to allow Cynthia a long life, as to ensure that at her death they will
be reunited in love.

    quamvis te longae remorentur fata senectae,   17
    though long may delay you the fate of old age,

The first word, *quamvis*, is mildly ambiguous—the first sense seems to be
"However long may delay you the fate of old age," but there is also the possible meaning "Though the fate of long old age may detain you," which will
be confirmed as the main sense by *tamen*, "nevertheless," in the next verse.[61]
This is a practical remark—of course Cynthia may long outlive Propertius—but it thrusts aside the parallel between Cynthia and the short-lived
Laodamia.

          cara tamen lacrimis ossa futura meis.   18
          still, beloved, to my tears your bones will be beloved.

A *very* Propertian line. *Cara*, "beloved," we attach to Cynthia, following
upon the direct address to her (*te*) in the preceding verse; and *tamen*, "nevertheless," picks up the preceding *quamvis*, "although." *Lacrimis* means "to
tears" or "for tears"—tears are very familiar in love poetry, but the mean-

---

[59] Williams 1968: 771, in a long and detailed comment on the parenthesis.
[60] So Boyle 1974: 905.
[61] So the translators (Goold 1990: 103; Lyne 1980: 141; Hodge and Buttimore 1977: 56;
Williams 1968: 769).

ing here is not at first clear. Then *ossa futura*, "bones will be . . . ," seizes our attention. *Cara* now becomes ambiguous, or, better perhaps, polysemic—in our minds, it is still Cynthia who is "beloved," but grammatically *cara* can be a neuter plural instead of a feminine singular, so the "bones" are "beloved," too; defying grammatical logic, we must understand "beloved Cynthia will be beloved bones."[62] There is some degree of shock.[63]

And *ossa* conveys, besides the idea of Cynthia's death, the idea of love, for in Latin poetry the bones are the seat of love. A later Propertian poem, composed after Cynthia's death, concludes with her reproachful shade saying to him, *nunc te possideant aliae: mox sola tenebo: | mecum eris, et mixtis ossibus ossa teram* (4.7.93–94)—something like, "Now other women may possess you: soon I alone shall hold you. | With *me* will you be, and I shall rub bone on entwining bone"—which has even more erotic connotations in Latin than in English (Robert Lowell translated it, "Others can have you, Sextus; I alone | Hold: and I grind your manhood bone on bone").[64] And finally, *meis* "my," clarifies the "tears," though the meaning is still complex: Propertius (both alive and as a shade) sheds tears because of Cynthia while she lives (cf. *felix, qui potuit praesenti flere puellae; | non nihil aspersis gaudet Amor lacrimis*, "Happy is he who can weep in his mistress' presence—| much does Love rejoice in tears shed!" 1.12.15–16), and the thought of her death might also invoke his tears. So we conclude with something like, "Nevertheless, beloved Cynthia, for my tears you will be beloved bones." However long-delayed Cynthia's death may be, she will still be loved all her life by the dead Propertius—and of course after her death, too, for that must be one of the ideas carried by *ossa*.

But what are Propertius' "tears" *for*? As he is imagining the situation, he will not be a mourner at her funeral, and in fact, since her death will mean the possibility of their reunion, he should not grieve at it. They must be, as usual, the tears of unfulfilled love, which have overwhelmed Propertius's shade during its long wait for her coming. The poet's tears will *end*, not begin, at Cynthia's death—a neat inversion of the usual meaning.[65] And by saying "your bones" instead of "your death, your shade," he has added a further symbol of love and of unity in the physical aspects of death, one that goes back in poetry as far as (once again) Homer, who in both his mighty

---

[62] The syntactical ambiguity is pointed out in Edwards 1961: 131; Boyle 1974: 905; Lyne 1980: 143 (he calls it "transient ambiguity"—though it is not transient, but continuing).

[63] Well brought out by Hodge and Buttimore 1977: 198–199.

[64] Propertius also mingled the bones of Antigone and Haemon in their tomb (2.8.23); see Commager 1974: 18 n. 39. Cf. also 3.17.9–10: *hoc mihi, quod veteres custodit in ossibus ignes, | funera sanabunt aut tua vina malum*, "This evil [i.e., love], which has long kept a long-lasting fire in my bones, | my death will heal, or your wine, [Bacchus]."

[65] Lyne (1980: 141 and 144) translates "tears of welcome," which seems to me too restrictive.

epics tells of the mingling of the bones of Achilles and his friend Patroclus after their deaths. (Actually, from a later poem of Propertius [4.7], we know that Cynthia died before him, and he did *not* pay proper honor to her at her funeral—he tells us so in sorrowful detail.)

> quae tu viva mea possis sentire favilla!   19
> *If only you, alive, these my feelings could discern from my ashes!*

"This you, alive, from me, if only you could feel it, from my ashes!" The intertwined word order makes difficult English but simple, direct, and powerful Latin. "If only you, while still alive, could share my feelings when I am dead," or something like that.[66] *Mea favilla* is hard to define, though the general sense is clear enough (the nineteenth-century Latin scholar J. P. Postgate, whose appreciation of Propertius' peculiarities of diction is still the best there is, had the sense to throw up his hands in despair in classifying Propertius' use of the ablative case—this particular instance he grouped with cases where the "connexion with the main idea of the sentence is far from obvious").[67]

> tum mihi non ullo mors sit amara loco.   20
> *Then, for me, nowhere would death be bitter.*

After the beginning, "Then, for me," there comes a slight ambiguity in *non ullo . . . loco*, which may mean "not in any place [where I might die]" (but Propertius here seems not to be contemplating any foreign journey), "not in any place [where I might find myself after death]," which fits the context well, or best perhaps the more comprehensive "not under any circumstances," which can include the sense "not at any time" (cf. Horace's familiar *dulce est desipere in loco, Odes* 4.12.28).[68] *Amarus,* "bitter," is often used by Propertius for nights spent away from Cynthia, and for the goddess Isis when her demands keep her away from him,[69] so it carries here almost a technical sense, "death would not be a separation from you."

> quam vereor, ne te contempto, Cynthia, busto   21
>   abstrahat a nostro pulvere iniquus Amor,   22
> *How much I fear that scorning my tomb, Cynthia,*
>   *you may be dragged from my ashes by harsh Love,*

[66] Hodge and Buttimore (1977: 199) suggest that *quae* might also be taken to refer to *ossa,* which I think is possible.

[67] Postgate 1881: c. Camps (1966: 92) also calls it "a very free use of the ablative" and suggests "at my ashes" (i.e., his tomb) or "on account of my ashes"; Williams (1968: 773) tries "over my embers." Hodge and Buttimore (1977: 196) suggest it is locatival, "in my ashes."

[68] Boyle (1974: 907) points out the "potent semantic ambiguity" of this line, giving the two meanings "the coming of death whenever it occurs" and "the state of death wherever my abode is"; Williams (1968) translates "in whatever circumstances." For *locus* as "situation, circumstances," see *Oxford Latin Dictionary* s.v., §22 and §25.

[69] E.g., 1.1.33, 2.17.3, 2.33.6.

Propertius now returns to the ideas of the first lines, repeating *vereor* in *quam vereor,* "How much I fear," and painting (with *contempto . . . busto,* "[my] tomb scorned"; *contemno* is often used of scorning the offer of love[70]) a more vivid and direct—almost violent—picture of Cynthia's feared desertion of him after his death; the position of *Cynthia* between *contempto* and *busto* makes it clear that it is her scorn he fears, not Love's. Now he blames, not her possible faithlessness or levity, but other less reprehensible causes. *Abstrahat,* in the emphatic position, is a fairly violent word, "drags you away," and its subject remains for a moment unstated (a brutal rival lover?) as we read *a nostro pulvere,* "from my ashes"; then we find it is *iniquus Amor* (or *amor*), "harsh Love (or love)." *Amor* often seems to be personified, and probably we should think of the love-god Cupid (the Greek Eros) himself here—though since Propertius did not capitalize an initial letter, it is modern editors and printers who have to make the decision, not the poet or his readers (or listeners). The adjective *iniquus,* "harsh," is essentially proleptic—Love is harsh *because* he is dragging Cynthia away (Propertius has Aurora apply the term to all the gods as she left her beloved Tithonus to bring dawn to the world, 2.18.13).[71]

> cogat et invitam lacrimas siccare cadentīs!   23
> *and forced, unwilling, to dry your falling tears!*

Another initial verb conveying violence (*cogat,* "compels"), followed by (perhaps) a touch of sympathy in *et invitam,* "even though you may be unwilling," before *lacrimas siccare cadentis,* "[your] tears to dry [as they] fall"; but the verses have been taken as quasi-humorous and ironical, which may be right.[72] Perhaps, though it is not explicit, we may think again of the *heroinae,* the women captured at the fall of a city and dragged away from the corpses of their menfolk and sexually violated;[73] there must have been such slave-women in many a Roman household.

> flectitur assiduis certa puella minis.   24
> *She is turned aside by incessant threats, even a steadfast woman.*

A third successive violent verb in the emphatic initial position (*flectitur,* "is bent, turned aside"). *Assiduis,* "incessant," might well, in this context, lead us to expect *precibus,* "entreaties," as at 1.8.28,[74] or *blanditiis,* "flatteries," as at 1.9.30, and the actual word (postponed to line-end) *minis,* "threats," comes as a shock. Propertius in his characteristic way lays inordinate stress

---

[70] Cf. 1.5.13, 1.10.25, 1.13.9, 2.25.19.
[71] "*L'iniquus Amor* corrisponde al δεινὸς Ἔρως della tradizione ellenistica" (Fedeli 1980: 452).
[72] By Boyle 1974: 908.
[73] Suggested by Boyle (ibid.).
[74] Suggested by Hodge and Buttimore (1977: 200).

on a single word, *certa*, "true," which here must mean "even if she wants to be faithful"; the mannerism is like that in *non tamen illa meos fugit <u>avara</u> sinus*, "nevertheless she did not flee my embrace, tempted by greed."[75] The "threats" are those of *iniquus Amor*, which may include (one supposes) those of a lover (including threats of what he may do to himself if rejected[76]), of her husband, or of her family.

> quare, dum licet, inter nos laetemur amantes: 25
> *So, while we may, with each other let's enjoy love;*

Even eternity with Cynthia in the underworld would not be long enough for Propertius' love; and *dum licet*, "while we may," "so long as we can," may suggest not only "while we both are still alive," but also perhaps the poet's constant uneasiness—"while you still love me" (the uneasiness typical of his love).[77] *Inter nos*, "with each other," goes closely with both *laetemur* (meaning "enjoy ourselves together") and *amantes* (meaning "loving each other"). *Laetemur*, "let us be happy," coupling poet and his beloved together, is the only first-person-plural verb in the poem.

> non satis est ullo tempore longus amor.   26
> *never enough at any time, never long enough is love.*

The poet surfaces a little from the depths of emotion, and returns to the present, though keeping very much in mind the future stretching indefinitely before them. After *non satis est*, "not enough is . . . ," *ullo tempore*, "at any time" (like *inter nos* in the previous line) bridges the mid-verse caesura (the break between words that usually falls in the middle of the line), perhaps unconsciously suggesting the unbreakable tie the poet longs for. The sentiment has been compared to Horace's familiar *carpe diem*, "enjoy the present moment" (*Odes* 1.11.8),[78] but I think this is wrong: Horace's feeling is, "We know nothing about the future, so don't worry about it—take the here and now," whereas Propertius *knows* that the future, whatever it may be, cannot be long enough for this love of his (even if Cynthia remains faithful as Laodamia)—a love (no longer personified and deified, as in 22, but *real*) that need not *now* be enjoyed only, like Protesilaus', *falsis . . . palmis*, "with insubstantial hands" (9).

The essential point in reading poetry in the original language is to savor to the full the poet's intent, to be able to appreciate the feelings he wants to communicate to us without the inaccuracies, omissions, supplements, and

---

[75] See Postgate 1881: lxii, cxxi; and Edwards 1961: 141–142.
[76] So Camps 1966: 93.
[77] Suggested by Boyle 1974: 909.
[78] By Papanghelis 1987: 15.

other assorted distractions that inevitably result from translating his poem into another language. When the original language is Latin, we must take special care to observe its particular poetic virtues—the flexibility of its word order (and hence the possibilities for position emphasis and word juxtaposition), its indeterminacy (because it has no definite or indefinite articles, and is sparing of possessive pronouns), its frequent ambiguity. These qualities are very different from those of English, and the unfamiliarity may be a handicap in comprehending the skills of a Latin poet, or a virtue if we make the effort to see how he is manipulating his own language and hence find more and more substance to be rendered (if possible) in our translation.

This kind of approach is productive, and essential, for any Latin poet. Propertius may well provide the best examples. He is not primarily concerned with the aspects of his poetry that commentators often focus on—with the ancient myths he uses, with the gods, or even with eschatology. He is struggling to express his personal feelings and his ideas about love and death, and exploiting the nature of the Latin language to compress as many meanings as possible into his verses. Any uncertainty over exactly how a word or a phrase is to be understood should make us realize that we should not try to limit the meaning, that we should accept all viable possibilities and be glad of the richness this gives us. And any unusual word order, any unexpected juxtaposition of words should be noted and evaluated—not dismissed as a result of the requirements of the meter, but regarded as potentially another of the poet's means of conveying to us what he wants us to feel.

AFTERWORD

I HOPE this book will have some value in helping teachers of ancient Greek and Latin poetry to keep up the freshness of their approach, and to avoid having their work in translating with students become routine or mechanical. These chapters aim at encouraging readers to look at the text they read in new ways—or rather, in ways that, even if familiar, are not so often employed as they could be: ways of paying greater attention to how words in Homer draw emphasis from their position in the verse, and how they are arranged so that the sense can be easily followed by a listener; how Homeric narrative varies between scenes and summaries, and how changes of location are contrived with as little interruption as possible to a listener's attention; how even a general idea of what meter a dramatic poet is using in a choral song, and what emotions it usually conveys, can give the modern reader a more vivid feeling of what the author intended to be presented to the eyes and ears of his own audience; and how taking care to interpret Latin words *in their context*, that is, with reference both to allowing other meanings besides the surface one, and to noting how a word may be interacting with its neighbors in the line, can enrich the sense and the poetry.

Good students will be attracted by observation and discussion of such points. And introducing such emphases is not difficult. Mostly, all that is involved is carefully looking at a text in a certain way, and not resting content after identifying and translating the most evident sense of the ancient words. Lyric meters in Greek drama may seem to be a complicated issue that need not be added to the plentiful problems of translating the choruses, but the facts about the nature of the meter in any given choral song are available in any annotated edition of the text and should not be neglected. Especially prominent uses of a striking meter—the insistent, exotic ionics throughout the *Bacchae*, the frequent dochmiacs on the more agitated occasions in Aeschylus, the dramatic variations of meter in Sophocles' πολλὰ τὰ δεινὰ ode (*Antigone* 332–375), the even more dazzling metrical exploits and pounding rhythms of Aristophanes—much of this can in fact be made accessible to students. I know this because in past years readings of Greek drama (and of Plautus) were popular in my own department, largely because of the enthusiasm and hard work of Professor Helene Foley, a junior faculty member at that time. With some preparation, the performance of the choral meters by even undergraduate beginners was often surprisingly good.

One can also draw students' attention more closely to the refinements of expression in Greek and Latin poetry by encouraging them to prepare a written translation of a poem or passage, emphazing particular angles. They must be aware that they are being asked not just "What does this mean?" but "Why does the poet say this in this way?" and "How can you produce a similar effect in English?" They must be made to notice the different positions in which emphatic words in the sentence—the "new information"—are placed in different languages. It will also improve students' familiarity with lyric meters, relatively painlessly, if they are introduced to English verse composed in such meters (stress replacing vowel quantity) and encouraged to write such verse themselves (whether translating the original or composing their own). Frost's hendecasyllables, Bunting's renderings of Horace and Nims' of Sappho and Pindar (discussed in Appendix D), are potentially valuable for this purpose. Similarly, a feeling for the essential nature of Homeric word order, with its ever-changing positioning of breaks between clauses, its significant enjambment, its emphatic runover words, can be directly conveyed by studying a passage from Tennyson's *Morte d'Arthur* (along with an appreciation for the sound of fine English verse).

Even when the reading is being done in translations, in addition to the usual discussions of the general thematic content and value of the material, it is of course good for the students to be reminded that although something of the power of the original is inevitably lost to them, nevertheless many of the stylistic features used by the ancient poet can be quite satisfactorily observed in the translation before them and warrant the same approaches that they would use for a novel or a drama composed in English. In famous passages of the *Iliad*, for instance, it is not hard to bring students to realize the emotional power of Hector's conversation with Andromache, or Achilles' with Priam. But it engages their intellect, as well as their emotions, when it is pointed out that the first of these scenes is written (if one may use the word) like a drama, with successive speech introductions almost as bald as mere indications of change of speaker, whereas in the second the poet describes at length the feelings of both men before passing on to their direct speech[1]—and that in other cases Homer's narrator (sometimes wrongly thought to be objective) goes further still in commenting on the action he is describing. Not only will he sometimes interject, "The fool, for [doing X]" as one of the characters does something unwise, but he will even directly address his characters (e.g., "Then, Patroclus, the end of your life appeared," *Iliad* 16.787) or his audience (in "gentle reader" style: "You would not think . . . ," *Iliad* 4.429, etc.).[2] Similes, too, draw the narrator and his audience closer together, as side-by-side they watch the heroic action and compare it to scenes that they commonly witness in everyday life.[3] A

[1] E.g., *Iliad* 24.477–484, 507–516.
[2] These usages are summarized in Edwards 1987: 33–38 and Edwards 1991: 2–7.
[3] See Edwards 1987: 102–110; 1991: 34–37; and references there.

closer reading can also be encouraged by showing students that the "books" into which their translated *Iliads* and *Odysseys* are divided are not actually like a novel's chapter divisions—though they may for purely instructional purposes similarly serve as breaking-off points—and that Homer's way of carrying his audience with him from one scene-locale to another is very different from those of Dickens or Henry James, for good reasons.

The richness to be sought out in the masterpieces of Greek and Latin literature is inexhaustible. How much of this can be opened up to an undergraduate depends, of course, on the natures of both the particular undergraduate and the particular teacher. I hope this book may do a little to stimulate—I would rather say "restimulate"—teachers by suggesting certain ways in which they may see familiar works with fresh eyes, and so be reinvigorated in their honorable, exacting, and never-finished task.

Appendix A

TENNYSON'S *MORTE D'ARTHUR*

I HAVE NOTED above (p. 14) Tennyson's knowledge of Greek from boyhood and his love for Homer. Another characteristic that contributed to his poetry—very certainly to the following piece—was his attention to sound and familiarity with reading or reciting his poems aloud.[1] This is evident not only in his care for alliteration and assonance, which give his verse great sonority, but also in the frequency of monosyllables, which (because they facilitate a stress on successive syllables) give the verses slowness and weight (this is discussed more fully in Appendix D). One cannot tell how much it was an instinct for clarity, how much the constant awareness of a listening audience, and how much an equally constant (perhaps unconscious) imitation of Homeric sentence structure that produced the remarkable fluidity and melodiousness of Tennyson's verse here; but close attention to the ways the poem works will, I think, help us to identify the similar features in Homer.

In the following commentary I note anything in the style that seems particularly reminiscent of Homeric epic, and anything about the metrics or the sound that seems to me particularly effective as English poetry. I do not, however, always note the reversal of stress in the first two syllables of these iambic pentameters (e.g., "Clóthed ìn . . . ," compared to the usual "Amóng . . ."), as this is so common in any poet's work in this meter in English.[2]

MORTE D'ARTHUR

So all day long the noise of battle roll'd

The poem begins with four stressed syllables (two spondees), the first three with long vowel-sounds and the fourth lengthened (in effect) by the nasal consonants: "Só áll dáy lóng. . . ." There is another long diphthong in "noise," and a long vowel followed by slow consonants in "roll'd"; between

---

[1] Levi (1993: 41), speaking of the teenage Tennyson's love for the coastal hamlet of Mablethorpe, says, "It was also at Mablethorpe that the sound of the *Iliad* became inextricably mingled for him with the noises of the sea." The development of Tennyson's metrical practices is examined in Hanson 1992: 166–176.

[2] Cf. D. Gioia in Baker 1996: 88: "The inverted first foot is common to all English iambic measures and has been universally accepted by prosodically conservative poets like Ben Jonson or Alexander Pope, who abhor triple feet and allow themselves few other metrical liberties," quoting Marlowe's "Cút ìs | thè bránch |. . . ."

these words comes the clatter of "battle" (is Tennyson anachronistically thinking of rifle-fire?). The sense is complete at the end of the line.

> Among the mountains by the winter sea;
> Until King Arthur's table, man by man,
> Had fallen in Lyonesse about their Lord,
> King Arthur: then, because his wound was deep,   5

The exegetical lines first give the location (and begin the theme of coldness), then identify the characters and their circumstances. Arthur's name is first introduced mid-verse and peripherally, then anticipated by "their Lord," and finally repeated in the most emphatic position possible (a runover followed by a pause, at the beginning of the line, and in the "Focus" position at the end of the [English] sentence). The enjambment of a title and name is not (I think) Homeric, though in devising the title Tennyson may well be thinking of "Lord of men Agamemnon," ἄναξ ἀνδρῶν Ἀγαμέμνων. In line 4 I take "fallen" to be scanned as a monosyllable.

> The bold Sir Bedivere uplifted him,

The name-epithet formula is Homeric enough (cf. verse 39 and comment), but such formulas are not common in this position in Homer (a nominative beginning verse and clause), though they sometimes occur (for instance, | Ἕκτωρ Πριαμίδης is found mid-sentence at *Iliad* 16.828 and 17.449). The Focus word is the verb, and Tennyson wants to place it in the final (normal) position.

> Sir Bedivere, the last of all his knights,

This kind of repetition of a proper name from one verse to the beginning of the next (*anaphora, epanalepsis*) is common in Homer, with the amplification both in the form of a patronymic (e.g., ἔνθα δὲ Σίσυφος ἔσκεν, ὃ κέρδιστος γένετ᾽ ἀνδρῶν, | Σίσυφος Αἰολίδης [*Iliad* 6.153–154]) or a relative clause (e.g., ἀλλ᾽ ὁ μὲν Αἰθίοπας μετεκίαθε τηλόθ᾽ ἐόντας, | Αἰθίοπας, τοὶ διχθὰ δεδαίαται, ἔσχατοι ἀνδρῶν [*Odyssey* 1.22–23]).[3]

> And bore him to a chapel nigh the field,
> A broken chancel with a broken cross,

In Homer, when adjectives are repeated, as "broken" is here, there is usually a contrast (at least slight) marked by the particles μέν and δέ, and often the adjectives are in different cases (*polyptoton*); for example, τώ κ᾽ ἀγαθὸς μὲν ἔπεφν᾽, ἀγαθὸν δέ κεν ἐξενάριξε, "A brave man would have killed, and

---

[3] See Edwards 1991: 59–60 and 331 (*ad* 371–372); Macleod 1982: 50–53. The second example is quoted (as "palliliogy") by ps.-Plutarch, *Essay on the Life and Poetry of Homer* 32 (Keaney and Lamberton 1996: 101) with the remark, "This figure both reveals the emotion of the speaker and deeply affects the listener."

a brave man he would have slain" (*Iliad* 21.280). Tennyson's effect is pathetic, but Greek would have expressed the meaning a little more strongly (perhaps, "A broken chancel, broken, too, the cross").

That stood on a dark strait of barren land.   10

The middle stresses are reversed in "òn à dárk straít," giving a mournful emphasis to the two long-vowelled stressed monosyllables.

On one side lay the ocean, and on one

The analepsis is like Homer's threefold πολλὰ μὲν ἄρ μάστιγι θοῇ ἐπεμαίετο θείνων, | πολλὰ δὲ μειλιχίοισι προσηύδα, πολλὰ δ' ἀρειῇ (*Iliad* 17.430–431). Here μέν and δέ would fit beautifully. Closest, perhaps, is *Odyssey* 12.235–236: ἔνθεν γὰρ Σκύλλη, ἑτέρωθι δὲ δῖα Χάρυβδις | δεινὸν ἀνερρύβδησε θαλάσσης ἁλμυρὸν ὕδωρ.

Lay a great water, and the moon was full.

For a solemn conclusion of this descriptive passage, the stresses are irregular in both halves of the verse: in the first, two weighty long-vowelled syllables follow the reversed initial stresses ("Láy à greát wátèr"); and in the second, the first stress is lightened ("ànd thè . . . ," not "ánd thè . . .").

Then spake King Arthur to Sir Bedivere:

This kind of formulaic speech introduction precedes virtually every speech in Homer, but rarely are two proper names included, not only because of metrical difficulties but also because normally one of the characters is already in our minds (the Topic) and his name is not needed.[4] The verse is repeated at 66. A close parallel is *Iliad* 17.237 = 651, καὶ τότ' ἄρ' Αἴας εἶπε βοὴν ἀγαθὸν Μενέλαον. Later, Tennyson writes, "Then *spoke* King Arthur . . ." (my italics; 113, 153), probably because the king's growing weakness makes the more formal (because more archaic) form "spake" less appropriate there.

"The sequel of to-day unsolders all
The goodliest fellowship of famous knights   15
Whereof this world holds record. Such a sleep
They sleep—the men I loved. I think that we

The third verse (16) has in effect five consecutive long solemn syllables, "Whèreóf thís wórld hólds récord," for it is natural to pronounce even the short-vowelled "this" slowly before the following *w*. Like Homer, Tennyson likes to begin a new sentence late in the verse and run it over into the

---

[4] On such formulas, see Riggsby 1992: 102–109; Edwards 1968: 15–16; and chapter 2, pp. 57–58.

next, often in order to emphasize the words that are thus brought to the beginning of the verse, and here he combines it with another Homeric technique, a cognate noun and verb in analepsis, like πόλεμον πολεμίζειν, βουλὴν βουλεύσῃ, and others (*Iliad* 2.121, 9.75).[5]

> Shall never more, at any future time,
> Delight our souls with talk of knightly deeds,
> Walking about the gardens and the halls   20
> Of Camelot, as in the days that were.

The runover genitive noun ("Of Camelot," 21) gives emphasis, and in Homer often introduces a following exegetical clause or phrase.

> I perish by this people which I made,—

One-verse gnomic statements like this are common in Homeric speeches. Hector, facing Achilles, imagines the Trojans saying of him mockingly, " Ἕκτωρ ἧφι βίηφι πιθήσας ὤλεσε λαόν," " 'Hector trusted his own might and destroyed his people'" (*Iliad* 22.107).

> Tho' Merlin sware that I should come again
> To rule once more—but let what will be, be,

Homer played with tenses even more ostentatiously in his description of the prophet Calchas, ὃς ἤδη τά τ' ἐόντα τά τ' ἐσσόμενα πρό τ' ἐόντα, "who knew what was, and what was to be, and what was before" (*Iliad* 1.70). The fatalism is of course pervasive among Homer's characters (on the lips of Hector, *Iliad* 22.130, and Achilles, 22.365–366); Tennyson may have been thinking of Διὸς δ' ἐτελείετο βουλή, "Zeus' will was accomplished" (*Iliad* 1.5), and the other occurrences of forms of the verb τελέω, perhaps the many phrases ending (at verse-end) τετελεσμένον ἔσται, "it will come about."

> I am so deeply smitten thro' the helm   25
> That without help I cannot last till morn.
> Thou therefore take my brand Excalibur,
> Which was my pride: for thou rememberest how
> In those old days, one summer noon, an arm

"Thou therefore take . . ." is better Greek word order than English (e.g., σὺ δὲ σύνθεο . . . , *Iliad* 1.76). In line 28, I would scan "rememb'rest." The last verse, with two separate phrases before the final enjambing words, is further slowed by three consecutive stressed, long-vowelled syllables in the first phrase ("Ìn thóse óld dáys"), perhaps followed by two more ("one" can easily be stressed too, because of the time taken to pronounce it here).

[5] Several other examples are given in P. Chantraine, *Grammaire homérique*, vol. 2 (Paris, 1963), 41 §50; and Edwards 1991: 56–57.

Rose up from out the bosom of the lake,   30

Compare 143–144 (see p. 16 above), ". . .rose an arm | Clothed in white samite . . ."; here the wording is arranged so that the (long-vowelled and stressed) emphatic word "rose" stands at the head of the verse, whereas in the later passage the heaviest emphasis falls on the description of the arm, not just the fact of its appearance. This kind of adjustment is very like Homer.

Clothed in white samite, mystic, wonderful,

On similar runover adjectives in Homer, see above, p. 17.

Holding the sword—and how I row'd across

The participial phrase picks up from the verb in 30. Three consecutive verses begin with the stressed heavy vowel ō, picked up yet again in "row'd" (and "told" and "known" are to come soon). Tennyson liked these "hollow oes and aes" (see p. 15 above).

And took it, and have worn it, like a king:
And, wheresoever I am sung or told

Like Homer, Tennyson takes care to vary the placing of the main pauses in his verse, and includes the occasional "threefolder" like the first verse above. Again the repeated, listener-friendly "and," for δέ.

In aftertime, this also shall be known: 35
But now delay not: take Excalibur,

A simple, heavily significant new sentence stands complete in the last five syllables of the second verse. There are many Homeric parallels, some formulaic (e.g., οὐδέ με πείσεις, "you will not persuade me," six times *Iliad*, once *Odyssey*), some specific to one occasion (e.g., εἵλετο δ' ἔγχος, "he seized his spear," *Iliad* 10.24).[6]

And fling him far into the middle mere:
Watch what thou seëst, and lightly bring me word."

Double alliteration occurs in the first verse, and Old English–style alliteration on *w* in the second. Arthur personifies his sword ("him"), just as the weapon has a personal name: this is heroic enough, but not Homeric. Despite the diaeresis, I think "seëst" is scanned as one syllable here, though it counts as two in 256.

To him replied the bold Sir Bedivere:

This is as close as Tennyson can come to the recurrent Homeric τὸν δ' ἀπ-αμειβόμενος προσέφη (πόδας ὠκὺς Ἀχιλλεύς) ("To him replied [swift-

---

[6] See Edwards 1966: 170.

footed Achilles]"), found thirty-six times in the *Iliad* and seventy in the *Odyssey*, with various name-epithet formulas following the verb. His own formula, "The bold Sir Bedivere," will end the verse again, in alternative formulas, four times (69, 120, 165, 231).

"It is not meet, Sir King, to leave thee thus,   40

"Sir King" is Homeric ἄναξ, often found like this in the vocative with or without an accompanying proper name.

Aidless, alone, and smitten thro' the helm.

A line in enjambment and apposition, exegetical of the preceding, in the same style as "Clothed in white samite . . ." (31). The sound of the first two words is reminiscent of the common repetition of alpha-privative in Greek: Tennyson may have in mind ἀθάνατος καὶ ἀγήραος, "deathless and ageless" (nine times in Homer, in various forms).

A little thing may harm a wounded man.

Here is another direct-speech gnome; cf. 22.

Yet I thy hest will all perform at full,

The word order (subject-object-verb) is un-English: why did he not write, "Yet I will all perform thy hest at full"? Because Tennyson, knowing more than he realized about the conclusions of Functional Grammar on English word order and emphasis, wanted to locate the predicate "will all perform at full" in the final (Focus) position, instead of the already understood (Topic) "thy hest."

Watch what I see, and lightly bring thee word."

This line is a variation on verse 38, with change of person. Homer often does this for many consecutive verses when a message is entrusted to an envoy and later delivered in virtually the same words.

So saying, from the ruin'd shrine he stept   45

A Homeric close to the speech (ὣς ἔφατ') indicates to the listener the resumption of the narrative.

And in the moon athwart the place of tombs,
Where lay the mighty bones of ancient men,
Old knights, and over them the sea-wind sang

The last verse shows a runover phrase in apposition, followed by a Homeric-style parataxis "and over them . . ." for "over whom."

Shrill, chill, with flakes of foam. He, stepping down

Runover adjectives and a descriptive phrase (cf. 31, 41 above) are emphasized by rhyme, alliteration, and consecutive initial stresses, each followed
by a pause. These are *very* slow lines, appropriate to the knight's reluctance
to leave his king.

> By zig-zag paths, and juts of pointed rock,   50
> Came on the shining levels of the lake.

The first verse is rough with consonants, the second smooth with long vowels and liquid alliterating *l*'s, conveying the contrast between the rugged de-
scent and the calm plane of the water. Later (lines 189–192) Tennyson
spreads the same contrasting sounds over four verses. Homer, too, manip-
ulates such effects—the best-known examples are the tearing of Odysseus'
sails, which the wind τριχθά τε καὶ τετραχθὰ διέσχισεν (*Odyssey* 9.71), and
the quiet cattle pasture lying πὰρ ποταμὸν κελάδοντα, παρὰ ῥοδανὸν δονα-
κῆα (*Iliad* 18.576).[7]

> There drew he forth the brand Excalibur,
> And o'er him, drawing it, the winter moon,

Here "him" is Sir Bedivere, "it" the sword, which in Arthur's mouth was
personified as masculine (37). Tennyson cleverly avoids ambiguity, and
keeps the narrator detached.

> Brightening the skirts of a long cloud, ran forth

The first word reverses the stresses, but probably does not bring in an extra
syllable ("Bríght'nìng thè skírts . . ."); then another stress-reversal causes
the line to end in four stressed syllables (". . .òf à lóng clóud, rán fórth | . . . ,"
perhaps to suggest the motion of the moon emerging from the cloud.

> And sparkled keen with frost against the hilt: 55
> For all the haft twinkled with diamond sparks,
> Myriads of topaz-lights, and jacinth-work
> Of subtlest jewellery.

The description runs on after the structure of the sentence is clear, the exotic foreign words adding to the decoration. Similar descriptions in Homer
(usually without obviously foreign words) include of course the richly or-
namented armor of Achilles and Agamemnon, and the finery of Hera deck-
ing herself out to catch her husband's eye.[8] Tennyson does not attempt to
imitate Homer's way of describing the action of the craftsman in making
the artifact (most notably with the Shield of Achilles, *Iliad* 18.482–607).
The sparkling of the jewels is imitated by the irregular stresses of "twínklèd

---

[7] On Homer's sound effects, see Edwards 1987: 117–119; 1991: 57–58; and Packard 1974.
[8] *Iliad* 18.483–607, 11.24–44, 14.178–185, respectively.

wìth díâmònd spárks," and perhaps "mýrìàds," too (though this, and "dia-monds," might possibly be taken as dissyllables).

> He gazed so long
> That both his eyes were dazzled, as he stood,

That "both" his eyes were dazzled hardly seems worthy of note in English; perhaps Tennyson was influenced by Homer's almost invariable use of the Greek dual number for eyes (e.g., δεινὼ δέ οἱ ὄσσε φάανθεν, *Iliad* 1.200).[9]

> This way and that dividing the swift mind,   60

Tennyson clearly imitates *Iliad* 1.188–189, ἐν δέ οἱ ἦτορ | στήθεσσιν λα-σίοισι διάνδιχα μερμήριξεν, rendered by Lattimore "and within | his shaggy breast the heart was divided two ways, pondering | whether. . . ."[10] Writing "thè swíft mínd," instead of "his . . . ," more easily throws the stress onto "swift"—"his," taking longer to pronounce because of the collision of the two *s*'s, might lead to the erroneous "hís swìft mínd."[11]

> In act to throw: but at the last it seem'd
> Better to leave Excalibur conceal'd
> There in the many-knotted waterflags,

Tennyson's omniscient narrator, like Homer's, can tell us the characters' thoughts. "Many-knotted" recalls the innumerable Homeric adjectives compounded with πολυ- (four columns in Cunliffe's *Lexicon*). Tennyson, as Homer often does, gives first a brief account of Sir Bedivere's perplexity and final decision, then later amplifies the scene at greater length (lines 85–111).[12]

> That whistled stiff and dry about the marge.

The poet reinforces the onomatopoeic "whistled" with the assonance of "stiff."

> So strode he back slow to the wounded King.   65

The repeated long *o* sounds and the two reversed stresses on the monosyl-lables ("Só stróde hè báck slów . . .") drive home Sir Bedivere's troubled and deliberate return. Tennyson used a similar effect in *The Lady of Shalott*: ". . . slide the heavy barges trail'd | Bỳ slów hórsès; ànd únhaíl'd | . . ." (Part I, stanza 3, v. 3).

---

[9] Ὄσσε is dual; ὀφθαλμός appears in both dual and (more commonly) plural forms.
[10] Gray (1998: 100) calls this "an echo of Virgil . . . (*Aeneid* 4.285)," but (if one must choose) I think the Homeric passage the more likely source.
[11] Cf. Appendix D, p. 169 below.
[12] On this technique in Homer, see p. 19 above.

Then spake King Arthur to Sir Bedivere:
"Hast thou perform'd my mission which I gave?
What is it thou hast seen? or what hast heard?'

The first verse (66) is identical to verse 13. In the second verse (67), "my mission" (instead of normal English "the mission which I gave"), completes the sense before the explanatory and emphatic "which I gave," like the grammatically similar phrase in line 123, "I see thee what thou art." Perhaps, too, it is influenced by Greek (e.g., γέρας δέ μοι, ὅς περ ἔδωκεν, *Iliad* 9.367). The sound of the third verse recalls 38 and 44, "'Watch what thou *seëst*, and lightly bring me *word*'."

And answer made the bold Sir Bedivere:

At verse 39 Tennyson had used, "To him replied the bold Sir Bedivere"; the form used here is repeated at 115 and 151, and is perhaps made slightly less formal by the introductory "And." Tennyson may have noticed that Homer himself uses several different verbs in his "answering" formulas (e.g., ἀπαμειβόμενος προσέφη, ἠμείβετ' ἔπειτα, αὖτε προσέειπε, and others).[13]

"I heard the ripple washing in the reeds,   70
And the wild water lapping on the crag."

Onomatopoeia occurs again in many of the words, suggesting the splashing of the waves against the rocky shore (cf. 116–117).

To whom replied King Arthur, faint and pale:

Tennyson repeats the answering formula he had used at verse 39, adding an unformulaic descriptive phrase to the name. In true Functional Grammar style, the Homeric equivalent places the new information in second place in the sentence, the English verse last: τὸν δ' ὀλιγοδρανέων προσέφη κορυθαίολος Ἕκτωρ (*Iliad* 15.246 = 22.337).

"Thou hast betray'd thy nature and thy name,

There is powerful alliteration and assonance in "nature . . . name."

Not rendering true answer, as beseem'd
Thy fëalty, nor like a noble knight: 75
For surer sign had follow'd, either hand,
Or voice, or else a motion of the mere.
This is a shameful thing for men to lie.

The concluding gnomic statement is given prominence by the enjambment of the two preceding couplets.

[13] See Edwards 1968: 4.

Yet now, I charge thee, quickly go again
As thou art lief and dear, and do the thing   80
I bad thee, watch, and lightly bring me word."

The last line (81) has a very Homeric adaptation and shortening of verses 38 and 44: "'Watch what thou seëst, and lightly bring me word'."

Then went Sir Bedivere the second time

The end-of-verse name-epithet formula is displaced by the significant adverbial phrase.[14]

Across the ridge, and paced beside the mere,
Counting the dewy pebbles, fix'd in thought;
But when he saw the wonder of the hilt,   85
How curiously and strangely chased, he smote
His palms together, and he cried aloud,

The positions of the pauses in the verse (marked by punctuation) vary constantly, as they do in Homer. The soliloquy that follows, spoken aloud, is obviously modeled on the decision-making monologues in Homer, especially perhaps the best known, Hector's pondering whether to stand and face Achilles (*Iliad* 22.98–130). Tennyson does not attempt to imitate Homer's formulas for beginning the monologue, ὤ μοι ἐγών, and for introducing the actual decision, ἀλλὰ τί ἤ μοι ταῦτα φίλος διελέξατο θυμός;[15]

"And if indeed I cast the brand away,
Surely a precious thing, one worthy note,
Should thus be lost for ever from the earth,   90
Which might have pleased the eyes of many men.
What good should follow this, if this were done?
What harm, undone? deep harm to disobey,
Seeing obedience is the bond of rule.
Were it well to obey then, if a king demand   95
An act unprofitable, against himself?

Verse 95 is probably intended to be pronounced "Wert well t'obey . . . ," and hence is rhythmically regular. But verse 96 has four consecutive unstressed syllables (". . . ùnprófitàblè, àgaínst . . ."), a phenomenon that Tennyson and other poets (see chapter 3, p. 66) use to indicate suffering or wrongdoing, and this may well be his intent here.

---

[14] Janko (1992) has collected a number of Homeric instances where a formula that normally ends the verse has been displaced by another more significant in the context: see his Index s.v. "formulae: displaced."

[15] On these Homeric monologues, see Edwards 1991: 72 (*ad* 90–105) and references there (adding R. L. Fowler, *Harvard Studies in Classical Philology* 91 [1987]: 20–23).

The King is sick, and knows not what he does.
What record, or what relic of my lord
Should be to aftertime, but empty breath
And rumours of a doubt? but were this kept,   100

The last verse ends with three strongly stressed monosyllables, to show the speaker's intensity (the last two vowels are short, but the syllables are slowed by the clustered consonants: see Appendix D, p. 169).

Stored in some treasure-house of mighty kings,
Some one might show it at a joust of arms,
Saying, 'King Arthur's sword, Excalibur,
Wrought by the lonely maiden of the Lake.
Nine years she wrought it, sitting in the deeps   105
Upon the hidden bases of the hills.'
So might some old man speak in the aftertime
To all the people, winning reverence.

The inset imaginary direct speech, with its introduction ("Some one might show it . . . | Saying . . .") and conclusion ("So might some old man speak . . .") closely follows a familiar Homeric model, the *tis*-speech (ὧδε δέ τις εἴπεσκεν . . . , ὣς ἄρα τις εἴπεσκεν . . . , *Iliad* 4. 81, 85: "Someone might say . . . | . . . | So might someone speak . . ."). Homer uses the device (for example) to give the thoughts of Greeks and Trojans alike as they watch the preparations for the duel between Paris and Menelaus (twice, *Iliad* 3.297–301 and 319–323), and antiphonally to present the desperate resolve of each battle-line as they struggle over the body of Patroclus (*Iliad* 17.414–423).[16] In line 107 the last words are probably to be pronounced "in th' aftertime."

But now much honour and much fame were lost."
So spake he, clouded with his own conceit,   110
And hid Excalibur the second time,
And so strode back slow to the wounded King.

Cf. "So strode he back slow to the wounded King" (65); here Tennyson modifies the phrase and slows the verse even more with four consecutive stresses (or five, if "And" is included because of its consonant cluster).

Then spoke King Arthur, breathing heavily:
"What is it thou hast seen? or what hast heard?"
And answer made the bold Sir Bedivere: 115

The familiar Homeric speech introduction with adverbial phrase; cf. the comment on verse 72. The next two verses repeat 68–69.

[16] On such *tis*-speeches, see de Jong 1987b. She finds seventeen examples in the *Iliad*.

"I heard the water lapping on the crag,
And the long ripple washing in the reeds."

Compare "I heard the ripple washing in the reeds, | And the wild water lapping on the crag" (70–71); Tennyson keeps the onomatopoeic effects but changes the order of the verses. (If Homer ever did this, emendation would eventually have made the two couplets identical.)

To whom replied King Arthur, much in wrath:

See the comment on 73 above, and τὴν δὲ μέγ᾽ ὀχθήσας προσέφη νεφελη-γερέτα Ζεύς (*Iliad* 1.517, etc.).

"Ah, miserable and unkind, untrue,
Unknightly, traitor-hearted! Woe is me!   120

Homeric reproachful terms are limited to one verse (e.g., *Iliad* 1.149, 3.39). "Woe is me!" is of course the Homeric ὦ πόποι, which, however, always begins the verse.

Authority forgets a dying king,
Laid widow'd of the power in his eye

The metaphor "widow'd" is Homeric, though there applied (more appropriately) to the streets of Troy: Ἰλίου ἐξαλάπαξε πόλιν, χήρωσε δ᾽ ἀγυιάς (*Iliad* 5.642).

That bow'd the will. I see thee what thou art,
For thou, the latest-left of all my knights,

On 123, see the note on 67. "Latest-left" is perhaps influenced by ὀψίγονος, "late-born," found five times in Homer, including two verses ending with the formula ὀψιγόνων ἀνθρώπων.

In whom should meet the offices of all,   125
Thou wouldst betray me for the precious hilt;
Either from lust of gold, or like a girl
Valuing the giddy pleasure of the eyes.
Yet, for a man may fail in duty twice,
And the third time may prosper, get thee hence: 130
But, if thou spare to fling Excalibur,
I will arise and slay thee with my hands."

"Yet" in 129 is the very common Homeric verse-initial ἀλλ(ά), occasionally followed (as here) by γάρ, "for"; cf. *Iliad* 23.607 ἀλλὰ—σὺ γὰρ δὴ πολλὰ πάθες . . . , "But—for you have suffered much. . . ."

Then quickly rose Sir Bedivere, and ran,
And, leaping down the ridges lightly, plunged

Among the bulrush-beds, and clutch'd the sword,   135
And strongly wheel'd and threw it. The great brand
Made lightnings in the splendour of the moon,
And flashing round and round, and whirl'd in an arch,
Shot like a streamer of the northern morn,
Seen where the moving isles of winter shock   140
By night, with noises of the northern sea.
So flash't and fell the brand Excalibur:
But ere he dipt the surface, rose an arm
Clothed in white samite, mystic, wonderful,
And caught him by the hilt, and brandish'd him,   145
Three times, and drew him under in the mere.

For comment on 133–146, see chapter 1, pp. 14–18 above.

And lightly went the other to the King.

"Lightly" goes Sir Bedivere, relieved that he has at last performed his mission; but it may be borrowed from Tennyson's formula "'. . .lightly bring me word'" (38, 44, 81), or may just be a favorite adverb (cf. 134).

Then spoke King Arthur, drawing thicker breath:

This is the same speech introduction as at 113, with a different (but metrically identical) qualifying phrase (see on 167 below).

"Now see I by thine eyes that this is done.
Speak out: what is it thou has heard, or seen?"   150

The first verse is especially easy to recite impressively, for the first six syllables have long vowels, four of them successive *-ai-* diphthongs; the couplet is entirely composed of monosyllables, making possible a very slow delivery of the dying man's words. The final sentence is shortened from 68 (= 114), "'What is it thou hast seen? or what hast heard?'" Why has the poet not followed the pattern and written, "'What is it thou hast seen, or heard?'" Is it because he does not wish to evoke a commonplace English phrase such as "Children should be seen and not heard"? Or is it just to match the king's final vowel sound of the speech to the second?

And answer made the bold Sir Bedivere:

The verse was used at 69 (see comment there) and 115.

"Sir King, I closed mine eyelids, lest the gems
Should blind my purpose, for I never saw,
Nor shall see, here or elsewhere, till I die,
Not tho' I live three lives of mortal men,   155

More slow, heavy verses, mainly monosyllables with long vowels or short vowels followed by clustered consonants ("lids," "lest," "gems"). The last verse recalls the phrasing Homer uses for Nestor's longevity (*Iliad* 1.250–252).

> So great a miracle as yonder hilt.
> Then with both hands I flung him, wheeling him;
> But when I look'd again, behold an arm,
> Clothed in white samite, mystic, wonderful,
> That caught him by the hilt, and brandish'd him   160
> Three times, and drew him under in the mere."

Excalibur is personified again. The last three lines are repeated from 144–146, and "Clothed . . ." follows three different phrases (". . .an arm | Rose up from out the bosom of the lake" [29–30], ". . .rose an arm" [143], and this). Tennyson may have known the *Iliad* well enough to be aware that Homer's pathetic line describing Patroclus' corpse, stripped of armor by Hector (γυμνοῦ· ἀτὰρ τά γε τεύχε' ἔχει κορυθαίολος Ἕκτωρ), follows three different verses as the calamity is narrated in turn by Menelaus to Ajax, Menelaus to Antilochus, and Antilochus to Achilles (*Iliad* 17.121, 17.692, and 18.20).

> And answer made King Arthur, breathing hard:

Tennyson has previously used the phrase, "To whom replied King Arthur . . ." to accommodate final three-syllable adverbial expressions at 72 and 118. Here he changes to the synonymous and metrically identical, "And answer made King Arthur . . . ," which has been previously used three times for ". . . the bold Sir Bedivere" (69 = 115 = 156). This appears a violation of Milman Parry's principle that there should be only one formula to represent the same meaning in the same metrical shape. However, even Homer sometimes allows variety: usually each character is allotted just one of the three main "he answered" formulas (τὸν δ' ἠμείβετ' ἔπειτα . . . , τὸν δ' ἀπαμειβόμενος προσέφη . . . , τὸν δ' ἀπαμειβόμενος προσεφώνεε . . .), even if the available name-epithet formulae would allow alternatives, but there are exceptions—and in fact, "Helen answered him" is expressed in three different ways within sixty lines (*Iliad* 3.171, 199, 228).[17] After the other speech-introduction formula "Then spoke King Arthur . . ." (*not* "he answered": 113, 153), the adverbial expressions are two syllables longer.

> "My end draws nigh; 'tis time that I were gone.
> Make broad thy shoulders to receive my weight,

Both verses begin with four long-vowelled monosyllables (the short-vowelled syllable "end" is protracted by the four consonants following the vowel).

[17] See Edwards 1969.

And bear me to the margin; yet I fear   165

The rhythm is slightly changed in the second foot ("Ànd beár mé tò thè márgìn").

My wound hath taken cold, and I shall die."

Three heavy syllables end the verse. As before, almost all of the sinking king's words are slow, heavy monosyllables.

So saying, from the pavement he half rose,

The rhythm changes (". . .pávemènt hè hálf róse"), perhaps to reflect the movement.

Slowly, with pain, reclining on his arm,
And looking wistfully with wide blue eyes
As in a picture. Him Sir Bedivere   170

The second verse ends with three stressed syllables, the third begins with three unstressed ones. The inverted word order of the final phrase sounds Greek, but actually τὸν δ᾽ Ἀγαμέμνων (for instance) does not occur at verse-end. Placing the object "him" so early allows it to be taken more easily with both the following verbs "regarded" and "took."

Remorsefully regarded thro' his tears,
And would have spoken, but he found not words,
Then took with care, and kneeling on one knee,
O'er both his shoulders drew the languid hands,
And rising bore him thro' the place of tombs.   175
   But, as he walk'd, King Arthur panted hard,
Like one that feels a nightmare on his bed
When all the house is mute. So sigh'd the King,
Muttering and murmuring at his ear, "Quick, quick!"

There is a striking contrast of sound between the mumbling at the beginning of the last verse and the sharp consonants at the end. Similar effects are common in Homer.[18]

I fear it is too late, and I shall die."   180
But the other swiftly strode from ridge to ridge,

Verse 181 is doubtless to be recited "Bùt th' óthèr. . . ."

Clothed with his breath, and looking, as he walk'd,
Larger than human on the frozen hills.
He heard the deep behind him, and a cry
Before. His own thought drove him, like a goad.   185

[18] See references in note 7 above.

The last line is impressive in its unexpected enjambment, and in the inter-woven different-quality long *ō* sounds.

> Dry clash'd his harness in the icy caves
> And barren chasms, and all to left and right

Striking alliteration and assonance appears again, culminating in the almost unpronounceable (and hence prominent) monosyllable "chasms."

> The bare black cliff clang'd round him, as he based

Five stressed syllables sound in succession, three of them with short vowels lengthened by consonant clusters ("bláck clíff cláng'd") between two with long vowels. Homer matches "clang'd" with *kanachē*, notably in what are perhaps his noisiest lines: . . . βάλλοντες· δεινὴν δὲ περὶ κροτάφοισι φαεινὴ | πήληξ βαλλομένη καναχὴν ἔχε, βάλλετο δ᾽ αἰεὶ . . . (*Iliad* 16.104–105; something like, ". . .Whacking; terribly around his head the blazing | whacked casque crashed, whacked again and again . . .").[19]

> His feet on juts of slippery crag that rang
> Sharp-smitten with the dint of armed heels— 190
> And on a sudden, lo! the level lake
> And the long glories of the winter moon.

The change from the sharp sounds of the first two lines to the smoothness of the second two is very obvious: Tennyson has already produced this ef-fect in a single couplet (50–51). In the last line, the two long powerful syl-lables "lóng glór-" are made prominent by being preceded by two short syl-lables and followed by three more.

> Then saw they how there hove a dusky barge,
> Dark as a funeral scarf from stem to stern,
> Beneath them; and descending they were ware 195
> That all the decks were dense with stately forms
> Black-stoled, black-hooded, like a dream—by these
> Three Queens with crowns of gold—and from them rose
> A cry that shiver'd to the tingling stars,
> And, as it were one voice an agony 200
> Of lamentation, like a wind, that shrills
> All night in a waste land, where no one comes,
> Or hath come, since the making of the world.

These verses contain further examples of alliteration, assonance, effective enjambment, compound adjectives grouped in the runover position, and

[19] Besides the repetition of βαλλ- and the rattle of πήληξ and καναχήν, the first syllable of κροτάφοισι, "temples," must have suggested κροτέω, κροταλίζω, "rattle." On Homer's sound effects, see note 7 above.

consecutive stressed syllables at beginning and end of the verse. Verse 202 emphasizes the words of desolation with two initial stressed syllables, two unstressed, and again two stressed, the regular rhythm being recovered only in the last foot ("Áll níght ìn à wáste lánd, whére nó òne cómes").

Then murmur'd Arthur, "Place me in the barge,"

The half-verse speech conveys the king's faintness. Such half-verses occur in Homer, but very rarely (e.g., Hector's prayer for his son, "καί ποτέ τις εἴποι 'πατρός γ' ὅδε πολλὸν ἀμείνων'," "And sometime, someone may say, 'He's much better than his father'" [*Iliad* 6.479]).

And to the barge they came. There those three Queens 205
Put forth their hands, and took the King, and wept.
But she, that rose the tallest of them all
And fairest, laid his head upon her lap,
And loosed the shatter'd casque, and chafed his hands,
And call'd him by his name, complaining loud, 210
And dropping bitter tears against his brow

The varying of pause positions (i.e., punctuation) is noteworthy (the second verse is like a Homeric "threefolder"). "And" is again repeated over and over as an equivalent for Greek δέ, and (as in Homer—and in conversation) the continuously linked sentences are easy for a listener to follow.

Striped with dark blood: for all his face was white
And colourless, and like the wither'd moon
Smote by the fresh beam of the springing east;
And all his greaves and cuisses dash'd with drops 215
Of onset; and the light and lustrous curls—
That made his forehead like a rising sun
High from the dïas-throne—were parch'd with dust;
Or, clotted into points and hanging loose,
Mix'd with the knightly growth that fringed his lips. 220
So like a shatter'd column lay the King;
Not like that Arthur who, with lance in rest,
From spur to plume a star of tournament,
Shot thro' the lists at Camelot, and charged
Before the eyes of ladies and of kings. 225

There are several elaborate negative similes in Homer ("Not so great was X . . . as . . ."),[20] but Tennyson is more likely to be thinking of the vaunt of the Greeks over the dead Hector ("Ah, look here—| how much softer he is to handle now, this Hector, | than when he gutted our ships with roaring fire!" [*Iliad* 22.373–374, trans. Fagles]).

[20] See Edwards 1991: 28–29.

> Then loudly cried the bold Sir Bedivere,
> "Ah! my Lord Arthur, whither shall I go?
> Where shall I hide my forehead and my eyes?
> For now I see the true old times are dead,
> When every morning brought a noble chance,   230
> And every chance brought out a noble knight.
> Such times have been not since the light that led
> The holy Elders with the gift of myrrh.
> But now the whole ROUND TABLE is dissolved
> Which was an image of the mighty world;   235
> And I, the last, go forth companionless,
> And the days darken round me, and the years,
> Among new men, strange faces, other minds."

The emotional change in rhythm in the penultimate line ("Ànd thè dáys dárkèn . . .") is all the more noticeable because the previous verses have been mainly endstopped and unusually free of mid-verse pauses. In verse 238 nearly every syllable is stressed.

> And slowly answered Arthur from the barge:
> "The old order changeth, yielding place to new,   240

The second line has an extra syllable (because although Tennyson might have defended himself by claiming "Th' old . . ." counted as one syllable, no one would actually pronounce it so here), and after the iambic start the rhythm is marked and impressively slowed by the heavy trochaic words ". . . órdèr chángèth, yiéldìng. . . ."

> And God fulfils Himself in many ways,
> Lest one good custom should corrupt the world.
> Comfort thyself: what comfort is in me?
> I have lived my life, and that which I have done

As at 240 above, it seems best to admit a small change in rhythm ("Ì hàve líved . . .") rather than "I've. . . ."

> May He within Himself make pure! but thou,   245
> If thou shouldst never see my face again,
> Pray for my soul. More things are wrought by prayer

Skillful use of enjambment brings the emphatic word "Pray" to the beginning of the verse (after an interposed clause); then it is picked up again at the verse-end.

> Than this world dreams of. Wherefore, let thy voice
> Rise like a fountain for me night and day.
> For what are men better than sheep or goats   250
> That nourish a blind life within the brain,

Reversed stress on "à blínd lífe" is further emphasized by the assonance of the long vowels.

> If, knowing God, they lift not hands of prayer
> Both for themselves and those who call them friend?
> For so the whole round earth is every way
> Bound by gold chains about the feet of God. 255

Heavy stresses are intensified by long vowels on "whóle roúnd eárth" and "Boúnd bỳ góld chaíns."

> But now farewell. I am going a long way

As in 240 and 244, we should probably read (recite) "Ì àm góing" rather than "I'm going." There are effective stresses on "à lóng wáy."

> With these thou seëst—if indeed I go—
> (For all my mind is clouded with a doubt)
> To the island-valley of Avilion;

Once more, possibly (but not probably) "To th' island. . . ."

> Where falls not hail, or rain, or any snow, 260
> Nor ever wind blows loudly; but it lies
> Deep-meadow'd, happy, fair with orchard-lawns
> And bowery hollows crown'd with summer sea,
> Where I will heal me of my grievous wound."

Once more the poet clusters adjectives and descriptive phrases in enjambment, Homeric-style—the *oral* style. The absence of snow, rain, and wind is, of course, reminiscent of Olympus and the Elysian Fields (*Odyssey* 6.42–46, 4.565–568 respectively), the meadows, orchards, and summer sea very English.

> So said he, and the barge with oar and sail 265
> Moved from the brink, like some full-breasted swan
> That, fluting a wild carol ere her death,
> Ruffles her pure cold plume, and takes the flood
> With swarthy webs. Long stood Sir Bedivere

There are many instances here of successive stressed syllables, slowing the movement of the verse in harmony with the sense.

> Revolving many memories, till the hull 270

The alliteration in "many memories" weighs against the more metrical "mem'ries."

> Look'd one black dot against the verge of dawn,

Four initial monosyllables culminate in the powerfully stressed "dot," which somehow seems to gather additional weight from its unexpectedly short sound. This is a virtuoso effect of sound reflecting meaning.

And on the mere the wailing died away.

A skillful final assonance of the diphthongs in "wailing" and "away," separated by another long diphthong, "died." As he concludes his narrative, Tennyson allows the universal deathbed scene of which this is in some ways an allegorization to emerge more clearly.

Appendix B

CONTINUITY IN *MRS. DALLOWAY*

SEYMOUR CHATMAN stresses the elimination of summaries from Virginia Woolf's *Mrs. Dalloway*, and comments on "the abruptness and speed of the urban experience" (above, p. 59). From our own viewpoint, even more interesting than the omission of summaries are the ways in which Woolf changes the focus from one character to another, or moves the setting of the action. She makes much use of of Richardson's first category of Homeric scene-change technique: the narrator "lets himself be led from from scene to scene by one of his characters" (above, p. 54). Peter Walsh takes us from Mrs. Dalloway's drawing-room to Regent's Park, where we resume acquaintance with other characters (pp. 51–59),[1] much as Homer takes us from Olympus to Calypso's island in the company of Hermes, seeing with him the wide expanses of the sea and afterward smelling the welcoming warmth of the fire in Calypso's comfortable cave-dwelling and admiring with him her lovely garden and grounds (*Odyssey* 5.50–75). Woolf also employs the Homeric device of having the action we are leaving watched by a character whose response introduces the new action (above, p. 54), sometimes on a small scale, as in, "As he [Septimus] sat smiling at the dead man in the grey suit the quarter struck—the quarter to twelve. [¶] And that is being young, Peter Walsh thought as he passed them" (p. 76), or sometimes on a larger scale, as when (early in the novel) Woolf makes much use of events—the mysterious backfiring motor car, the skywriting airplane—to which the thoughts of watching characters react in succession.

As in Homer (above, p. 55), Woolf's characters may be linked by hearing: "Happiness is this, he said, as he entered Dean's Yard. Big Ben was beginning to strike, first the warning, musical: then the hour, irrevocable. Lunch parties waste the entire afternoon, he thought, approaching his door. [¶] The sound of Big Ben flooded Clarissa's drawing-room, where she sat, ever so annoyed, at her writing-table; worried; annoyed" (p.127). Woolf also naturally expands this technique to cover transitions by means of the *thoughts* of one character about another: "but the door was ajar, and outside the door was Miss Kilman, as Clarissa knew; Miss Kilman in her mackintosh, listening to whatever they said. [¶] Yes, Miss Kilman stood on the

---

[1] Page references to *Mrs. Dalloway* are to the Harvest Book edition (San Diego, New York, and London, 1997).

landing, and wore a mackintosh. But she had her reasons. First, it was cheap; second, she was over forty; and did not, after all, dress to please" (p. 133); "[Clarissa thought] . . . any horror was better than people wandering aimlessly, standing in a bunch at a corner like Ellie Henderson. . . . Gently the yellow curtain with all the birds of Paradise blew out. . . . Was it draughty, Ellie Henderson wondered? She was subject to chills" (p. 183).

Rarely, Woolf may make an intentionally abrupt transition, the link becoming clear a little later on. After the shell-shocked ex-soldier Septimus has jumped from a window and killed himself, his drugged wife, in her bedroom, looks at the doctor ("So that was Dr. Holmes"), and after a line-space we move to the heavy irony of Peter Walsh (in the street) thinking repeatedly of "the triumphs of civilization" as he hears the "light, high bell" of the same ambulance speeding "swiftly, cleanly" to pick up the corpse "instantly, humanely" (p. 164). Once (at a line space) there is a leap from Peter Walsh "entering the house, the lighted house, where the door stood open" (p. 179) to Lucy the maid "running full tilt downstairs"; it is Lucy's thoughts and reports about the dinner we then follow for several pages, but the location is the same and the time of Walsh's and Lucy's actions is presumably simultaneous.

Woolf knew Greek, as is clear from her essay "On Not Knowing Greek" (in *The Common Reader: First Series* [New York, 1925] 24–39), where she writes about the Greek of Greek tragedy and the *Odyssey* It is doubtful, however, that Homer had any influence on her narrative technique. She was probably interested more in creating something new than in making her action sequences easier for a listener for follow, but her "stream of consciousness" method provides an unbroken continuity that is very like Homer's.[2]

[2] It is interesting that when she began working on the book that became *Mrs. Dalloway*, Woolf had not yet figured out its distinctive technique, but described her project as "a short book consisting of six or seven chapters, each complete separately. Yet there must be some sort of fusion! And all must converge upon the party at the end" (quoted in *Mrs Dalloway's Party: A Short Story Sequence by Virginia Woolf*, ed. Stella McNichol [New York and London, 1973], 15).

Two modern novels have been inspired by *Mrs. Dalloway*. Michael Cunningham's *The Hours* (New York, 1998) is structured differently, divided into chapters that follow the experiences of different characters at different times, converging at the end. In his *Mr. Dalloway* (Louisville, 1999) Robin Lippincott sometimes imitates Woolf's techniques, sometimes uses sharper breaks. The 1997 movie based on Woolf's book (directed by Marleen Gorris for First Look Pictures) does not attempt to keep her sequence or connect its scenes as she does.

Appendix C

THE PERFORMANCE
OF HOMERIC EPISODES

THE *Iliad* and the *Odyssey* are mighty poems, intended to be sung or recited by a bard and listened to by an audience, but each is far too long to be performed without intermissions, or at least changes of singer. However, as has been shown in chapter 4, they have no apparent breaks in continuity, no obvious breaks in the action. This poses several questions.

How were breaks for intermissions found? First, it has been doubted if the poems were ever performed as wholes. Some years ago Walter Burkert wrote, "This much is certain for simple practical reasons, though it is not always acknowledged: there never could be a question of reciting the complete text of the *Iliad* at a rhapsodic contest. To recite the whole of the *Iliad* alone, not to mention the *Odyssey* and all the other works still attributed to Homer, would take thirty to forty hours, more than the time available for all the tragedies and comedies at the Great Dionysia."[1] Even if the poems were divided into three (or more) large sections, as some leading scholars now think, how were the obviously necessary minor breaks—surely required every hour or so by both singer and audience—handled?

The only indication I know of is an inconclusive analogy from another culture. Albert Lord discussed this question in the case of the South Slavic oral poetic tradition, and found that "the Yugoslav singer, when not interfered with by his audience, will pause at almost any point in the narrative to rest himself or to put off singing to another occasion." He also notes that "because of the progressive style of composition, the addition of theme upon theme, the singer has no difficulty in finding places to pause." After the intermission, the South Slavic singer had what Lord calls "the ordinary formulaic lines to take up the song:

Where were we, where did we leave
Our little song of times long past?"

Lord extended the analogy to Homer: "Homer could have stopped almost anywhere without impairing his story."[2] More recently, J. M. Foley looked

---

[1] Burkert 1987: 49. See also Ford 1997; Dowden 1996: 50–51, and references there.
[2] Lord 1936. The quotations are from pp. 106, 110, 111, and 113 respectively.

at further instances in South Slavic songs, and found that "the singer will not resume his song at just any point; rather . . . he 'backtracks' to the last traditional boundary and, after a brief proem for continuance, begins anew from there. This usually means reverting to the last thematic or subthematic structure and identifying it as a starting point."[3] The singer Foley quotes breaks off saying, "That isn't the end; I'll rest a little," and restarts with the resumptive verses quoted by Lord. Presumably the Homeric bard could manage something similar.

But what was done when not the entire epics, but just extracts from them were performed? We are told that rhapsodes presented parts of the poems in this way.[4] We also know that at an early date parts of the poems were referred to by the titles of episodes, not precisely corresponding to our book divisions—for example, "The Aristeia of Diomedes," "The Battle by the Ships," "The Prayers," "The Games for Patroclus," "The Ransoming," "What Happened in Pylos," "The Story to Alcinous," "The Bath Scene," "The Killing of the Suitors"—but our information is not detailed enough to let us identify the precise places at which these sections began and ended.[5] Did a performance of "The Games for Patroclus" (Ἐπὶ Πατρόκλῳ ἆθλα) begin (as does *Iliad* 23) with a summary of the mourning in Troy (ὣς οἳ μὲν στενάχοντο κατὰ πτόλιν), which the listeners have not heard? Did "The Ransoming" (Λύτρα) include the ending of the games, as described in our Book 24.1–3?

Hermann Fränkel claimed that Homeric singers had "a developed art of beginning, or of beginning anew after an interruption" (Fränkel 1973: 14), and he gave a full reconstruction of the circumstances of presentation of an episode from an epic. According to Fränkel's plan, the poet's recital began with a prayer or hymn, like those which survive in the collection known as the Homeric Hymns. This invocation of the relevant deity would be followed by what Fränkel calls a "set proem" relevant to the particular singer and the particular occasion, which would contain, in sequence:

a) a formal address to the host and others present;
b) praises of the pleasures of the hospitable board, including listening to a singer;
c) the many sufferings and heroic deeds that the singer knows how to describe;
d) how all these things came about by the will of the gods;
e) the general area of the coming song (e.g., the Trojan War);

---

[3] Foley 1990: 284. I am grateful to Professor Foley for helpful correspondence on this matter.

[4] See Burkert 1987: 48–50; Nagy 1996: 60–74.

[5] On these ancient divisions, see N. Richardson 1993; Stanley 1993: 282–284; and Nicolai 1973: 139–40. Some of the names are listed in Aelian *Varia Historia* 13.12.14; they are included in van Leeuwen's editions of the epics (1912–1913, 1917).

f) the particular theme of the night's recitation, announced by requesting the Muse to sing of it; after which the narrative begins.

Fränkel constructed this scenario on the basis of scenes described in the *Iliad* and the *Odyssey:* partly on their proems, partly on the episodes they contain where tales are told by the characters. He was using, in particular, Odysseus' words to his host and the rest of the company in Phaeacia as he prepares to enter upon the tale of his wanderings; and there are several other occasions where we can see what interests us particularly, the transition between what Fränkel calls the proem and the beginning of the actual story, where the storyteller closes in on the special theme of the occasion. Helen, preparing to entertain her husband Menelaus and young Telemachus at dinner with a story, begins (*Odyssey* 4.240–244):

Everything I could not tell you or enumerate by name,
not all enduring-hearted Odysseus' exploits.
But a thing like this, that he accomplished and endured, that mighty
man,
in the Trojans' country, where you suffered miseries, you Greeks.
His own body with degrading blows he disfigured.

She first states the general area of her tale (Odysseus' exploits), then narrows it down (something he did at Troy), then describes the initial actions of her narrative (Odysseus' disguise before his incursion into Troy). This is much like a paraphrase of the kind of prospective summary found at the beginning of a new episode (see above, pp. 42–46).

A fairly similar picture has been more recently presented by Andrew Ford (1992: 18–31). In Ford's view, the singer gives an invocation to the Muse, in which he establishes a relationship between himself and his expectant audience by praying to the goddess to tell a story, which will be overheard by the audience. This invocation includes a kind of "title" (such as "The Wrath of Achilles") and a kind of list of contents (as in the first few lines of the *Odyssey*). After this invocation, a character enters, and the action begins. This invocation Ford sees as preceded by a proem, of which the largest surviving example is the first 104 lines of Hesiod's *Theogony*.

The transition into the narrative would doubtless have been simple enough when the singer was an *aoidos*, a composer in the oral tradition when every performance was different, where the singer would create the song as he went along, shaping its length and its content to the needs of the moment. But what about the situation where a ready-made section of an epic is excerpted by a rhapsode from a huge fixed whole? To form an idea of the possible options, we can examine the surviving examples of the ways in which an invocation or a proem might be attached to a section of narrative epic. Such invocations, followed by narrative, survive in the initial and subsequent invocations in the *Iliad* and the *Odyssey*, in Hesiod's *Theogony* and *Works and Days*, in the Homeric Hymns, and in Apollonius of Rhodes' *Argonautica*.

APOLLONIUS, *ARGONAUTICA*

This is the simplest case. It has been noted that the invocations to the Muse with which Books 3 and 4 of the *Argonautica* begin "are ornamental: take them away, and you lose nothing in coherence" (Campbell 1983: 154; Fränkel 1968a: 22 says that Apollonius did not take the book division very seriously). Starting the third book, the invocation is:

Come now, Muse Erato, stand beside me, and tell me   3.1
How from there to Iolchus he brought back the Golden Fleece, Jason
    did,
By Medea's love. For you in Aphrodite's power
Have a share, and the unwedded with love-sickness you charm,
The maidens; and so to you, too, an *erotic* name has been attached.[6]   5

If this invocation is omitted and the two books are printed consecutively, the text runs like this:

                              So by Argus' advice, Jason   2.1281
high up he ordered them to drag the ship, with prow-anchors,
driving into a shady slough; this was close by
as they advanced. There they encamped for the night.
Dawn not long afterward to their expectant eyes appeared.   2.1285
So the heroes, out of sight in the thick rushes,   3.6
Waited in ambush; but they were noticed by
Hera and Athena.[7]

---

[6]   εἰ δ' ἄγε νῦν Ἐρατώ, παρ' ἔμ' ἵστασο καί μοι ἔνισπε
       ἔνθεν ὅπως ἐς Ἰωλκὸν ἀνήγαγε κῶας Ἰήσων
       Μηδείης ὑπ' ἔρωτι· σὺ γὰρ καὶ Κύπριδος αἶσαν
       ἔμμορες, ἀδμῆτας δὲ τεοῖς μελεδήμασι θέλγεις
       παρθενικάς· τῷ καί τοι ἐπήρατον οὔνομ' ἀνῆπται.   5
[7]   Ἄργου δ' αὖτε παρηγορίῃσιν Ἰήσων
       ὑψόθι νῆ' ἐκέλευσεν ἐπ' εὐναίῃσιν ἔρυσθαι,
       δάσκιον εἰσελάσαντας ἕλος· τὸ δ' ἐπισχεδὸν ἦεν
       νισσομένων. ἔνθ' οἵγε διὰ κνέφας ηὐλίζοντο·
       ἠὼς δ' οὐ μετὰ δηρὸν ἐελδομένοισι φαάνθη.   2.1285
       ὣς οἱ μὲν πυκινοῖσιν ἀνωίστως δονάκεσσιν   3.6
       μίμνον ἀριστῆες λελοχημένοι, αἱ δ' ἐνόησαν
       Ἥρη Ἀθηναίη τε.

This is exactly like a Homeric scene-change, with summarizing "So they . . . , but (the others) . . ." (ὣς οἳ μὲν . . . , αἱ δ᾽ . . .) before the focus shifts to persons watching the scene and their reactions (see above, pp. 43–45).[8] Apollonius does exactly the same at the joint between Books 3 and 4: if the invocation is removed (it is bracketed and italicized below), the text runs smoothly, with a Homeric-style change of focus:

So then Lord

Aeëtes' heart was visited by heavy grief.
He went back to the city, returning together with the Colchians,
troubled about how against them [the heroes] he might most swiftly
   go.
The day ended, and for him [Jason] the contest was
   completed.   3.1407
[*Do you yourself now, goddess, the troubles and wiles of the maiden*   4.1
Of Colchis describe, Muse, daughter of Zeus; for surely within me
Dumbly my heart whirls, as I consider
Whether the madness of lovesick grief I should call it, or
Disgraceful flight, in which she abandoned the people of Colchis.]   4.5
Surely then *he*, with the men of his people, all the best of them,
All night long, sheer treachery against them was devising
In his palace, with fierce anger in his heart about the contest—
Aeëtes was, furiously angry. Nor did he at all without
His daughters think this had happened.   4.10
But into *her* heart grievous fear was cast by Hera.[9]

---

[8] Hunter (1989: 97) notes on 6–7: "A continuation from the conclusion of Book 2 . . . in imitation of a Homeric structure, cf. *Il.* 9.1, 20.1."

[9]   ὣς τότ᾽ ἄνακτος
Αἰήταο βαρεῖαι ὑπὸ φρένας ἦλθον ἀνῖαι·
ἤιε δ᾽ ἐς πτολίεθρον ὑπότροπος ἄμμιγα Κόλχοις   3.1405
πορφύρων ᾗ κέ σφι θοώτερον ἀντιόῳτο.
ἦμαρ ἔδυ, καὶ τῷ τετελεσμένος ἦεν ἄεθλος.
[αὐτὴ νῦν κάματόν γε θεὰ καὶ δήνεα κούρης   4.1
Κολχίδος ἔννεπε Μοῦσα, Διὸς τέκος· ἦ γὰρ ἔμοιγε
ἀμφασίη νόος ἔνδον ἑλίσσεται, ὁρμαίνοντι
ἠὲ τόγ᾽ ἄτης πῆμα δυσιμέρου ἦ μιν ἐνίσπω
φύζαν ἀεικελίην ᾗ κάλλιπεν ἔθνεα Κόλχων.]   4.5
ἤτοι ὁ μὲν δήμοιο μετ᾽ ἀνδράσιν ὅσσοι ἄριστοι
παννύχιος δόλον αἰπὺν ἐπὶ σφίσι μητιάασκεν
οἷσιν ἐνὶ μεγάροις, στυγερῷ ἐπὶ θυμὸν ἀέθλῳ
Αἰήτης ἄμοτον κεχολωμένος, οὐδ᾽ ὅγε πάμπαν
θυγατέρων τάδε νόσφιν ἑῶν τελέεσθαι ἐώλπει·   4.10
τῇ δ᾽ ἀλεγεινότατον κραδίῃ φόβον ἔμβαλεν Ἥρη.

Here, too, the scene of Aeëtes' plotting continues from book to book, and is summarized (4.6–10, beginning ὁ μὲν) before the focus shifts from his thoughts to the subject of his thoughts, his daughter and her fears.[10]

We note that these two detachable invocations have the same basic structure: a call to the Muse for help; a prospective summary of the topic to be sung ("how Jason . . ."; "Medea's labors . . ."); a compliment to the Muse (her power in love; the poet's *aporia* without her)—this is what Janko, in his analysis of the Hymns, calls an "Attribute" (see below); and the narrative, continuing exactly as we have seen in Homer.

Apollonius was not, of course, an oral poet in the sense that Homer was, but he may have known something about how rhapsodes used to begin and end their recitations of Homer. His own epic was itself far too long for uninterrupted recitation, and he may well have intended it to be presented as separate episodes, with introductions like these insertable invocations which we find beginning his Books 3 and 4; he may have modeled them on the introductions used for episodes from Homeric epic. This idea is further supported by the ending of Apollonius' poem:

> Be gracious, you blessed ones;[11] and these songs of mine,   4.1773
> year after year may they be sweeter to sing
> among humankind; for now I have reached the glorious end
> of your labors.[12]

This is an obvious reminiscence of the closure tradition found in the Homeric Hymns (see below, pp. 160–161). Apollonius has taken over the salutation and prayer to the divinity, and adapted (in his way) the traditional mention of future songs into an assertion that *his* song is now over.[13]

---

[10] Apollonius begins his epic with an exact copy of a standard Homeric Hymn (see below), i.e., an invocation to a deity (Apollo) and a general summary of the topic ("ancient heroes' famous deeds"), leading on (with a hymn-like relative pronoun) to a more specific prospective summary (1.2–4), which introduces the narrative through a pronoun ("Such was the oracle Peleus had heard," 1.5). See Albis 1996: 6–8; Goldhill 1991: 286–287. At the end of his first book, he brings his heroes to land at sunrise, and at the beginning of the second continues directly with, "Here were the oxstalls and farm of Amycus, | the Bebrycians' haughty king, whom once a nymph | bore." The scene goes on with Amycus visiting and haranguing the heroes. There is no break, but the relative clause beginning after the king's "titles" is characteristic of the Homeric Hymns (see Janko 1981: 10–11). See also Campbell 1983: 154–155, and on sunsets and sunrises in Apollonius generally, de Jong 1996 and Van Sickle 1984.

[11] Translating Fränkel's emendation ἀριστῆες for the manuscripts' ἀριστήων (rejected by Goldhill 1991: 294 n. 31 and others).

[12] Ἵλατ᾿ ἀριστῆες, μακάρων γένος, αἵδε δ᾿ ἀοιδαὶ
εἰς ἔτος ἐξ ἔτεος γλυκερώτεραι εἶεν ἀείδειν
ἀνθρώποις· ἤδη γὰρ ἐπὶ κλυτὰ πείραθ᾿ ἱκάνω   4.1775
ὑμετέρων καμάτων.

[13] See Albis 1996: 39, who suggests also that the poet's direct address to his characters in

The *Iliad* and the *Odyssey*

At the beginning of each of the two major epics, the narrative proper is preceded by an invocation, which is connected to it by the methods we have already seen.[14] The *Iliad* begins with a call to the Muse, a topic ("The wrath of Achilles . . ."), which is then expanded by a summary of the disaster it caused (1.2–5) and followed by a further definition of where the tale is to begin ("since the time when . . . ," 1.6–7). Then comes a rhetorical question ("Who then. . . ?" 1.8), which is a variation of the "Who first. . . ?" trope found in the other *Iliad* invocations (e.g., 11.219: see below).[15] Next is a prospective summary ("Apollo: for he sent a plague, because Agamemnon dishonored Chryses . . . ," 9–12a); and finally the narrative begins with a linking pronoun ("For he came to the ships . . . ," 1.12b).[16] All the usual aspects have been included, and all runs very smoothly.

The initial *Odyssey* invocation follows the same pattern, with a call to the Muse, a topic ("The hero . . . ," 1.1a), which is considerably expanded by a summary of the experiences of Odysseus and his men (1.1b–9) and ends with a definition of where the song is to begin ("from some point . . . ," 1.10). Then the narrative is introduced, this time by a retrospective summary ("By then everyone else . . . | was home . . .": ἔνθ' ἄλλοι μὲν πάντες . . .| οἴκοι ἔσαν, 1.11), which leads as usual to a contrasting idea ("But *this* man alone . . . ," τὸν δ' οἶον . . . , 1.13), which is then developed in the subsequent narrative. This phrasing forms a smooth transition, and is very common in both poems (it has been discussed above, p. 45).

Prominent within the *Iliad* is the long, expanded invocation that introduces the "Catalogue of Ships." This in many ways resembles the invocations in Apollonius, and like them could be removed from the text without interruption of the narrative. It begins with a call to the Muses (2.484) and

---

the last line of the epic (εἰσαπέβητε, 1781) "is typical of the closing of a hymn." Goldhill 1991: 294–295 also discusses this.

[14] For the extensive bibliography on these two invocations, see especially Heubeck et al. 1988: 67–69, and Race 1992: 20–22. Minchin 1995a gives an excellent up-to-date account of the effects of the appeal to the Muse on the audience.

[15] See de Jong 1987a: 49–50. Race (1992: 21) has a slightly different explanation.

[16] Commentators (e.g., Kirk 1985: 54; Edwards 1966: 135; Bassett 1926: 125) have felt harshness here, since the pronoun ὅ must refer not to the immediately preceding Ἀτρεΐδης but to τὸν Χρύσην . . . ἀρητῆρα in the previous verse. Functional Grammar can now show this apprehension to be false. In the preceding sentence, both the Greek word order (see above, pp. 9–13) and the sense show that Ἀτρεΐδης is only the Topic, repeating the significance of βασιλῆϊ in line 9: the Focus, the new information, is τὸν Χρύσην . . . ἀρητῆρα, and the pronoun naturally enough refers back to the more significant name (Chryses), not to the nearest one (Agamemnon).

continues with a compliment to them (2.485–486: in the Homeric Hymns this would be called an "Attribute," see below), a topic ("Who were the chiefs of the Greeks?" 2.487), a declaration of *aporia* like that of Apollonius ("The multitude I could not tell of or name . . . ," 2.488–492), and a reiteration of the topic ("I will tell of the leaders and the count of the ships," 493). Finally the narrative continues, "Of the Boeotians, Peneleos and Leïtos were the leaders." If the invocation were not there, the sequence of thought would be normal enough:

> Such Atreus' son was presented by Zeus that day,
> outstanding amid the host, and conspicuous among the heroes.   2.483
> Of the Boeotians, Peneleos and Leïtos were the leaders.[17]   494

Of course, it is hard to imagine the mighty list that follows without the dignified prelude it now has—which would also serve as an impressive introduction to a separate recitation of the "Catalogue"—but the fact that the continuity would not be spoiled by omitting the invocation shows how closely the catalogue is linked to the narrative that precedes and follows it.

Elsewhere within the course of the *Iliad* there are four short invocations to the Muses (2.761, 11.218, 14.508, 16.112). These take (with minor variations) the form "Tell me now, Muses of Olympus, | who first came against Agamemnon" (ἔσπετε νῦν μοι Μοῦσαι Ὀλύμπια δώματ᾽ ἔχουσαι | ὅς τις δὴ πρῶτος Ἀγαμέμνονος ἀντίον ἦλθεν, 11.218–219), going on to name the next significant character (often in asyndeton). These are unlike the two intermediate invocations in Apollonius, and (as de Jong 1987a: 51 has pointed out) they are really emphatic variants of the trope often used to introduce a duel, as in "First Antilochus killed one of the Trojans, a warrior" (πρῶτος δ᾽ Ἀντίλοχος Τρώων ἕλεν ἄνδρα κορυστὴν, 4.457). Minchin (1995a: 27–28) has rightly said that they serve to get the audience's attention before a special moment. Hence they are not separable from the text, but might perhaps serve as introductions to a detached episode: they include, though very briefly, a call to the Muse and a prospective summary of the topic to be entered upon, followed by the continued narrative.

In the *Odyssey*, there is no subsequent invocation of the Muse by the poet himself, but his shadow-figure Demodocus keeps to the same format. In his first song, the Phaeacian bard begins with the Muse's help ("The Muse stirred him to sing," 8.73), the topic is specified ("the famous deeds of heroes," 8.73) and then the starting point ("[that part] of the story . . . , | the quarrel of Odysseus and Achilles," 8.74–75).[18] Then the narrative starts

---

17 τοῖον ἄρ᾽ Ἀτρεΐδην θῆκε Ζεὺς ἤματι κείνῳ   2.482
ἐκπρεπέ᾽ ἐν πολλοῖσι καὶ ἔξοχον ἡρώεσσιν.   483
Βοιωτῶν μὲν Πηνέλεως καὶ Λήϊτος ἦρχον.   494
18 For this rendering of οἴμη, cf. Heubeck et al. 1988: 351: "Probably partitive genitive, . . .

with, "How once they contended . . ." (8.76). In his second song, he again "begins with the goddess" (8.499)[19] on the topic that has already been requested by Odysseus (the Wooden Horse: 8.492–493); the starting-point is described in some detail ("beginning from where . . . ," 8.500–504), and then the narrative proper takes over with our familiar retrospective summary ὡς ὁ μὲν ἑστήκει . . . (see above, pp. 43–45), "So [the Horse] stood there . . . ," and a contrasting clause with δέ ("But they [the Trojans] endlessly talked," τοὶ δ᾽ ἄκριτα πόλλ᾽ ἀγόρευον, 8.505).

Needless to say, whatever ending a bard may have appended to Homer's epics has long ago disappeared. In the *Odyssey*, the closures of Demodocus' songs are similar to each other, running, "So the famous bard sang; but Odysseus . . ." (ταῦτ᾽ ἄρ᾽ ἀοιδὸς ἄειδε περικλυτός· αὐτὰρ Ὀδυσσεὺς | . . .), but this is a normal retrospective summary and contrasting continuation that tells us nothing of real-life practice. One suspects that a few lines of salutation and prayer, like those which end the Homeric Hymns and the *Argonautica*, would normally form the conclusion of a recitation of the whole or a part of these epics, too.

The Homeric Hymns

The structure of the Homeric Hymns has been carefully analyzed in Janko 1981, and is fairly standard despite the Hymns' great differences in length.[20] Our present interest, however, the invocation of the Muse, Janko considers the one irregular factor. The Muse is invoked at the start of eleven of the Hymns in various forms, which (like the *Iliad* and *Odyssey*) include the subject of the song in the first line: examples are, "Muse, sing for me the works of golden Aphrodite" (Μοῦσά μοι ἔννεπε ἔργα πολυχρύσου Ἀφροδίτης, Hymn 5.1), and "Of Castor and Polydeuces sing, sweet-voiced Muse" (Κάστορα καὶ Πολυδεύκε᾽ ἀείσεο, Μοῦσα λίγεια, Hymn 17.1 ≈ 20.1). In the other Hymns, the poet ignores the Muse and instead declares in the first person his intention to sing of a particular deity, again in various phrases, often taking a form like, "Of Demeter the lovely-haired, awesome goddess, I begin to sing" (Δήμητρ᾽ ἠΰκομον σεμνὴν θεὰν ἄρχομ᾽ ἀείδειν, Hymn 2.1: the initial verses of Hymns 11, 13, 16, 22, 26, and 28

---

since the Homeric poet thinks of the bard as taking up the narrative *from* a certain point in the tale"; Finkelberg 1998: 51; and N. Richardson 1974: 136.

[19] I take θεοῦ ἤρχετο together and ὁρμηθείς absolutely, with Hainsworth in Heubeck et al. 1988: 379. Finkelberg, however, prefers, "The bard was stirred by the god and began his performance . . ." (1998: 53).

[20] On the nature and origin of these Hymns, see Clay 1997; and N. Richardson 1974: 3–12; and on their openings, Race 1992: 19–22.

are similar). The invocation of the Muse is thus either vestigial or absent altogether. Janko refuses to commit himself to the theory that the call to the Muse belonged in whatever work the Hymn was used to introduce, not in the Hymn itself (Janko 1981: 11).

Following the line or two of introduction, the substance of the Hymn is usually led into by a relative pronoun, and may consist of a Myth (told in the past tense, and often relating the birth of the deity), a listing (in the present tense) of the deity's Attributes (powers, spheres of activity, etc.), or both. After this section, which is responsible for the enormous variation in the length of the Hymns, comes the Conclusion, which Janko divides into three elements (the last two of which may be omitted): a Salutation (with χαῖρε or ἵληθι); a Prayer (often with reference to the song); and the "Poet's Task," a reference to moving on to another song (Janko 1981: 15).[21]

If these Hymns were used as preludes to the recitation of an episode from the great epics, it is not clear how the connection was usually made. Two hymns alone, those to Helios and Selene (31 and 32), have endings where in similar wording, after a salutation and prayer, the poet explicitly announces a coming song of heroes: "Be gracious,[22] Lord, and willingly endow me with heart-warming sustenance. | Having begun with you, I will celebrate the race of human men, | the demi-gods [= heroes] whose deeds the deities [= the Muses] have displayed to mortals" (χαῖρε ἄναξ, πρόφρων δὲ βίον θυμήρε᾽ ὄπαζε· | ἐκ σέο δ᾽ ἀρξάμενος κλήσω μερόπων γένος ἀνδρῶν | ἡμιθέων ὧν ἔργα θεοὶ θνητοῖσιν ἔδειξαν, Hymn 31.17–19, cf. Hymn 32.17–19). The mention of the Muses in the last line of each of these hymns suggests the possibility of a continuation (as in the *Theogony*, see below) in which they were invoked (cf. κλείετε . . . , *Theogony* 105) and the topic more clearly specified (perhaps, too, the point at which it was to begin, as in the *Iliad* and *Odyssey*) before the transition to the narrative. The date of these two hymns is uncertain—they have been called both pre-Alexandrian and Neoplatonic[23]—but in any event they are archaizing in style, and so the form of their endings may go back to at least the classical period.

In the other hymns, it is perhaps most likely that the almost universal salutation to the deity at the hymn's conclusion, and the accompanying prayer, could be followed either with a similar "Sing, Muse . . ." continuation, or by the reference to "another song," which would in practice mean

[21] This ending pattern is much elaborated in the well-known "blind man of Chios" passage at the end of the Hymn to Delian Apollo (Hymn 3.165–178), where the poet unabashedly calls upon the chorus of Delian maidens to vote for him as the best singer, and promises that he will never cease singing the god's praises.

[22] On the meaning of χαῖρε, cf. Race 1982: 8–10.

[23] By van der Valk 1976: 434–445 and Gelzer 1987: 166, respectively, with references to others. I share Albis' doubts (1996: 7 n. 25) that *Argonautica* 1.1–2 are derived from Hymn 32.18—the expressions are too commonplace (but the idea is accepted by Ardizzoni 1967: 99).

the recitation would not immediately continue.²⁴ In our collection of hymns, five longer hymns end with an "another song" formula compared with two that do not, and ten of the shorter hymns do so (not counting 31 and 32) compared with fourteen that do not, which of course is far from conclusive.²⁵

HESIOD, *WORKS AND DAYS* AND *THEOGONY*

Both of Hesiod's poems begin in the style of the Hymns. The *Works and Days* starts with a call to the Muse, and passes on to give Zeus as the topic and proceed in the usual way, via a relative pronoun, to a list of his Attributes.²⁶ After this, there is no closing salutation, but a prayer to the god: "Hear [me], as you see and listen, and keep judgments straight with justice."²⁷ Then he refers to himself, "*I*, for my part, Perses, would like to tell the truth" (ἐγὼ δέ κε, Πέρση, ἐτήτυμα μυθησαίμην, 10b),²⁸ as bards often do in the Hymns (the "Poet's Task" element),²⁹ and continues into his narrative: "So, then, not single was the lineage of the Strifes, but . . ." (οὐκ ἄρα μοῦνον ἔην Ἐρίδων γένος, ἀλλ᾽ . . . , 11). As Minton pointed out, "the truth"

²⁴ On the uncertainty about whether this formula literally implies a further song is to follow immediately, see N. Richardson 1974: 324–325, and the references in Clay 1997: 493 and Nagy 1990: 353–354.

²⁵ Five longer hymns (2, 3, 4, 5, 19) and ten shorter hymns (6, 9, 10, 18, 25, 27, 28, 29, 30, 33) end in either αὐτὰρ ἐγὼ καὶ σεῖο (or ἐγὼν ὑμέων) καὶ ἄλλης μνήσομ᾽ ἀοιδῆς or σεῦ δ᾽ ἐγὼ ἀρξάμενος μεταβήσομαι ἄλλον ἐς ὕμνον; the shorter hymns 31 and 32 give the topic of a song to follow without using these formulas. No such formula or other announcement is found in two longer (2 [probably long] and 7) and fourteen shorter hymns (8, 11, 12, 13, 14, 15, 16, 17, 20, 21, 22, 23, 24, 26).

²⁶ For bibliography, see West 1978: 136–137, and Race 1992: 31–32.

²⁷ Instead of χαῖρε the poet uses κλῦθι, which is closer to a prayer than a salutation (so Verdenius 1985: 9). Commentators agree that the word refers to Zeus, not to Perses.

²⁸ West (1978: 142) and Verdenius (1985: 11–12) prefer to read the dative Πέρσῃ. It seems to me, however, that this ignores the full sense of ἄρα in 11, and makes the transition to the narrative unusually abrupt. In his fine account of the sense of ἄρα, Bakker quotes *Iliad* 16.787, "There, then, Patroclus, appeared the end of your life" (ἔνθ᾽ ἄρα τοι Πάτροκλε φάνη βιότοιο τελευτή), and says, "Patroklos literally *is* there, and the poet's addressing him creates . . . a maximum of presence in the epic performance" (Bakker 1993: 23). I think the same effect appears here, and suggests it is better to read the vocative of Perses' name, which is supported by the parallel τύνη δ᾽, ὦ Πέρση, ἔργων μεμνημένος εἶναι . . . at *Works and Days* 641.

I have not translated τύνη here (10), as I find it hard to believe it refers to Zeus; in its six occurrences in the *Iliad* it seems to have an intimate or familiar tone—Achilles to Patroclus, Thetis to Achilles, Hermes to Priam after he has revealed himself to be a god—which would be much more appropriate from Hesiod to Perses (as at 641), though the present text does not seem to allow this.

²⁹ Cf. καὶ σὺ μὲν οὕτω χαῖρε Διὸς καὶ Λητοῦς υἱέ· | αὐτὰρ ἐγὼ καὶ σεῖο καὶ ἄλλης μνήσομ᾽ ἀοιδῆς (Hymn 3.545–546).

(ἐτήτυμα) takes the place of the usual question (or specification) of the place at which the story is to begin, and the account of the two Strifes provides the answer: "These final lines . . . fulfill precisely the same function as the usual closing question: they provide a transition from the body of the proem to the specific point at which the poem begins" (Minton 1962: 198).

The beginning of the *Theogony* is much longer and much more complex, as can best be seen in Janko's study (1981: 20–22).[30] For our present purpose, it is enough to note that the first of the two hymns of which it consists (1–34) calls upon the Muses of Helicon, and after a description of their attributes and the possible subjects of their song (2–21), Hesiod presents, in the place of a myth, an account of how the Muses appeared to him on Helicon and gave him the gift of song (22–34). There is no closing salutation, but the final "They bade me . . . of themselves first and last to sing" (καί μ' ἐκέλονθ' . . .| σφᾶς δ' αὐτὰς πρῶτόν τε καὶ ὕστατον αἰὲν ἀείδειν, *Theogony* 33–34) sounds like an adaptation of the "Poet's Task."

After a proverbial expression (*Theogony* 35), apparently intended as a kind of transition (Janko refers to it as "the unconvincing device," 1981: 20),[31] the second hymn speaks of the Muses living on Olympus and continues through the usual hymnic relative pronoun to another description of their Attributes and the subjects of their song (36b–52). Then comes the myth of their birth, and after further Attributes, the myth of their entry to Olympus, their names, and yet more Attributes (53–103). Finally there is a brief, hymnlike salutation and prayer: "Be gracious, daughters of Zeus, and grant [us] a lovely song" (χαίρετε τέκνα Διός, δότε δ' ἱμερόεσσαν ἀοιδήν, 104). However, this is not the end by any means, for the poet once more calls upon the Muses (κλείετε . . . , 105), giving (in hymnic style) a topic leading through a relative pronoun to a short myth (the birth of the gods): then he does the same thing yet again (εἴπατε . . . , 108), this time defining the topic (again the birth of the gods) with a Homeric phrase we have mentioned above, "how first . . ." (ὡς τὰ πρῶτα . . . , 108 and repeated in 113), winding up with a couplet containing two further calls to the Muses ("These things tell me, Muses on Olympus, | from the beginning, and relate what was their first origin"; ταῦτά μοι ἔσπετε Μοῦσαι Ὀλύμπια δώματ' ἔχουσαι | ἐξ ἀρχῆς, καὶ εἴπαθ', ὅτι πρῶτον γένετ' αὐτῶν, 114–115). Then at long last the narrative begins, expounding the topic that has been so many times announced: "First then Chaos there was;[32] then next . . ." (ἤτοι μὲν πρώτιστα Χάος γένετ'· αὐτὰρ ἔπειτα . . . , 116).

The whole unique conglomeration of beginning-motifs has presumably been put together to form a specially impressive introduction to a mighty

[30] See also Race 1992: 22–23; Hamilton 1989: 10–14; Minton 1970; West 1966: 150–151.

[31] See also Hamilton 1989: 108 n. 8 and references there; Minton (1970: 369) and Race (1980: 6–7) find the line appropriate enough.

[32] Or "Chaos came to be"; cf. Bussanich 1983: 213.

poem (like the collection of similes and the long Muse invocation before the "Catalogue of Ships"). The transition from the end of the first invocation to the beginning of the second tells us nothing about how invocations led to narrative (especially since the salutation is omitted). At the end of the second invocation, however, the way in which the salutation and prayer (104) are immediately followed by κλείετε and the other words for "Sing!" (another conglomeration for impressiveness!) is almost identical with the ending of Hymns 31 (κλήσω . . .) and 32 (ᾄσομαι ἡμιθέων ὧν κλείουσ᾽ ἔργματ᾽ ἀοιδοί), which employ the same verb (though here in the first person). The (very broad) definition of the topic is also like that found in these two Hymns: there, the deeds of heroes, here the γένος (perhaps "generation" rather than "race") of the gods. The two Hymns break off before further specification of the topic has been made, but here in the *Theogony* several dependent clauses provide this (οἳ . . . , 106; ὡς τὰ πρῶτα . . . , 108; οἵ τε . . . , 111;[33] ὥς τε . . . , 112; ἠδὲ καὶ ὡς τὰ πρῶτα . . . , 113; ὅ τι πρῶτον . . . , 115) until the narrative begins the answers to all these questions, picking up all the τὰ πρῶτα (etc.) with ἤτοι μὲν πρώτιστα . . . and the familiar contrasting continuation αὐτὰρ ἔπειτα . . . (116; cf. *Iliad* 3.315, 4.424, and often in Homer).

SUMMARY AND CONCLUSIONS

This survey of the ways in which a section of narrative epic can be introduced by an invocation or proem results in examples of the following:

• Invocations standing at the head of a poem, including a prospective summary of what is to come, an expansion of it, a statement of the point at which the narrative is to begin, and a standard link to the first scene of the narrative (*Iliad* 1.1–12a; *Odyssey* 1.1–11, 8.73–76, 8.499–505).

• Invocations, including a prospective summary (= brief topic, subject), inserted within a Homeric-type narrative at what would otherwise be a normal change of focus, showing that such an invocation could easily precede recitation of a detached episode (*Argonautica* 3.1–5, 4.1–5; *Iliad* 2.484–493).

• Hymns to a deity (at whose festival they are presumably sung), in which the singer may begin by calling upon the Muse for aid or simply announce himself as the singer; including celebration of the deity by listing his or her Attributes and/or relating a relevant myth at greater or lesser length; and concluding (almost always) with a salutation to the deity, sometimes with a prayer, too, and sometimes also with a mention of the poet's laudatory func-

[33] This line is probably interpolated; see West 1966: 190.

tion (or "Task"), without any apparent link to a continuing narrative (most of the Homeric Hymns, and the ending of the *Argonautica*).

• Two hymns to a deity of the above pattern, but concluding not only with a salutation and prayer but also with an explicit summary of a following celebration of heroic stories; and a greatly elaborated introduction to a long poem that ends with a section following the same model as these two hymns (but also greatly elaborated), and ending with a summary of the stories of divinities which are to come, the narrative of which then smoothly begins (Hymns 31 and 32; the *Theogony*).

• A long poem that begins like a hymn, modifies the salutation into a prayer, outlines the general topic (with both a first-person and a second-person address), and then begins the narrative (*Works and Days*).

• Short mid-stream invocations that serve to emphasize the coming scene (whose subject they summarize) and are an integral part of the continuous narrative; such invocations may well be modeled upon initial invocations, but since their purpose is emphasis *within* the course of an episode, they are unlikely to have *introduced* the recitation of an episode (*Iliad* 2.761, 11.218, 14.508, 16.112).

It seems likely that there were two main ways in which recitation of an episode excerpted from a long epic might have been introduced. In one, which is like the *Iliad* and *Odyssey* introductions, the poet would call upon the Muse(s), name a general topic, go on to define it more specifically, say at what point it was to begin, then, after retrospective and/or prospective summaries, lead smoothly into the narrative, much as the epics we know pass from one action or focus to the next.[34] Alternatively, the singer might first invoke the deity whom he wishes to honor (probably on the occasion of his or her festival), continue the celebration with a list of the deity's Attributes and/or a myth about him or her, and after this give a salutation (χαῖρε) to the deity concerned, a prayer, and a reference to his own responsibilities, after which the first sequence outlined above would be followed. Where the myth was very long, as in some of the hymns, the poet may well have used the formulaic verse about "another song, too," to signal an intermission before the epic extract began.

Just what was done must have varied according to the nature of the occasion, the locality, the period, and so on. But clearly various options were available for beginning a song and leading smoothly into an episode from one of the long epics, without forcing us to try to believe in a poet starting off with "So he spoke . . . ," or "She came to the ships" (when we do not know who "she" is), or "When they reached the ford. . . ."[35] If we look at

---

[34] This is much like what Ford says (1992: 18–31), except that I see problems in his division beween invocation and proem.

[35] The beginning words of *Iliad* 7, 19, and 21; see above, pp. 39 and 47.

the episodes marked by titles in van Leeuwen's texts, some begin with a prospective summary and would fit reasonably well after the kind of invocation we have been considering, such as *The Aristeia of Diomedes* with its "Then to Diomedes Pallas Athena | gave strength and courage" (*Iliad* 5.1–2, following the retrospective summary at 4.543–544), or *The Ransoming of Hector* with "The games ended, and the men, each to his own ship, | scattered. *They* were thinking of eating and sleep; but Achilles | . . ." (24.1–3), or *What Happened in Pylos* with daybreak (*Odyssey* 3.1–3). But van Leeuwen allows abrupt beginnings, hard to envision directly following an invocation, such as, "In answer said crafty Odysseus" (*Odyssey* 9.1) for *The Story to Alcinous*, and, "Then she addressed him, did wise Penelope" (19.308) for *The Bath Scene*. In such cases some intermediary verse(s) would have been required.

Appendix D

CLASSICAL METERS
IN MODERN ENGLISH VERSE

THE QUANTITIVE BASIS of classical metre runs athwart the principle of stress that mainly governs English verse rhythm, and this has doomed virtually all the brave efforts to transplant classical metres in English," say the editors of a recent collection of classical verse in translation (Poole and Maule 1995: xliii–xliv). Many have made the attempt; J. F. Nims lists fourteen names, making no attempt to be comprehensive (Baker 1996: 176).[1]

In a special group are classicists who have attempted "isometric" translations, reproducing both the meaning and (syllable by syllable) the rhythm of the original. George Thomson included such a version with his *Oresteia* text and commentary (Thomson 1938, vol. 1), declaring boldly, "Since the choral rhythms form an integral part of the whole composition, a translation which ignores them is defective" (xii); I have found this useful in making my own renderings, though I found I seldom liked his versions well enough to plagiarize them.[2] My old teacher H.D.F. Kitto published a translation of Sophocles' *Antigone* in which the choral songs are rendered isometrically (Kitto 1962), with another brave statement: "Sophocles' own lyric rhythms in this play are so dramatic that it seemed presumptuous to try to find better ones; therefore I have followed them as closely as the English language permits" (v). Their efforts have not, I think, attracted much notice, because few readers are familiar with the meter of the Greek originals, and the modern authors did not explain in detail the effects they were attempting to reproduce.[3]

---

[1] Older poets who experimented with classical meters are discussed by Carne-Ross 1990: 122–131; Attridge 1974; and (with special emphasis on vowel quantity) Hanson 1992: 188–216.

[2] The distinguished scholar C. M. Bowra must have known of Thomson's attempt when he wrote, "Nobody has succeeded in the smallest degree in turning Greek choral meters into English" (foreword to Robert Fagles' translation of Bacchylides [New Haven and London, 1961], xiii).

[3] I made an amateurish effort to reproduce Homeric hexameters in isometric English in my *Homer: Poet of the* Iliad (Edwards 1987: 46–47). The only *poet* I know of who sometimes approximates Greek meters in a translation of the *Agamemnon* is Robert Browning. In the introduction to his version (1877), Browning speaks about his attempt to be literal, but not about his meters. In fact, his varying-length lines (rhymed) recall Greek choral practice (e.g., his rendering of *Agamemnon* 160–166, the "Hymn to Zeus," in his own 172–179), but he does not

However, even in the twentieth century, poets sometimes make use of classical meters, especially when translating or imitating an ancient Greek or Latin poem. The Greek or Latin vowel quantity is usually replaced by the English stress accent, which is clearly marked and easy to identify.[4] It has been said that two successive stressed syllables, to match spondees in Greek and Latin, are uncommon in English,[5] and D. Attridge (1995: 29) points out that in such cases, one of the stresses becomes secondary, as on the second syllable in "groundhog" and "backslash," and the secondary and primary stresses may shift according to the rhythmical context; he suggests we would normally say "sìxteén beliévers" but "síxteèn ánecdótes" (30), "the únknown soldier" but "this unknówn clarinétist" (39). This instinct to avoid consecutive stressed syllables in polysyllables naturally discourages spondees. However, by skillful use of stressed *mono*syllables, skillful poets have produced not only spondees but even longer sequences of stressed syllables rivaling those found in classical quantitative meters.[6] An examination of some of these modern poems also reveals a correspondence between English stress and English "quantity."

In chapter 3 I quoted a stanza from Ezra Pound's version of Sophocles' *Women of Trachis* (Pound 1957: 9). Here it is again, with scansion marked as I see it (stressed syllables with an acute, unstressed with a grave):

Párdòn ìf Í rèpróve theè, Ládỳ,   1
Tò sáve theè fálse hópes dèláyed.   2
Thínkst thoú thàt mán whò diés,   3

---

imitate the original meter or observe strophic responsion. On other aspects of Browning's version, see Carne-Ross 1990: 120–121; Steiner 1992: 329–333; and Brower 1966b: 186–189; Browning's version of *Agamemnon* 278–316 is printed in Stoneman 1982: 284–287, that of 184–248 in Poole and Maule 1995: 127–129. Richmond Lattimore, despite his disclaimer, "Necessarily, then, my translation fails to reproduce the Greek meter" (in Brower 1966a: 55), seemed unable to resist a fair imitation of Aeschylus' paeons (*Eumenides* 328–333: "Òver thè beást doòmed tò thè fíre | thìs ìs thè chánt, scàttèr òf wíts . . ." [Lattimore 1953: 146]).

[4] There is an admirably succinct and authoritative outline of stress and quantity in English in Lewis 1939. Leishman 1956: 42–59 also has a good discusssion. He includes (54–55) an isometric translation of Horace *Odes* 1.35.1–4, in which I am afraid the meter would be hard to recognize if we had not been told it was there (e.g., "in" and "and" are counted as stressed). Guy Lee has recently published an isometric translation of Horace's *Odes* and *Carmen saeculare* (Lee 1998), which came to my attention only after my manuscript was virtually complete.

The rules for stress and secondary stress in English are given by L. P. Turco in Baker 1996: 259; cf. Fussell 1979: 8–9; Attridge 1995: 26–34. (My markings of stress are explained in chapter 3, note 9 above.)

[5] E.g., by T. Steele in Baker 1996: 231–232; Fussell 1979: 20 uses the example "humdrum," Hanson and Kiparsky 1997: 30 "mandate" and "deathbed." Yvor Winters was especially opposed to the concept of spondees in English: "The truly spondaic foot is extremely rare in English. . . . The true spondee is a violent aberration" (Winters 1957: 90). The theoretical basis is discussed in Kiparsky 1977: 196–201.

[6] Spondees are easily produced by placing a stressed monosyllable before a word with initial stress: Lewis 1939: 123 uses as examples "HARD HAYmaking," "BRIGHT QUICKsilver," etc.

Sháll fròm Kíng Chrónòs táke   4
    únvárièd [*or* ùnvárièd] háppìnèss?   5
Nór yét's áll paín.   6

Matching English stresses to Greek quantities, this would become basically an iambic rhythm, scanned: (1) two iambic metra (the first a choriamb) + one syllable; (2) two iambic metra (the second in the form of a cretic); (3) spondee + iamb; (4) two iambic metra (both cretics); (5) iambic metron + two short syllables;[7] (6) two spondees. Though I do not think he had genuine Greek quantitative meter in mind here, Pound uses a number of indubitable spondees ("false hopes," "Thinkst thou," "King Chron[os]"), and in the clausula in the final verse two in succession. Shakespeare managed the same effect with monosyllables ("Love's not Time's fool"), and in fact a fully spondaic verse ("And with old woes new wail my dear time's waste" (*Sonnets* 30.4).[8] So did Yeats (among others, "Why should I blame her that she filled my days . . . ," and "What made us dream that he could comb grey hair?") and Frost ("Now no joy but lacks salt").[9]

Take the other example quoted above (p. 68):

Dárk às thè níght fálls   1
thè wíntèr fálls dárkèr (*or* dárkér)   2
stíll: yiélds stárs   3
ìnnúmèràblè, fiérce ànd cléar.[10]   4

The Greek metrical equivalent (basically iambic again) would be: (1) iambic metron (choriamb) + one syllable;[11] (2) iamb + trochee (or possibly spondee); (3) spondee + long syllable; (4) two iambic metra (the first with the final long syllable resolved into two shorts, the second a cretic). The third

---

[7] Despite the lack of a capital letter beginning the fifth verse, the setting on Pound's printed page suggests that this verse is not continuous with the fourth and divided for the printer's convenience, as there would have been ample space to include "unvaried" on the same line as the rest of the fourth verse. Either way, my "Greek" scansion would not be affected.

[8] Quoted as such by J. F. Nims in Baker 1996: 189. Of the same verse, R. Pinsky says, "In [this] line some of the iambs are made of two syllables so close in prominence ('old woes,' 'new wail') that they are practically equal, though I like hearing the slight change of pitch throbbing through them" (1998: 57); later he says, "It makes sense to call the rhythm 'spondaic'" (ibid.: 65). Shakespeare, of course, produced some of his finest effects with monosyllables (stressed or not), such as Juliet's "When he shall die | Take him and cut him out in little stars | And he will make the face of heaven so fine | That all the world will be in love with night."

[9] From Yeats' "No Second Troy" and "Robert Gregory" respectively, and Frost's "To Earthward" (*New Hampshire* [1923]). The first line of Tennyson's *Morte d'Arthur* (cf. Appendix A) begins with four heavy syllables (= two spondees): "So all day long. . . ." It ends ". . .the noise of battle roll'd," which might well be an anachronistic rattle of gunfire and boom of cannon.

[10] Quoted by C. O. Hartman in Baker 1996: 118. I thank Professor Hartman for informing me that he composed the verses himself, and for other comments.

[11] In the rhythmic context, this seems preferable to dactyl + spondee.

verse is composed of three successive monosyllables, all of them impossible to pronounce except with a long, heavy stress (though the vowel of the first is short).

The English stress accent is often reinforced by the extended time taken to pronounce a syllable. Sometimes this protraction is caused by a long vowel or a diphthong, and sometimes by the extra time taken up by a cluster of consonants following a vowel that itself is short. This was clearly stated by C. S. Lewis: "In order to write Alliterative verse it is therefore necessary to learn to distinguish not only accented from unaccented syllables, but also long from short syllables . . . A long syllable is one which contains *either* a long vowel (as *fath[er], fame, seek, pile, home, do*); *or*, a vowel followed by more than one consonant (as *punt, wind, helm, pelt*)" (Lewis 1939: 119– 120). (The same thing occurs, of course, with Greek and Latin syllable quantity.) An exaggerated example might be the two short-vowelled but long syllables of "sixth-string." In Pound's stanza quoted above, long, heavy vowels increase the stress on "I," "reprove," "save," "false," and so on (and probably the clustered consonants that follow the last three of these help, too); and certainly the multiple consonants ending the short-vowelled syllables "Thinkst," "King," and "yet's" (and perhaps others) prolong the time of pronunciation and thus the emphasis. (Tennyson uses consonant clusters in the same way to prolong short vowels: cf. "bláck clíff cláng'd" in *Morte d'Arthur* 188.) In the second stanza just quoted, weight is often given by impressively long vowels (three in the first line, and the diphthongs in "fierce" and "clear"), and in the third line the multiple consonants, in one place five together—musical enough, since they are mainly liquids and sibilants—extend not only the long vowels but also the short one in "still."

Among English poets, this phenomenon was most clearly discussed (and observed) by Gerard Manley Hopkins; in a recent detailed study, Paul Kiparsky remarks that "instead of making a futile attempt to dismantle stress-based meter and rebuild it on the basis of syllable quantity, as the Elizabethans had tried to do, Hopkins retained the basic accentual system of English verse and refined it by quantitative restraints."[12] Others have accepted the point with less systematic understanding. George Thomson referred, without elaboration, to quantity in English ("In reproducing [Greek choral rhythms] I have made a somewhat more systematic use of quantity than is usual in English verse," 1938: xii), and some recent scholars have drawn attention to the phenomenon. Rolfe Humphries, the translator of Virgil, Ovid, and Juvenal, said, "The difficulty of converting quantitative to

---

[12] Kiparsky 1989: 338. There are full linguistically based treatments of light and heavy syllables in English meter in Hanson and Kiparsky 1997: 23–30 and 1996: 289–301, and Hanson 1992: 5–57. On Pound's ideas about, and use of, English quantities, see S. J. Adams' article in *Essays in Literature* 4 (1977): 95–109 (I thank Professor C. O. Hartman for this reference).

accentual meters . . . is greatly exaggerated" (in Brower 1966a: 57), and points out that English accent and classical rules of quantity agree in marking as heavy the first five syllables in Keats' "Robs not one light seed from the feather'd grass" (ibid.: 58–59). Carne-Ross asks, "What part does quantity play in English verse?" and after a brief discussion concludes, "Must we then rely on our ear? In fact, yes, we must."[13] Among those primarily concerned with English poetry, Fussell (1979: 36), speaking of Pope's famous "When Ajax strives some rock's vast weight to throw | The line too labours, and the words move slow," notes, besides the spondaic-for-iambic substitutions, "the contribution of cacaphony (that is, the effect of strain or difficulty resulting from the collocation of consonants difficult to pronounce rapidly)"; he might also have noted that only two words in the couplet are not monosyllables. Gunn, commenting on the lines from Bunting's *Brigflatts*, "Rainwater from the butt | she fetches and flannel | to wash him inch by inch," says "The short lines have to be read slowly for the sake of clarity—we must pause a moment after the word *fetches*, to prevent it from seeming part of a parallel construction with *flannel*; 'to wash him inch by inch' can not be hurried over because of the closeness of the *sh* and *ch* sounds" (Gunn 1993: 62). B. Weller (in Baker 1996: 267–268) has said: "Quantity or length—though not necessarily reckoned by classical rules— also has some effect on how readily a semantically insignificant syllable receives a positional accent. . . . In English or American terms the rule of thumb is that sounds which are difficult to pronounce will slow down the poem . . . and any poet (or reader) who disregards this phenomenon and relies solely on stress to determine or describe a poem's movement will ignore something almost as fundamental as meter."[14]

Thus with careful use of monosyllables, the unforced English rhythm, based on the natural stress of the language, corresponds easily enough to the strings of heavy syllables that occur in standard Greek quantitative metrical patterns. However, a series of light syllables is (if short) difficult or (if long) impossible, as the natural English word stress inevitably falls upon some of them: even in Hopkins, the most "spectacular example" Kiparsky can find is a series of four unstressed syllables ("Bóth are in an únfáthomable, áll is in an enórmous dárk").[15] In my isometric translations in chapter 3, I have done my best to minimize this problem by marking the syllables I want to be stressed and (more important) those I do *not* want to be stressed

---

[13] Carne-Ross 1967: 223; see also Carne-Ross 1990: 130–131.

[14] T. Steele (in Baker 1996: 244–245) holds that the length of a syllable in English depends not on the length of the vowel but on whether it ends in a voiceless or voiced consonant, "beat" (like "bit") being short whereas "bead" is long, as is the short-vowelled "jazz."

[15] Kiparsky 1989: 314, from Hopkins' "Heraclitean Fire" (I have ventured to replace Kiparsky's underlining of the beats in this six-beat line by the acute accents I use elsewhere to mark stressed syllables).

(to match the Greek light syllables), though often this violates the normal English pronunciation.

With these points in mind, we can consider some self-conscious imitations or reproductions of classical meters (by stress accent) by modern English and American poets. The results can be very successful. The first sentence of Frost's short poem in hendecasyllabics, "For Once, Then, Something,"[16] may be scanned like this (the hendecasyllabic poems of Frost's model Catullus scan ⌄ ⌄ - - ⌄ ⌄ - ⌄ ⌄ - ⌄ ⌄ - ⌄, the first two syllables usually being heavy):

> Óthèrs taúnt mè wìth hávìng knélt àt wéll-cúrbs
> Álwàys wróng tò thè líght, sò névèr seéìng
> Deépèr dówn ìn thè wéll thàn whére thè wátèr
> Gíves mè báck ìn à shínìng súrfàce píctùre
> Mé mysélf ìn thè súmmèr heávèn, gódlíke,
> Loókìng oút òf à wreáth òf férn ànd cloúd púffs.

Frost keeps to the natural stress, which often falls on a short-vowelled syllable ("óthers," "hávìng," "néver"), sometimes I think weighted by following consonants ("knélt," "wéll-cúrbs," "gíves," etc.). Syllables with a long vowel sometimes carry the stress ("taúnt," "wróng," "líght," etc.), sometimes are unstressed and must be pronounced quickly ("mè," "álwàys" [probably], "sò," "mysélf," and later in the poem "Ì" [vv. 8, 10], "lày" [13]). At least one long diphthong in an unstressed position resists shortening and remains emphatically unmetrical: "clear" in "Wátèr cáme tò rèbúke thè toó cleár wátèr" (11); and the syllable in that same position—light in Catullus—also carries emphasis and stress in the poem's final culminating phrase, "Fòr ónce, thén, sómethìng" (15).[17]

Of particular interest to us here are cases where poets have employed the

---

[16] Quoted from *The Poetry of Robert Frost*, ed. Edward Connery Lathem, copyright © 1969 by Henry Holt and Company. Reprinted by permission of Henry Holt. J. F. Nims notes (Baker 1996: 176) that Frost "gloated over the fact that 'none of my Latin people recognized it.'" Metrically the poem seems to me very good, and much better than Tennyson's well-known "Look, I come to the test, a tiny poem | All composed in a metre of Catullus." Fussell 1979: 102–103 is good on Frost's "The Vantage Point," which changes rhythm as speaker turns over—"And if by noon I have tóo múch of these, | I háve / bùt tò / túrn òn / mỳ árm, / ànd ló, | . . . ." There is an excellent appreciation of the "hidden effects" of Frost's meters by Brad Leithauser in *The New York Review of Books*, 43, 13, 8 August 1996, 40–43 ("There's the poet who delights in the fabrication of slight irregularities—in twisting the form without snapping it outright," ibid.: 41). There are also many good comments on Frost's versification in Pinsky 1998.

[17] Though in the verses quoted above Frost always begins with the equivalent of a trochee (- ⌄), two of the later verses begin with a spondee (- -), as usually in Catullus ("Ónce, whén trỳing . . ." [7, Frost's italics], and "Óne dróp féll . . ." [12]). Dudley Fitts remarked that in rendering classical quantitative meters into English, the hendecasyllable is "particularly troublesome" (in Brower 1966a: 41–42).

same meters as Aeschylus did in the choral songs discussed in chapter 3. Basil Bunting, an English poet who was very familiar with Ezra Pound and his work, completed translations from a number of different languages, including several of Horace's *Odes*. Bunting once remarked: "I suppose I really got going when I started playing about with quantity. I don't mean direct imitations of Greek quantity. That won't do. English is another language. English is full of long syllables and there is hardly one of the classical metres that you can adapt into English without making your syntax totally impossible. So you've got to invent new metres in quantity if you want to do anything with them. . . . Very few poems in modern times have been written in quantity. They are written instead in stress patterns copied from the quantity patterns of the ancient Greeks."[18] In a volume published in 1931, he rendered the ionics of one of Horace's odes into the English equivalent.[19] The Horace begins:

> miserarum est neque amori dare ludum neque dulci
> mala vino lavere, aut exanimari metuentis
>   patruae verbera linguae

(Odes 3.12.1–3)

and is scanned:

ᵕᵕ – – ᵕᵕ – – ᵕᵕ – – ᵕᵕ – – (twice)
          ᵕᵕ – – ᵕᵕ – –

Bunting's version of this goes:

> Yes, it's slow, docked of amours, docked of the doubtless efficacious
> bottled makeshift, gin: but who'd risk being bored stiff
> every night listening to father's silly sarcasms?

(Bunting 1994: 132)

This is very natural English, far from "translationese," and yet the ionic rhythm is easily perceptible, without the reader's having to make any effort to impose it on the words. Some of the syllables bearing the stress have a long vowel (e.g., "slow"), some a short vowel followed by a consonant cluster (e.g., "docked," "risk"). Besides using monosyllables where he needs successive stressed syllables, Bunting finds several genuinely spondaic words: "makeshift," with first vowel long and second protracted by consonants; "father's," with two long vowels (the second, normally lightly

---

[18] Quoted by D. Reagan in Terrell 1981: 237. On Bunting's translations, see especially V. M. Forde in ibid.: 301–342; and Gordon 1980.

[19] In his *Overdrafts*, recently republished in Bunting 1994: 129–150. This is the only Horatian ode in this meter. In his recent isometric translation, Guy Lee skillfully renders the lines "It's a girl's fate not to let love | Have its due fling nor with sweet wine | Wash away all her afflictions or to lose heart being frightened | Of the tongue-lash of an uncle" (Lee 1998: 127).

stressed, is weighted by the following consonants, as is also the case with "doubtless"). Sometimes the natural stress on a syllable must be suppressed slightly where it falls in an unstressed position (e.g., the first syllables of "bottled," "silly," in both of which the short vowel may help the lightening). Occasionally there is a real metrical flaw, as with "gin," which bears a heavy stress in the sentence but is metrically unstressed.[20]

Bunting also tried his hand at Horace's Second Asclepiadeans (a glyconic verse followed by a lesser asclepiad). Horace's

> cum tu, Lydia, Telephi
> > cervicem roseam, cerea Telephi
> laudas bracchia, vae meum
> > fervens difficili bile tumet iecur

(Odes 1.13.1–4)

scanned

```
_ _ _ ∪ ∪ _ ∪ ×

    _ _ _ ∪ ∪ _ _ ∪ ∪ _ ×
```

becomes

> Please stop gushing about his pink
> neck smooth arms and so forth, Dulcie, it makes me sick,
> badtempered, silly: makes me blush.
> Dribbling sweat on my chops proves I'm on tenterhooks.

(Bunting 1994: 133)

In this colloquial English, Bunting easily manages the required stresses (largely by using stressed monosyllables—"Please, stop . . ."), but correspondence loosens at the trisyllable in the third verse ("bádtémpéred, síllỳ: mákes mè blúsh," perhaps?).[21] A few other Horatian odes were rendered by

---

[20] Gordon (1980: 78) marks scansion on some of Bunting's verses in this poem, but not that on "gin"; he says, "With a certain looseness in some of his lines, [Bunting] invents a convincing English cadence that adapts the *ionic a minore* to the stresses of his line." In the remainder of Bunting's poem, there is "looseness" in his line 8, which (to keep the meter) would have to be scanned as "of that goódloókìng àthléte's glístenìng wèt shoúldérs"; line 10, which seems to lack two syllables ("-ing ànd stánds | tówellìng hìmsélf [´] ìn fúll view"?). His last line (16) is also erratic, perhaps for a vivid matching of sound to sense: "whèn thè dríven tígèr àppeárs súddenlỳ àt [or "súddènlỳ àt"?] árms'-léngth."

[21] Gordon (1980: 81) scans "bádtémpéred, sìllỳ: mákes mè blúsh," which follows the Latin meter but violates the English lack of stress on the third syllable. I would also challenge his scanning of verse 6, "úngóvérnàblè cúb cértaìn tò bíte oùt á" (again the third syllable must be unstressed, and the stresses on the last two reversed), and verse 7, "pérmánént mèmòrándùm ón," where the second syllable must be unstressed. Guy Lee's isometric translation (Lee 1998: 23) renders the lines "When you, Lydia, praise Tèlephus | *And* his neck (rosy pink!), Tèlephus *and* his arms | (Wax-smooth!) yuk, I can feel it, my | Liver boiling with sour bile and oedema-

Bunting into freer English forms, which are interesting as poems but not so relevant to our purpose here.[22]

Another modern poet who has translated widely from different languages, including ancient Greek and Latin, is the American John Frederick Nims. In his *Sappho to Valéry*, a volume of translations, he writes: "What we generally settle for, in translating from Greek and Latin, is a transposition of long and short syllables into stressed and unstressed—which may give us as good a notion of the movement of Sappho's verse as we are ever likely to have" (Nims 1990a: 10). He renders five poems of Sappho into English Sapphics (ibid.: 376–385), and one that includes glyconic lines like those found in our Aeschylean choral songs, Sappho's well-known

ὤιμ᾽ ὡς δεῖνα πεπ[όνθ]αμεν,	4
Ψάπφ᾽, ἦ μάν σ᾽ ἀέκοισ᾽ ἀπυλιμπάνω.	5
τὰν δ᾽ ἔγω τάδ᾽ ἀμειβόμαν·	6
χαίροισ᾽ ἔρχεο κἄμεθεν	7
μέμναισ᾽, οἶσθα γὰρ ὥς σε πεδήπομεν·	8
αἰ δὲ μή, ἀλλά σ᾽ ἔγω θέλω	9
ὄμναισαι	10

(Sappho 94.4–10)

which is in stanzas composed of two glyconics followed by a glyconic expanded by an extra three syllables, - ˘ ˘ , as

⏓ ⏓ - ˘ ˘ - ˘ ⏓ (twice)
⏓ ⏓ - ˘ ˘ - ˘ ˘ - ˘ ⏓.

Nims renders this as:

"Sappho, this is our darkest day!	4
Heaven knows it's no wish of mine to be	5
leaving you!" and I answered her,	6
"Fare well, fare very well, and still	7
think of me, for you know you were cherished here.	8
Don't remember? Well, if you don't	9
I'd remind you of. . . ."[23]	10

(Nims 1990a: 389)

tous" (in the first line "Lydia" must presumably be scanned as two syllables only, and "praise" as an unstressed light syllable).

[22] Horace *Odes* 1.5, 1.9, 1.23, 2.5, 2.14: Bunting 1994: 203, 205, 204, 204, 143, respectively.

[23] From *Sappho to Valéry: Poems in Translation* by J. F. Nims, copyright © 1990 by John Frederick Nims. Reprinted by permission of the University of Arkansas Press. For clarity I have divided Nims' text into stanzas, as is usually done with Sappho's.

The Greek rhythm is clear and natural enough except in line 5, where "Heaven" and "it's" must be rather uneasily taken as two syllables each in order to fit: "Heávèn knóws ìt ìs nó wìsh òf míne tò bé." Nims, however, often uses as unstressed those syllables where the vowel is followed by a cluster of consonants ("darkèst day," "wìsh," "ànd still," "chérìshed").

Nims also translates a poem of Sappho's in a related aeolo-choriambic meter, greater asclepiads:

κατθάνοισα δὲ κείσηι οὐδέ ποτα μναμοσύνα σέθεν
ἔσσετ᾽ οὐδὲ †ποκ᾽† ὕστερον· οὐ γὰρ πεδέχηις βρόδων
τῶν ἐκ Πιερίας· ἀλλ᾽ ἀφάνης κἀν Ἀίδα δόμωι
φοιτάσηις πεδ᾽ ἀμαύρων νεκύων ἐκπεποταμένα.

(Sappho 55)

which scans like a glyconic with two additional choriambs in the middle, i.e.,

ˇ ˇ – ˘ ˘ – – ˘ ˘ – – ˘ ˘ – ˘ ˇ

This becomes:

You though! Die and you'll lie dumb in the dirt; nobody care,
    and none
Miss you ever again, knowing there's no rapture can stir your soul;
You've no love for the Muse, none for her flowers. Even in hell
    you'll be
Not worth anyone's glance, lost in the vague colorless drifting dead.

(Nims 1990a: 387)

In the same meter he renders an ode of Horace:

tu ne quaesieris, scire nefas, quem mihi, quem tibi
finem di dederint, Leuconoë, nec Babylonios
temptaris numeros, ut melius, quidquid erit, pati. . . .

(Horace, Odes 1.11)

This becomes:

Don't ask—knowing's taboo—what's in the cards, darling, for you,
    for me,
what end heaven intends. Meddle with palm, planet, séance, tea leaves?
—rubbish! Shun the occult. Better by far take in your stride what
    comes.

(Nims 1990a: 411)

This might appear to be a difficult rhythm to produce convincingly in English,[24] but Nims manages it successfully (except for "teà leáves"!), and in fact the infrequency of successive heavy (stressed) syllables in this meter avoids a common problem.

Nims' most sustained effort is the poem "Water Music," which is based on the metrical scheme of Pindar's first Olympian Ode, aeolo-choriambic (Pindar's lines are more varied than Aeschylus' aeolo-choriambic, discussed in chapter 3).[25] Though he does not translate Pindar's content, Nims matches Pindar's lines syllable-for-syllable, with three strophes, three corresponding antistrophes, and three epodes. His first five verses are (with my scansion markings):

> "Nóthìng nóblè às wátèr, nó,
>   ánd[26] thére's góld wìth ìts glámór. . . . "   1
> Píndàr òn trúmpèt—Fírst
>   feístỳ Òlýmpìàn Óde tò thè hórsemàn,   2
> Dárìng ús, àcróss thè yeárs: 3
> Loók tò éxcèllènce ónlỳ.   4
> Wátèr, yoú're púre wóndèr! hére's   5
> Fébrùárỳ, ...

The first line is a glyconic followed by a pherecratean; Pindar's second line is taken as a cretic with the first heavy syllable resolved into two lights, followed by a pherecratean expanded by two inserted dactyls (i.e., ⌣ - ⌣ - ⌣ - - ⌣ ⌣ - ⌣ ⌣ - ⌣ ⌣ - -), but Nims has chosen to begin with a stressed syllable and subdivided the line so that the second part is entirely dactylic; the third is simply a cretic followed by an iambic metron; the fourth is a pherecratean; the fifth is the same as the third (Nims' "pure," obviously stressed, replaces Pindar's short syllable).[27] In the whole eleven-verse strophe, Pindar has two consecutive long syllables only five times, which eases a little the task Nims has set himself, but nevertheless his retention of "Pindar's lattice" (as he

---

[24] Cf. Carne-Ross 1990: 129, who quotes from Swinburne's "Choriambs": "What sweet visions of sleep lured thee away, down from the light above. . . ." Guy Lee's isometric version of the three Horatian lines is very close to the original: "You are not to inquire (knowing's taboo) what limit Gods have set | To my life and to yours, Leuconoe. No Babylonian | Numerology! Far better endure whatever comes to pass" (Lee 1998: 19).

[25] Nims 1990b: 22–25 (with notes on 51). By John Frederick Nims, from *The Six-Cornered Snowflake and Other Poems*, copyright © 1990 by John Frederick Nims. Reprinted by permission of New Directions Publishing Corp.

The full metrical scheme is given in Kirkwood 1982: 44 and Maehler 1971: 1.

[26] Or "ànd"; I think the clustered consonants might justify the stress, but either is metrically admissible.

[27] Technically this is permissible if the syllable is considered the first of an iambic metron.

calls it) throughout the poem, without straining English idiom, is remarkable and probably unique.[28]

Nims also used ionics and anacreontics. His poem "The Young Ionia" (Nims 1960: 12–13) is in pure ionics, grouped in threes, with each group printed as a couplet with the line break occurring at different positions, as in:

> Òr à húshed tálk   bỳ thè fírepláce
>   Whèn thè ásh fláres
> Às à heárt coúld   (ìf à heárt woúld)   tò
>   Rècáll yoú,
> Tò rècáll áll   ìn à lóng
>   Loók,   tò ènwráp yoú
> Às ìt ónce hád   whèn thè raín streámed   òn thè
>   Fáll aír. . . .[29]

The variety and flexibility given here by the interplay between metrical feet and line breaks is remarkable. (Unsurprisingly, this poem contains a very high proportion of monosyllabic words.)

Since its meter resembles Aeschylus' anacreontics, Nims' rendering of Catullus' galliambics should be mentioned, though here he is less successful because the lines would be hard (I think) to read aloud unless one is already familiar with the rhythm. Catullus begins:

> Super alta uectus Attis celeri rate maria
> Phrygium ut nemus citato cupide pede tetigit
> adiitque opaca siluis redimita loca deae,
> stimulatus ibi furenti rabie, uagus animis
> deuoluit ili acuto sibi pondera silice. . . .[30]

(Catullus 63.1–5)

The galliambic is formed from an anacreontic followed (after an invariable word break) by a second anacreontic that lacks the final syllable and usually resolves one of its medial long syllables into two shorts:

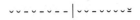

In Nims this becomes:

---

[28] Actually Nims' biggest problem, as he admits (1990b: 51), is the eighth verse, which Pindar begins with seven short syllables: perhaps his closest attempt is "Logy, disoriented."

[29] Nims 1960: 12 lines 3–10, with stress markings and spaces between ionic metra added. By John Frederick Nims, from *Knowledge of the Evening*, copyright © 1960 by Rutgers, The State University. Reprinted by permission of Bonnie Larkin Nims.

[30] This is the text printed by Nims 1990a: 396.

> Over oceans sped he, Attis, in the speediest of the ships,
> Till ashore by Phrygian forests, feet impetuous with desire,
> He drew near the gloomy purlieus of the goddess within the wood,
> There, his mind at sixes, sevens, he, hysterical in his zeal,
> With a flintstone cropped his pendules, the appurtenance of his groin.
>
> (Nims 1990a: 397)

Metrically the translation is a tour de force, and sometimes the anacreontics in the first half of the verse are natural enough (cf. the penultimate verse, "Spare my home your visitation; I've no relish to be possessed"), but in the lines quoted above an inexperienced reader might well be led astray into hearing three syllables in "Phrýgìàn" for the required disyllable "Phrýgiàn," "dréw neár" for "drèw neár," and perhaps "Wìth à flíntstóne" for ". . . stòne."[31]

The reader—perhaps I should say the listener—will be the judge; but in my opinion the above examples demonstrate that highly regarded modern poets have had considerable success in making use of the basic rhythms of standard classical meters in composing their own poems (as well as in translating), by substituting English stress accent for the classical syllable length, sometimes aided by a regard for the time taken to pronounce the vowel of the English syllable and the consonants that follow it. This lends support to the conception of using an isometric translation to reproduce the expressive variations of which Aeschylus is a master.

---

[31] Nims also used a version of galliambics in his "Niagara" (Nims 1990b: 47–49, 51–52). Here the first half of the verse is usually close to the classical original, the second half less so. Tennyson's "Boädicea" is in adapted galliambics (see Carne-Ross 1990: 123–124), but his first syllable is almost always long, making the first half of the line trochaic in movement, and in the second half he usually has one or more extra syllables. His first line, "While about the shore of Mona those Neronian legionaries," illustrates this—though it could be transmuted into a passable galliambic by writing and scanning it "Whìle aboút thè shóre òf Móná | thòse Nèrónìàn *lègiònnaires*." In Tennyson's "Anacreontics," there is only one real anacreontic verse: "With a silken cord I bound it."

REFERENCES

Albis, R. V. 1996. *Poet and Audience in the* Argonautica *of Apollonius.* Lanham, Md.

Anderson, W. D. 1994. *Music and Musicians in Ancient Greece.* Ithaca, N.Y.

Ardizzoni, A. 1967. *Apollonio Rodio: Le Argonautiche Libro I.* Città del Castello.

Attridge, D. 1974. *Well-Weighed Syllables: Elizabethan Verse in Classical Metres.* London.

———. 1995. *Poetic Rhythm: An Introduction.* Cambridge.

Baker, D., ed. 1996. *Meter in English: A Critical Engagement.* Fayetteville, Ark.

Bakker, E. J. 1990. "Homeric Discourse and Enjambement: A Cognitive Approach." *Transactions of the American Philological Association* 120: 1–21.

———. 1993. "Discourse and Performance: Involvement, Visualization and 'Presence' in Homeric Poetry." *Classical Antiquity* 12: 1–29.

———. 1997a. *Poetry in Speech: Orality and Homeric Discourse.* Ithaca, N.Y.

———, ed. 1997b. *Grammar as Interpretation: Greek Literature in its Linguistic Contexts. Mnemosyne,* supp. 171. Leiden.

———. 1997c.: "The Study of Homeric Discourse." In Morris and Powell 1997: 284–304.

———. 1999. "How Oral Is Oral Composition?" In Mackay 1999: 29–47.

Bakker, E. J., and A. Kahane, eds. 1997. *Written Voices, Spoken Signs: Tradition, Performance, and the Epic Text.* Cambridge, Mass.

Bal, M. 1985. *Narratology: Introduction to the Theory of Narrative.* Trans. C. van Boheemen. Toronto.

Baldi, P. 1999. *The Foundations of Latin.* Berlin and New York.

Bassett, S. E. 1926. "The So-Called Emphatic Position of the Runover Word in the Homeric Hexameter." *Transactions of the American Philological Association* 57: 116–148.

———. 1938. *The Poetry of Homer.* Berkeley.

Beck, D. 1999. "Speech Introductions and the Character Development of Telemachus." *Classical Journal* 94, no. 2: 121–141.

Bolkestein, M. 1996. "Free but Not Arbitrary: 'Emotive' Word Order in Latin?" In R. Risselada, J. R. de Jong, and A. M. Bolkestein, eds., *On Latin: Linguistic and Literary Studies in Honour of Harm Pinkster,* 7–24. Amsterdam.

Boyle, A. J. 1974. "Propertius I, 19: A Critical Study." *Latomus* 33: 895–911.

Brower, R. 1966a. *On Translation.* Reprint of 1959 ed. Oxford.

———. 1966b. "Seven Agamemnons." In Brower 1966a: 173–195.

Bunting, B. 1994. *The Complete Poems.* Ed. R. Caddel. Oxford.

Burgess, J. S. 1996. "The Non-Homeric *Cypria.*" *Transactions of the American Philological Association* 126: 77–99.

Burkert, W. 1987. "The Making of Homer in the Sixth Century B.C.: Rhapsodes versus Stesichoros." In *Papers on the Amasis Painter and His World,* The J. Paul Getty Museum, 43–62. Malibu, Calif.

Burnyeat, M. F. 1997. "Postscript on Silent Reading." *Classical Review* 47: 74–76.

Burton, R.W.B. 1980. *The Chorus in Sophocles' Tragedies.* Oxford.

Bussanich, J. 1983. "A Theoretical Interpretation of Hesiod's Chaos." *Classical Philology* 78: 212–219.

Caddel, R., ed. 1994. *Basil Bunting: Three Essays.* Durham, N.C.

Campbell, M. 1983. "Apollonian and Homeric Book Division." *Mnemosyne* 36: 154–156.

Camps, W. A. 1966. *Propertius: Elegies Book I.* Cambridge.

Carne-Ross, D. S. 1967. "New Metres for Old: A Note on Pound's Metric." *Arion* 6, no. 2: 216–232.

———. 1990. "Jocasta's Divine Head: English with a Foreign Accent." *Arion*, 3d ser. 1, no. 1: 106–141.

Carne-Ross, D. S., and K. Haynes, eds. 1996. *Horace in English.* Harmondsworth.

Chafe, W. 1994. *Discourse, Consciousness, and Time: The Flow and Displacement of Conscious Experience in Speaking and Writing.* Chicago.

Chatman, S. 1978. *Story and Discourse: Narrative Structure in Fiction and Film.* Ithaca, N.Y., and London.

Clark, M. 1994. "Enjambment and Binding in Homeric Hexameter." *The Phoenix* 48: 95–114.

———. 1997. *Out of Line: Homeric Composition beyond the Hexameter.* Lanham, Md.

Clay, J. S. 1997. "The Homeric Hymns." In Morris and Powell 1997: 489–507.

Cole, T. 1988. *Epiploke: Rhythmical Continuity and Poetic Structure in Greek Lyric.* Cambridge, Mass.

Commager, S. 1962. *The Odes of Horace: A Critical Study.* New Haven.

———. 1974. *A Prolegomenon to Propertius.* Norman, Okla.

Contiades-Tsitsoni, E. 1990. *Hymenaios und Epithalamion: Das Hochzeitslied in der frühgriechischen Lyrik.* Stuttgart.

Dain, A. 1965. *Traité de métrique grecque.* Paris.

Dale, A. M. 1968. *The Lyric Metres of Greek Drama.* 2d ed. Cambridge.

———. 1969. *Collected Papers.* Cambridge.

———. 1971, 1981, 1983. *Metrical Analyses of Tragic Choruses.* Vol. 1, *Dactylo-epitrite;* vol. 2, *Aeolo-Choriambic;* vol. 3, *Dochmiac-Iambic-Dactylic-Ionic. Bulletin of the Institute of Classical Studies,* supp. 21.1–3. London.

Davis, G. 1991. *Polyhymnia: The Rhetoric of Horatian Lyric Discourse.* Berkeley, Los Angeles, and Oxford.

Denniston, J. D., and D. Page, eds. 1957. *Aeschylus: Agamemnon.* Oxford.

Devine, A. M., and L. D. Stephens. 1984. *Language and Metre: Resolution, Porson's Bridge, and Their Prosodic Basis.* Chico, Calif.

———. 2000. *Discontinuous Syntax: Hyperbaton in Greek.* Oxford and New York.

Dik, H. 1995. *Word Order in Ancient Greek: A Pragmatic Account of Word Order Variation in Herodotus.* Amsterdam.

Dik, S. C. 1981. *Functional Grammar.* 3d rev. ed. Dordrecht.

Dowden, K. 1996. "Homer's Sense of Text." *Journal of Hellenic Studies* 116: 47–61.

Edwards, M. W. 1960. "The Expression of Stoic Ideas in the *Aeneid.*" *The Phoenix* 14: 151–165.

———. 1961. "Intensification of Meaning in Propertius and Others." *Transactions of the American Philological Association* 92: 128–144.

———. 1966. "Some Features of Homeric Craftsmanship." *Transactions of the American Philological Association* 97: 15–179.

———. 1968. "Homeric Speech Introductions." *Harvard Studies in Classical Philology* 74: 1–36.

———. 1969. "On Some 'Answering' Expressions in Homer." *Classical Philology* 64: 81–87.

———. 1977. "Agamemnon's Decision: Freedom and Folly in Aeschylus." *California Studies in Classical Antiquity* 10: 17–38.

———. 1980. "Convention and Individuality in *Iliad* 1." *Harvard Studies in Classical Philology* 84: 1–28.

———. 1986–1988. "Homer and Oral Tradition: The Formula, Part I" and ". . . Part II." *Oral Tradition* 1–2: 171–230 and 3: 11–60.

———. 1987. *Homer: Poet of the* Iliad. Baltimore and London.

———. 1991. *The Iliad: A Commentary*. Vol. 5, *Books 17–20*. Cambridge.

———. 1992a. "Homer and Oral Tradition: The Type-Scene." *Oral Tradition* 7, no. 2: 284–330.

———. 1992b. "Character and Style: Achilles in *Iliad* 18." In J. M. Foley, ed., *De Gustibus: Essays for Alain Renoir*, 168–184. New York and London.

Fagles, R., trans. 1990. *Homer: The Iliad*. New York.

Fedeli, P. 1980. *Sesto Properzio: Il primo libro delle elegie*. Florence.

Fenik, B. C. 1968. *Typical Battle Scenes in the Iliad*. *Hermes*, supp. 21. Wiesbaden.

———, ed. 1978. *Homer: Tradition and Invention*. Leiden.

Ferrari, G. 1997. "Figures in the Text: Metaphors and Riddles in the *Agamemnon*." *Classical Philology* 92, no. 1: 1–45.

Finkelberg, M. 1998. *The Birth of Literary Fiction in Ancient Greece*. Oxford.

Fish, S. E. 1980. "Literature in the Reader: Affective Stylistics." In Tompkins 1980: 70–100.

Flaschenriem, B. 1997. "Loss, Desire, and Writing in Propertius 1.19 and 2.15." *Classical Antiquity* 16: 259–277.

Foley, J. M. 1990. *Traditional Oral Epic: The* Odyssey, Beowulf, *and the Serbo-Croatian Return Song*. Berkeley.

———. 1999. "What's in a Sign?" In Mackay 1999: 1–27.

Ford, A. 1992. *Homer: The Poetry of the Past*. Ithaca, N.Y., and London.

———. 1997. "The Inland Ship: Problems in the Performance and Reception of Homeric Epic." In Bakker and Kahane 1997: 83–109.

Fraenkel, E., ed. 1950. *Aeschylus: Agamemnon*. 3 vols. Oxford.

Fränkel, H. 1973. *Early Greek Poetry and Philosophy*. Trans. M. Hadas and J. Willis. New York and London.

———. 1968a. *Noten zu den Argonautika des Apollonios*. Munich.

———. 1968b: "Der homerische und der kallimachische Hexameter." In *Wege und Formen frühgriechischen Denkens*, 100–156. Munich.

Fussell, P., Jr. 1979. *Poetic Meter and Poetic Form*. Rev. ed. New York.

Gaisser, J. H. 1977. "Mythological *Exempla* in Propertius 1.2 and 1.15." *American Journal of Philology* 98: 381–391.

Gamel, M.-K. 1998. "Reading as a Man: Performance and Gender in Roman Elegy." *Helios* 25: 79–95.

Gelzer, T. 1987. "Bemerkungen zum homerischen Ares-Hymnus (Hom. Hy. 8)." *Museum Helveticum* 44: 150–167.

Genette, G. 1980. *Narrative Discourse: An Essay in Method.* Trans. J. E. Lewin. Ithaca, N.Y., and London.

Goldhill, S. 1991. *The Poet's Voice: Essays on Poetics and Greek Literature.* Cambridge.

Goold, G. P., ed. 1990. *Propertius: Elegies.* Loeb Classical Library. Cambridge, Mass.

Gordon, D. 1980. "A Northumbrian Sabine." *Paideuma* 9, no. 1: 77–87.

Gould, J. 1973. "*HIKETEIA.*" *Journal of Hellenic Studies* 93: 74–103.

Gray, E. 1998. "Tennyson, Virgil, and the Death of Christmas: Influence and the *Morte d'Arthur.*" *Arion*, 3d. ser., 6, no. 2: 98–113.

Griffin, J. 1986. "Homeric Words and Speakers." *Journal of Hellenic Studies* 106: 36–57.

Gunn, T. 1993. *Shelf Life: Essays, Memoirs, and an Interview.* Ann Arbor.

———. 1994. *Collected Poems.* New York.

Hainsworth, J. B. 1970. "The Criticism of an Oral Homer." *Journal of Hellenic Studies* 90: 90–98.

———. 1993. *The Iliad: A Commentary.* Vol. 3, *Books 9–12.* Cambridge.

Hamilton, R. 1989. *The Architecture of Hesiodic Poetry.* Baltimore and London.

Hannay, M. 1991. "Pragmatic Function Assignment and Word Order Variation in a Functional Grammar of English." *Journal of Pragmatics* 16: 131–155.

Hanson, K. 1992. *Resolution in Modern Meters. Dissertation Abstracts International* 53-02A: 481.

Hanson, K., and P. Kiparsky. 1996. "A Parametric Theory of Poetic Meter." *Language* 72, no. 2: 287–335.

———. 1997. "The Nature of Verse and Its Consequences for the Mixed Form." In J. Harris and K. Reichl, eds., *Prosimetrum: Crosscultural Perspectives on Narrative in Prose and Verse,* 17–44. Bury St. Edmunds.

Haslam, M. 1997. "Homeric Papyri and the Transmission of the Text." In Morris and Powell 1997: 55–100.

Heiden, B. 1998. "The Placement of 'Book Divisions' in the *Iliad.*" *Journal of Hellenic Studies* 118: 68–81.

Hellwig, B. 1964. *Raum und Zeit im homerischen Epos.* Spudasmata Band 2. Hildesheim.

Herington, J. 1985. *Poetry into Drama: Early Tragedy and the Greek Poetic Tradition.* Berkeley.

Heubeck, A., S. West, and J. B. Hainsworth. 1988. *A Commentary on Homer's Odyssey.* Vol. 1. Oxford.

Heubeck, A., and A. Hoekstra. 1989. *A Commentary on Homer's Odyssey.* Volume 2. Oxford.

Higbie, C. 1990. *Measure and Music: Enjambement and Sentence Structure in the* Iliad. Oxford.

Hodge, R.I.V., and R. A. Buttimore. 1977. *The "Monobiblos" of Propertius: An Account of the First Book of Propertius Consisting of a Text, Translation, and Critical Essay on Each Poem.* Cambridge.

Hooker, J. T. 1968. "The Sacrifice of Iphigeneia in the *Agamemnon.*" ΑΓΩΝ 2: 59–65.

Hunter, R. L., ed. 1989. *Apollonius of Rhodes: Argonautica Book III.* Cambridge.

Jacobson, H. 1974. *Ovid's* Heroides. Princeton.

Janko, R. 1981. "The Structure of the Homeric Hymns: A Study in Genre." *Hermes* 109: 9–24.

———. 1992. *The Iliad: A Commentary.* Vol. 4, *Books 13–16.* Cambridge.

———. 1998. "The Homeric Poems as Oral Dictated Texts." *Classical Quarterly* 48: 1–13.

Jensen, M. S. 1999. "Report." In *SO Debate: "Dividing Homer: When and How Were the* Iliad *and the* Odyssey *Divided into Songs?"* *Symbolae Osloenses* 74: 5–35.

de Jong, I.J.F. 1987a. *Narrators and Focalizers: The Presentation of the Story in the Iliad.* Amsterdam.

———. 1987b. "The Voice of Anonymity: *Tis*-Speeches in the *Iliad.*" *Eranos* 85: 69–84.

———. 1996. "Sunsets and Sunrises in Homer and Apollonius of Rhodes: Book-Divisions and Beyond." *Dialogos: Hellenic Studies Review* 3: 20–35.

———. 1999. "Comment," In *SO Debate: "Dividing Homer: When and How Were the* Iliad *and the* Odyssey *Divided into Songs?"* *Symbolae Osloenses* 74: 58–63.

Keaney, J. J., and R. Lamberton, eds. 1996. *[Plutarch] Essay on the Life and Poetry of Homer.* Atlanta.

Kiparsky, P. 1977. "The Rhythmic Structure of English Verse." *Linguistic Inquiry* 8, no. 2: 189–247.

———. 1989. "Sprung Rhythm." In P. Kiparsky and G. Youmans, eds., *Phonetics and Phonology,* vol. 1: *Rhythm and Meter,* 305–340. San Diego.

Kirk, G. S. 1966a. "The Structure of the Homeric Hexameter." *Yale Classical Studies* 20: 76–104.

———. 1966b. "Verse-Structure and Sentence-Structure in Homer." *Yale Classical Studies* 20: 105–152.

———. 1985. *The Iliad: A Commentary.* Vol. 1, *Books 1–4.* Cambridge.

Kirkwood, G., ed. 1982. *Selections from Pindar.* Chico.

Kitto, H.D.F. 1942. "Rhythm, Metre, and Black Magic." *Classical Review* 56: 99–108.

———. 1955. "The Dance in Greek Tragedy." *Journal of Hellenic Studies* 75: 36–41.

———. 1962. *Sophocles: Three Tragedies (Antigone, Oedipus the King, Electra).* Oxford.

———. 1964. *Form and Meaning in Drama.* 2d ed. London.

Knox, B.M.W. 1968. "Silent Reading in Antiquity." *Greek, Roman and Byzantine Studies* 9: 421–35.

Korzeniewski, D. 1968. *Griechische Metrik.* Darmstadt.

Krischer, T. 1971. *Formale Konventionen der homerischen Epik.* Zetemata Heft 56. Munich.

Landels, J. G. 1999. *Music in Ancient Greece and Rome.* London and New York.

Latacz, J. 1996. *Homer: His Art and His World.* Trans. J. P. Holoka. Ann Arbor.

Lattimore, R., trans. 1951. *The Iliad of Homer.* Chicago.

———, trans. 1953. *Aeschylus I: Oresteia.* Chicago.

Lee, G., trans. 1998. *Horace: Odes and Carmen Saeculare with an English Version in the Original Metres, Introduction and Notes.* Leeds.

Leishman, J. B. 1956. *Translating Horace: Thirty Odes Translated into the Original Metres with the Latin Text and an Introductory and Critical Essay.* Oxford.

Levi, P. 1993. *Tennyson.* London.

Levin, D. N. 1969. "Propertius, Catullus, and Three Kinds of Ambiguous Expression." *Transactions of the American Philological Association* 100: 221–235.

Lewis, C. S. 1939. "The Alliterative Metre." In *Rehabilitations and Other Essays,* 119–132. Oxford. Reprinted in J. B. Bessinger Jr. and S. J. Kahrl, *Essential Articles for the Study of Old English Poetry* (Hamden, 1968), 305–316.

Lombardo, S., trans. 1997. *Homer: Iliad.* Indianapolis and Cambridge.

Lord, A. B. 1936. "Homer and Huso I: The Singer's Rests in Greek and Southslavic Heroic Song." *Transactions of the American Philological Association* 67: 106–113.

Lyne, R.O.A.M. 1980. *The Latin Love Poets from Catullus to Horace.* Oxford.

Mackay, E. A., ed. 1999. *Signs of Orality: The Oral Tradition and Its Influence in the Greek and Roman World. Mnemosyne,* supp. 188. Leiden and Boston.

Macleod, C. W., ed. 1982. *Homer: Iliad, Book XXIV.* Cambridge.

Maehler, H., ed. (post B. Snell). 1971. *Pindari Carmina cum Fragmentis.* Part 1, *Epinicia.* Leipzig.

Martindale, C., and D. Hopkins, eds. 1993. *Horace Made New: Horatian Influences on British Writing from the Renaissance to the Twentieth Century.* Cambridge.

Michie, J., trans. 1965. *The Odes of Horace.* New York.

Minchin, E. 1992. "Scripts and Themes: Cognitive Research and the Homeric Epic." *Classical Antiquity* 11: 229–241.

———. 1995a. "The Poet Appeals to his Muse: Homeric Invocations in the Context of Epic Performance." *Classical Journal* 91, no. 1: 25–33.

———. 1995b. "Ring-Patterns and Ring-Composition: Some Observations on the Framing of Stories in Homer." *Helios* 22, no. 1: 23–35.

———. 1996. "The Performance of Lists and Catalogues in the Homeric Epics." In I. Worthington, ed., *Voice into Text: Orality and Literacy in Ancient Greece, Mnemosyne,* supp. 157, 3–20. Leiden.

———. 1999. "Describing and Narrating in Homer's *Iliad.*" In Mackay 1999: 49–64.

Minton, W. W. 1962. "Invocation and Catalogue in Hesiod and Homer." *Transactions of the American Philological Association* 93: 188–212.

———. 1970. "The Proem-Hymn of Hesiod's Theogony." *Transactions of the American Philological Association* 101: 357–377.

———. 1975. "The Frequency and Structuring of Traditional Formulas in Hesiod's *Theogony.*" *Harvard Studies in Classical Philology* 79: 25–54.

Moritz, H. E. 1979. "Refrain in Aeschylus: Literary Adaptation of Traditional Form." *Classical Philology* 74: 187–213.

Morris, I., and B. Powell, eds. 1997. *A New Companion to Homer.* Leiden.

Morrison, J. V. 1999. "Homeric Darkness: Patterns and Manipulation of Death Scenes in the 'Iliad.'" *Hermes* 127: 129–144.

Murray, G., ed. 1955. *Aeschyli: Septem quae supersunt Tragoediae.* Oxford Classical Texts. 2d ed. Oxford.

Nagy, G. 1990. *Pindar's Homer: The Lyric Possession of an Epic Past.* Baltimore and London.

———. 1996. *Poetry as Performance: Homer and Beyond.* Cambridge.

Nicolai, W. 1973. *Kleine und große Darstellungseinheiten in der Ilias.* Heidelberg.

Nimis, S. A. 1999. "Ring-Composition and Linearity in Homer." In Mackay 1999: 65–78.

Nims, J. F. 1960. *Knowledge of the Evening*. New Brunswick, N.J.

———. 1990a. *Sappho to Valéry: Poems in Translation*. Fayetteville, Ark.

———. 1990b. *The Six-Cornered Snowflake and Other Poems*. New York.

Notopoulos, J. A. 1949. "Parataxis in Homer: A New Approach to Homeric Literary Criticism." *Transactions of the American Philological Association* 80: 1–23.

Oliver, R. P. 1966. "Apex and Sicilicus." *American Journal of Philology* 87: 129–170.

Olson, S. D. 1995. *Blood and Iron: Stories and Storytelling in Homer's* Odyssey. Leiden.

Packard, D. W. 1974. "Sound-Patterns in Homer." *Transactions of the American Philological Association* 104: 239–260.

Page, D. 1955. *The Homeric Odyssey*. Oxford.

———. 1972. *Aeschyli: Septem quae supersunt tragoedias*. Oxford Classical Texts. Oxford.

Palmer, A., ed. 1898. *P. Ovidi Nasonis Heroides*. Oxford.

Panhuis, D.G.J. 1982. *The Communicative Perspective in the Sentence: A Study of Latin Word Order*. Amsterdam.

Papanghelis, T. D. 1987. *Propertius: A Hellenistic Poet on Love and Death*. Cambridge.

Parry, M. 1971. *The Making of Homeric Verse: The Collected Papers of Milman Parry*. Ed. A. Parry. Oxford.

Pinkster, H. 1990. *Latin Syntax and Semantics*. Trans. H. Mulder. London and New York.

Pinsky, R. 1998. *The Sounds of Poetry: A Brief Guide*. New York.

Pohlsander, H. A. 1964. *Metrical Studies in the Lyrics of Sophocles*. Leiden.

Poole, A., and J. Maule, eds. 1995, *The Oxford Book of Classical Verse in Translation*. Oxford.

Postgate, J. P. 1881. *Select Elegies of Propertius*. London.

Pound, E. 1957. *Sophokles: Women of Trachis: A Version by Ezra Pound*. New York.

Prins, Y. 1991. "The Power of the Speech Act: Aeschylus' Furies and Their Binding Song." *Arethusa* 24, no. 2: 177–195.

Quinn, K. 1960. "Syntactical Ambiguity in Horace and Virgil." *AUMLA: Journal of the Australasian Universities Language and Literature Association* 14: 36–46.

———. 1982. "The Poet and His Audience in the Augustan Age." In *Aufstieg und Niedergang der Römischen Welt* 2.30.1. 75–180.

Race, W. H. 1980. "Some Digressions and Returns in Greek Authors." *Classical Journal* 76: 1–8.

———. 1982. "Aspects of Rhetoric and Form in Greek Hymns." *Greek, Roman and Byzantine Studies* 23: 5–14.

———. 1992. "How Greek Poems Begin." *Yale Classical Studies* 29: 13–38.

Rash, J. N. 1981. *Meter and Language in the Lyrics of the* Suppliants *of Aeschylus*. New York.

Richardson, L., Jr. 1977. *Propertius: Elegies I–IV*. Norman, Okla.

Richardson, N. J. 1974. *The Homeric Hymn to Demeter*. Oxford.

———. 1993. *The Iliad: A Commentary*. Vol. 5, *Books 21–24*. Cambridge.

Richardson, S. 1990. *The Homeric Narrator*. Nashville.

Riffaterre, M. 1980. "Describing Poetic Structures: Two Approaches to Baudelaire's 'Les Chats'." In Tompkins 1980: 26–40.

Riggsby, A. M. 1992. "Homeric Speech Introductions and the Theory of Homeric Composition." *Transactions of the American Philological Association* 122: 99–114.

Rimmon-Kenan, S. 1983. *Narrative Fiction: Contemporary Poetics.* London.

Rosenmeyer, T. 1982. *The Art of Aeschylus.* Berkeley.

Scott, W. C. 1982. "Non-Strophic Elements in the *Oresteia.*" *Transactions of the American Philological Association* 112: 179–196

———. 1984. *Musical Design in Aeschylean Theater.* Hanover and London.

———. 1996. *Musical Design in Sophoclean Theater.* Hanover and London.

Scully, S. P. 1986. "Studies of Narrative and Speech in the *Iliad.*" *Arethusa* 19: 135–153.

Seaford, R. 1987. "The Tragic Wedding." *Journal of Hellenic Studies* 107: 106–130.

Shive, D. 1987. *Naming Achilles.* Oxford and New York.

Slings, S. R. 1997. "Figures of Speech and Their Lookalikes: Two Further Exercises in the Pragmatics of the Greek Sentence." In Bakker 1997b: 169–214.

Stack, F. 1985. *Pope and Horace.* Cambridge.

Stahl, H.-P. 1985. *Propertius: "Love" and "War."* Berkeley, Los Angeles, and London.

Stanley, K. 1993. *The Shield of Homer: Narrative Structure in the* Iliad. Princeton.

Steiner, G. 1992. *After Babel: Aspects of Language and Translation.* 2d ed. Oxford.

Stevick, P. 1970. *The Chapter in Fiction: Theories of Narrative Division.* Syracuse, N.Y.

Stoneman, R. 1982. *Daphne into Laurel: Translations of Classical Poetry from Chaucer to the Present.* London.

Sullivan, J. P. 1964. *Ezra Pound and Sextus Propertius: A Study in Creative Translation.* Austin.

Taplin, O. 1992. *Homeric Soundings: The Shaping of the* Iliad. Oxford.

Terrell, C. F., ed. 1981. *Basil Bunting: Man and Poet.* Orono, Maine.

Thomson, G. 1938. *The* Oresteia *of Aeschylus Edited with Introduction, Translation, and a Commentary in Which Is Included the Work of the Late Walter G. Headlam.* 2 vols. Cambridge.

Tomlinson, C. 1993. "Some Aspects of Horace in the Twentieth Century." In Martindale and Hopkins 1993: 240–257.

Tompkins, J. P. 1980. *Reader-Response Criticism: From Formalism to Post-Structuralism.* Baltimore.

van der Valk, M. 1976. "On the Arrangement of the Homeric Hymns." *L'Antiquité classique* 45: 419–445.

van Groningen, B. A. 1960. *La composition littéraire archaïque grecque: Procédés et réalisations.* 2d ed. Amsterdam.

van Leeuwen, J., ed. 1912–1913. *Ilias.* Leiden.

———, ed. 1917. *Odyssea.* Leiden.

van Nes Ditmars, E. 1992. *Sophocles' Antigone: Lyric Shape and Meaning.* Pisa.

Van Sickle, J. 1980. "The Book-Roll and Some Conventions of the Poetic Book." *Arethusa* 13: 5–42.

———. 1984. "Dawn and Dusk as Motifs of Opening or Closure, in Heroic and Bucolic Epos (Homer, Apollonius, Theocritus, Virgil)." *Atti del Convegno mondiale scientifico di studi su Virgilio: Mantova, Roma, Napoli 19–24 settembre 1981,* vol. 1, 125–147. Milan.

van Thiel, H. 1991. *Homeri Odyssea*. Hildesheim, Zurich, and New York.

———. 1996. *Homeri Ilias*. Hildesheim, Zurich, and New York.

Verdenius, W. J. 1985. *A Commentary on Hesiod* Works and Days, *vv. 1–382*. *Mnemosyne*, supp. 86. Leiden.

Webster, T.B.L. 1970. *The Greek Chorus*. London.

Wender, D. 1977. "Homer, Avdo Mededović, and the Elephant's Child." *American Journal of Philology* 98: 327–347.

West, D. 1967. *Reading Horace*. Edinburgh.

West, M. L., ed. 1966. *Hesiod: Theogony*. Oxford.

———, ed. 1978. *Hesiod: Works and Days*. Oxford.

———. 1982. *Greek Metre*. Oxford.

———, ed. 1991. *Aeschylus: Agamemnon*. Bibliotheca scriptorum Graecorum et Romanorum Teubneriana. Stuttgart.

———. 1992. *Ancient Greek Music*. Oxford.

———, ed. 1998. *Homeri Ilias*. Vol. 1, *Rhapsodias I–XII Continens*. Bibliotheca scriptorum Graecorum et Romanorum Teubneriana. Stuttgart and Leipzig.

Wiles, D. 1997. *Tragedy in Athens: Performance Space and Theatrical Meaning*. Cambridge.

Williams, G. 1968. *Tradition and Originality in Roman Poetry*. Oxford.

Winnington-Ingram, R. P. 1983. *Studies in Aeschylus*. Cambridge.

Winters, Y. 1957. "The Audible Reading of Poetry." In *The Function of Criticism*, 79–100. Denver.

INDEX

Achilles and Aeneas, 18; and Areïthoös, 34–35; and Demuchus, 21–22; and Deucalion, 31–33; and Dryops, 20–21; and Echeclus, 29–31; and Hector, 18, 20; and Laogonus and Dardanus, 23; and Lycaon, 19, 24, 25, 26–27; and Moulius, 28–29; and Rhigmus, 33–34; and Tros, 24–28
aeolo-choriambic meter: defined, 82; in English, 82, 173–176; feeling conveyed by, 83, 92, 97; occurrences of, 82–83, 92
Agamemnon, 71–72, 75–81, 88–89
ambiguity, 105–109; in Homer, 25; lexical, 109, 121; simultaneous, 107–108; syntactical, 108–109, 120; transient, 106–107, 111, 112–113, 113–114, 117–118, 119
anacreontic meter: defined, 79; in English, 79, 177–178; feeling conveyed by, 79, 95–96; occurrences of, 79–81, 86–87, 89–91, 92–93, 97
analepsis, 131, 132
anapaestic meter: defined, 71; in English, 71; occurrences of, 82, 98n
anaphora, 130
antistrophe, 69
Apollonius of Rhodes, 154–156
asclepiad meter, greater: defined, 175; in English, 175–176
asclepiad meter, lesser: defined, 82; in English, 173

bacchiac foot: defined, 75; occurrences of, 73n, 75, 76, 77, 79, 80, 82, 91, 92, 94n
Bakker, E., 10–12
Bassett, S. E., 8
Blake, William, 74
book division in Homer, 39–47, 60
Bowra, C. M., 104–105, 166n
Browning, Robert, 166n
bucolic diaeresis, 5, 15
Bunting, Basil, 82, 102, 172–174
Bussanich, J., 162n

caesura, feminine, 5
Catullus, 64, 80, 82n
Chafe, W., 9–10

Chatman, S., 59, 149
choriamb: defined, 77–78; in English, 77; feeling conveyed by, 77, 95; occurrences of, 73n, 77–78, 79, 80, 81, 82, 90–91, 92, 93, 94. *See also* aeolo-choriambic meter
Clytemnestra, 71,72, 81, 88
Conrad, J., chapter divisions in, 40
consonants, clustered, 67n, 129, 136, 139, 142, 169–170, 171, 172–173, 175, 176n
corresponsion. *See* responsion
cretic foot: defined, 75; occurrences of, 75, 76, 80, 82, 83, 85, 92

dactyl: defined, 2, 62; in Aeschylus' choruses, 72–74; in English, 4, 73n; feeling conveyed by, 73, 81, 95, 97; in Homeric hexameters, 2–5, 14, 62
de Jong, I.J.F., 43, 158
Devine, A. and L. Stephens, 11n
Dickinson, Emily, 106–107
dochmiac meter: defined, 96; feeling conveyed by, 68n, 96; occurrences of, 95–96
double recension, 52n

emphasis from verse-position, 14, 16
enjambment, 7, 14, 28, 130, 133, 134, 137, 144, 146, 147
episodes: defined, 49–50; in *Iliad* 1, 50–52; transitions between, 53–58
Euripides, metrical resolutions in, 67; use of ionics in, 79

Fagles, R., 19–35, 46n, 54n, 61n
Fish, S. E., 102
"Focus" of sentence, 9–10, 12–13, 15, 17, 21, 22, 23, 29, 35, 104–105, 130, 134
Foley, Helene, 125
Foley, John Miles, 151–152
Ford, A., 153, 164
formulas: in Homer, 5, 130, 133–134; in "Hiawatha," 6–7; in *Morte d'Arthur*, 14, 15, 16, 130, 131, 133–134, 138, 142
Fränkel, H., 1–5, 152–153
Frost, Robert, 63–64, 168n, 171

SOUND·SENSE AND RHYTHM

‖ ≣ ‖ ≣ ‖ ≣ ‖ ≣ ‖ ≣ ‖ ≣ ‖ ≣ ‖ ≣

LISTENING TO GREEK AND LATIN POETRY

MARK W. EDWARDS

Sound, Sense, and Rhythm concerns the way we read—or rather, imagine we are listening to—ancient Greek and Latin poetry. Through clear and penetrating analysis Mark Edwards shows how an understanding of the effects of word order and meter is vital for appreciating the meaning of classical poetry, composed for listening audiences.

The first of four chapters examines Homer's emphasis of certain words by their positioning; a passage from the *Iliad* is analyzed, and a poem of Tennyson illustrates English parallels. The second considers Homer's techniques of disguising the break in the narrative when changing a scene's location or characters, to maintain his audience's attention. In the third we learn, partly through an English translation matching the rhythm, how Aeschylus chose and adapted meters to